PRAISE FOR
WORTHLESS, IMPOSSIBLE, AND STUPID

"In this provocative book, Daniel Isenberg shatters stereotypes and clarifies the often misunderstood concept of entrepreneurship. His inspiring real-life examples prove that true value is often found where many can only see something that seems worthless, impossible, or stupid."
—Akin Öngör, former CEO, Garanti Bank

"Valuable, practical, and insightful, Daniel Isenberg's new book is a very helpful and illustrative guide to the entrepreneurial journey."
—Sir Ronald Cohen, cofounder and former Chairman, Apax Partners

"Entrepreneurship is so important for a healthy economy: It creates jobs, supports communities, and builds a better working world. *Worthless, Impossible, and Stupid* provides a sophisticated and provocative narrative on this crucial topic."
—Maria Pinelli, Global Vice Chair of Strategic Growth
Markets, Ernst & Young

"Daniel Isenberg's bottom-up insights are a must-read for policymakers around the world racing to build smarter environments for starting and scaling firms."
—Jonathan Ortmans, President, Global Entrepreneurship Week, and Senior Fellow, Ewing Marion Kauffman Foundation

"Entrepreneurs take note. Daniel Isenberg makes his contrarian point clear in this provocative book: Entrepreneurs need to be as innovative in finding ways to capture value as they are in creating it. This will be good for them individually and for the society that benefits from entrepreneurialism."
—Nick Lazaris, former CEO, Keurig

"Daniel Isenberg brings us back to the roots of entrepreneurship: It's all about identifying, creating, and capturing value, in areas not seen by others and that may seem worthless, impossible, and stupid. But there are real rewards for the hard-headed entrepreneur—and for the rest of us!"
—Mikko Kosonen, President, the Finnish innovation fund Sitra

"*Worthless, Impossible, and Stupid* is a thought-provoking book for anyone interested in understanding the deeply contrarian nature of many entrepreneurs. It challenges the status quo definitions of entrepreneurship with substantive examples from all over the world. A must-read for building start-up communities."
—Brad Feld, Managing Director, Foundry Group;
cofounder, TechStars; and author, *Startup Communities: Building an Entrepreneurial Ecosystem in Your City*

WORTHLESS, IMPOSSIBLE, AND STUPID

WORTHLESS, IMPOSSIBLE, AND STUPID

HOW CONTRARIAN ENTREPRENEURS
CREATE AND CAPTURE EXTRAORDINARY VALUE

DANIEL ISENBERG
with Karen Dillon

HARVARD BUSINESS REVIEW PRESS
BOSTON, MASSACHUSETTS

Library of Congress Cataloging-in-Publication Data

Isenberg, Daniel J.
   Worthless, impossible, and stupid : how contrarian entrepreneurs create and capture extraordinary value / Daniel Isenberg.
       pages cm
   ISBN 978-1-4221-8698-5 (alk. paper)
   1. Entrepreneurship.   2. Value.   3. Creative ability in business.   I. Title.
   HB615.I744 2013
   658.4'21—dc23

                                                                    2012047093

ISBN: 9781422186985
eISBN: 9781422186992

The paper used in this publication meets the requirements of the American National Standard for Permanence of Paper for Publications and Documents in Libraries and Archives Z39.48-1992.

CONTENTS

WHY YOU ARE READING THIS BOOK

The buzz of entrepreneurship is all around us these days. High-profile start-up movements have launched in dozens of countries. Social media companies are sprouting from nowhere to impact—or impinge on, depending on your perspective—our personal and professional lives. Millions of people in dozens of countries are participating in celebrations such as Global Entrepreneurship Week. Each summer in the United States, tens of thousands of schoolkids take part in Lemonade Days, a program organized to teach the kids how to do business. In almost every nation on every continent, presidents and prime ministers have the word *entrepreneurship* on their lips, usually in the same breath as *job creation*.

What does this mean for you and me? At home, entrepreneurship touches many of us even more directly: maybe you yourself have started a venture or worked for someone who did. Maybe, instead of continuing to work for your current employer, you have the urge to take that great idea your boss trashed and try to bring it to market yourself. Perhaps, ignoring the advice of family and friends, you want to attack some frustrating need, solve a big problem, or build a brand-new product that no one had the sense to have made and sold already. Maybe you and a college mate have a zany idea that has grown on you, and you can't wait to get working on it. Or you have a relative who went out and took over a ragged little business that the owners or banks had written off as hopeless, and is growing it. Or you might just be reading these words during a rare break from eighteen-hour days, getting your own nascent venture off the ground, dealing with the "tough bloody sh*t" that you will read about later in this book.

With certainty, none of these ventures has been, or will be a cakewalk. Spouses are naturally worried about the fallout at home in case you fail. Customers are few and hard to convert into sales. Investors are picky and won't return phone calls or e-mails. Getting a ready-for-prime-time product to market takes more sleepless nights than you had imagined, making this the best year of your life at the same time that it is your worst.

Why is that? The main reason is that you are swimming against the market's existing current, going against the grain. All entrepreneurs do that. If that were not the case, it would not be entrepreneurship. Because if you or your friends are entrepreneurs, you are doing something novel, bringing to the market a product or service that doesn't exist yet, except perhaps in your mind's eye. You are trying to tell people that what they are currently doing or buying is not good enough, that they need to change their behavior and pay *you* in order to make their lives better. That means you will almost surely be butting up against anything from apathy to scorn. But if you succeed in scaling that wall of resistance, you will have proven that that new product or service has value.

In *Worthless, Impossible, and Stupid,* you will learn that this adverse process is the norm for entrepreneurship, not the exception. It is a contrarian process that repeats itself in one form or another countless times a day all over the world. Its ubiquity underlies a key question at the heart of this book: how do people with contrarian ideas succeed in creating and capturing value that is extraordinary? And is it somehow possible that more of us are capable of this than we think?

Worthless is about how so many people from all around the world see hidden value in situations where others do not. These people then use that perception to successfully develop valuable products and services that customers usually initially don't think they want, and ultimately go on to realize extraordinary value for themselves.

I have seen this kind of entrepreneurship in every one of the forty-five countries I have visited or worked in. I have come to believe that entrepreneurship is part of the human experience, like art, music, theater, and literature. Although it may be statistically unusual (like the statistical rarity of the good artist), entrepreneurship can and does occur in virtually every society, not just the mythical hot spots (e.g., Silicon Valley).

A paradox: despite their statistical rarity in creating extraordinary value, most of the entrepreneurs in these pages will strike you as ordinary people like you and me. The differences between them and us are less a matter of who they are or what resources they have than of what and how they think.

Entrepreneurship and entrepreneurs in general have always been a pretty puzzling phenomenon, and the entrepreneurs described on these pages are no exceptions. They make us wonder where their aspirations come from, what they are striving to accomplish, what keeps them going, and, in many cases, how they actually achieve those extraordinary results. These puzzles, I hope, will stimulate you to think and will possibly inspire you to act.

Worthless is not another how-to or recipe book for entrepreneurs and their champions. We have plenty of such books; some are quite good and a few are based on broad research and practice. But ultimately, recipes for entrepreneurs are oxymoronic because of the nature of entrepreneurship itself. As I attempt to illustrate, the phenomenon of entrepreneurship is about contradicting our expectations, and so codification of the right or better or best way to be an entrepreneur will always possess an elusive quality. The instant that we think we have it, the entrepreneur's job is to prove us wrong. The potentially extraordinary value resides precisely in showing how violating (or simply ignoring) the common prescriptions can work, sometimes, amazingly well.

Indeed, in addition to the impressive amounts of money involved, one of our fascinations with entrepreneurs lies precisely in their defiance of our expectations. The entrepreneurial record is writ full of entrepreneurs who should succeed but don't; those who shouldn't succeed, but do; those who almost crashed and burned, only to barely survive and to take off; and those who were taking off, only to suddenly lose altitude and fall. Entrepreneurs' defiance of our expectations is so prevalent that it always has a surprising quality—if it weren't a surprise, typically greeted by a great deal of skepticism in the early stages, someone would be doing it already.

Nonetheless, even though *Worthless* is not a set of prescriptions, I believe it will be a worthwhile read as well as intrinsically interesting. For some of you, it may kindle an aspiration that has so far remained dormant. For others, it may inspire you to cross a threshold from curiosity or desire to action. For still others, it may give a vicarious sense of adventure, excitement, or achievement, or may help explain the entrepreneurial experiences of friends or family. And for yet others, it may help you form more effective policies and programs to foster entrepreneurship in your home regions.

So, *Worthless, Impossible, and Stupid* has two broad objectives: one is to catalyze entrepreneurial aspiration and help more of you to choose the path of entrepreneurship (which I call the *entrepreneurial choice*) by simply showing you that entrepreneurship—extraordinary value creation and capture—is possible even though it is extraordinary. Aspiration is a funny thing. I can't shake a silly joke I heard as a child; it went something like this: "Last night I had a dream that if I concentrated really hard, I could fly. It was so vivid that when I woke up, I concentrated really hard to try to fly. Alas, I could only get a few feet off the ground." Aspirations are not usually formed out of the blue; at least in part, they are inspired by our perceptions of what is in the realm of the possible. We aspire to what we think we can achieve, and what we think we can achieve is influenced by what we see others achieving. Conversely, we often dampen our ambitions if we think that something is unattainable or undoable.

The thought of becoming a professional basketball player at the age of sixty and at five feet ten doesn't even cross my mind; if I saw someone like me succeeding at it, my aspirations might change.

Sociologist Kurt Lewin is attributed with the statement "There is nothing as practical as a good theory." So *Worthless*'s second objective is to clarify murky concepts of entrepreneurship by reframing the phenomenon in terms of value creation and its capture, rather than business ownership *per se*. This reframing will in and of itself make it easier for practitioners and policy makers to have an impact. As we will see in the subsequent chapters of *Worthless*, there are quite a few important implications of this reconceptualization; these include the relationship between entrepreneurship and income inequality (they go together, to some extent), the role of the government and how it bears on the entrepreneur (not necessarily making entrepreneurship easier), and the minimal relevance of youth and inventiveness.

How the Book Came to Be

On August 31, 1987, I landed in Israel with my wife Tsvia and our two boys. For the six years prior, I had been a Harvard-trained social psychologist turned Harvard Business School assistant professor. At that time, with no small amount of ambivalence, I turned down a coveted promotion at HBS to make the move. Tsvia and I had met in 1972, when I visited Israel on a whim. I ended up living, working, and studying there from 1972 to 1976, at which time I came back to Harvard to enter the social psychology doctoral program under the mentorship of Robert Freed Bales. With Freed I was immersed for five years in observing and thinking about how people interact.

When I landed in Tel Aviv, I had no precise plan of what I was going to do there. While getting ready for the move, I had met up with a loosely organized group of about fifty Boston-based entrepreneurs, all but one of whom were Jewish. All of them wanted to help Israel by donating experience rather than money, and all of them were MIT alumni who were friends, mentees, investees, or former students of MIT professor Ed Roberts. Roberts was, and still is, a revered graybeard of technological entrepreneurship and a Route 128 icon, and I learned quite a lot from him and from the group.[1] Roberts and the others met with me, and apparently, I fulfilled their fantasies. So on August 31, 1987, I left for Israel as chief operating officer of the newly named Technion Entrepreneurial Associates (TEA).

In truth, as I think back, my fascination with entrepreneurship had begun in 1983 during a visit to Israel, when I first had lunch with Eitan Wertheimer outside Nahariya, a small village on the Mediterranean coast just south of the Lebanese border. Nahariya is where Wertheimer's father, Stef, had established a small metal-products shop in the 1950s. Ultimately, in 2006, Eitan and Stef sold 80 percent of Iscar, by then the leading metal cutting tools manufacturer in the world, to Warren Buffett's investment company for $4 billion. But back in 1983, Iscar was a small manufacturer with perhaps $15–$20 million in revenues, and Eitan, in his early thirties, about my age, had just joined the company while Stef was recovering from a serious car accident.

Stef is an iconoclastic visionary in the Israeli scene, an anomaly among anomalies. In the fall of 1984, I received a paid research leave from Harvard and spent six months in Nahariya with Tsvia and our boys (you will meet Itai, the eldest, later in the book). In my spare time, I was helping Stef develop Israel's first training program for entrepreneurs. The program was based in the Tefen Entrepark, Stef's innovative complex for cultivating new businesses using his unique get-a-customer strategy, which would probably today be called an incubator. In 1986, HBS colleague Dick Rosenbloom and I, with Stef's sponsorship and active personal involvement, spent a few days every month launching the first of a series of year-long courses in the Tefen Entrepreneurs Program, which was designed for practicing entrepreneurs. I knew nothing about entrepreneurship then, but it was beginning to fascinate me, and I learned on the fly.

So, in 1987 Roberts was pitching to an already somewhat receptive catcher as I moved with my young family to start a new life outside the United States and outside the comfortable university environment. As COO of TEA, I had free rein for two years to do whatever I thought relevant to help stimulate technology-based entrepreneurship in Israel, which in reality, unbeknownst to most of the world, had already been percolating for three decades or so. In fact, by 1987 Israel had numerous technology start-ups, one or two venture capital funds, several R&D centers of US–based multinationals (Intel, IBM, National Semiconductor, etc.), and a number of government programs to support export-oriented businesses, with an emphasis on high-growth ventures. No less important, starting with the Eastern European pioneers who began settling the swamps and deserts from the early 1900s, Israel had deep in its national character an irrepressible entrepreneurial spirit. By 1987, a dozen or so Israeli ventures, such as Scitex, Elbit, Elron, Biotechnology General, Fibronics, and Optrotech, were already listed thousands of miles away on NASDAQ, and several US and Israeli venture capitalists, most notably the funds run by Fred Adler, Bob Daly, and Dan Tolkowsky, had actually made money from their investments. By 1987, Uzia Galil, arguably the grandfather of Israeli entrepreneurship, was already a serial entrepreneur, as were others such as the Zisapel brothers (who ultimately founded over two dozen IT companies).

Between 1987 and 1989, I initiated various activities under the auspices of the TEA. We conducted the first two National Conferences on Entrepreneurship in Israel, with over three hundred attendees and an illustrious group of speakers, such as Klaus Nathusius, chairman of the European Venture Capital Association; Gerry Goldstein of Advanced Magnetics; Ed Roberts; Morris Weinberg of Fibronics; Uzia Galil; and many others. I set up the President's Club, a forum for practicing CEO-entrepreneurs to share experiences and learn from each other. I co-ran the Tefen Entrepreneurs Program. We brought several Israeli start-ups to Boston so that they could participate in an MIT enterprise forum-like program in which the entrepreneurs would present and get feedback from panels of experts. I conducted a survey of forty-eight Israeli start-ups to learn their challenges in growing and globalizing. With Bob Mast and Jay Paap of Venture Economics, I conducted a series of seminars on how to form international strategic alliances for new ventures under the auspices of the Israel Export Institute. Several of the TEA members, such as Sherman Wolfe, made direct angel investments (investments by someone who invests in an early-stage entrepreneurial venture, but who, more importantly, offers guidance and support) in Israeli start-ups. And I designed Israel's first university masters course on technological entrepreneurship, which I taught twice at TEA, itself the source of many dozens of successful technology entrepreneurs.

In 1989, it was time to move on, partly because I myself had become infected with the bug that I had been trying to infect others with. I soon established Triangle Technologies to help emerging, high-potential Israeli technology companies sell their products and technologies in Japan, then the second-largest economy in the world and growing great guns.

Between 1990 and 2005, my partners, Amir Pomerantz and Yoshi Oikawa, and I were involved in many dozens of projects with Israeli entrepreneurs who, like Archimedes, were trying to move the earth. In fact, from this small and isolated place in the conflicted Middle East, thousands of miles away from customers and markets, a few hundred Israeli entrepreneurs have indeed moved billions of lives around the globe. They have been responsible for such pioneering innovations as network firewalls, instant messaging, USB memory sticks, capsule endoscopy, and Shopping.com, as well as dozens of platform innovations invisible to the consumer's eye. I was fortunate to have a front-row seat from which to view these fascinating developments unfolding, and from time to time, I even got into the act myself. We worked closely with many of Israel's most interesting entrepreneurs and saw both successes and failures. For a time I even served as vice president of business development for Japan for Voltaire, which later went public on NASDAQ and was acquired by another very successful technology pioneer, Mellanox.

In 1997, I joined Jerusalem Venture Partners' first $75 million fund as one of four general partners, a position I served in until 2001, while still running Triangle. JVP was organized and led by Erel Margalit, along with general partners Yuval Cohen and Aharon Fogel. This was my first experience on the buy side of entrepreneurship. The JVP fund had an amazing performance, with a great financial return, Israel's largest exit to date (Chromatis Networks), and an unprecedented number of investments with positive exits. I consider my personal contribution to JVP's actual performance to have been marginal, but I rolled up my sleeves and learned the intimate details of how venture capital funds work, which uniquely enriched my perspective on entrepreneurship. I observed dozens of exciting ventures, and I learned a lot from Margalit. Although he was sometimes difficult to work with in those early days, I still consider Margalit one of the most visionary, brilliant, and gutsy venture capitalists I have met anywhere.

In 2005 HBS professors Bill Sahlman and Teresa Amabile invited me to join the entrepreneurship faculty at HBS, and over the next five years I had the opportunity to traverse the globe in search of interesting entrepreneurship case studies for my second-year elective course, International Entrepreneurship. I had taken over the course from Walter Kuemmerle, radically redesigned it, and taught it for four years (about six hundred students took my class then, and it continued to be taught after I left in 2009). Between 2005 and 2009, I visited close to a hundred ventures in twenty or so countries on five continents. My observations culminated in twenty-seven published case studies, each showing an entrepreneur facing a critical fork in the road, each one from inception coping with a unique set of global challenges and opportunities, and each one having a surprise or mind-boggle.

In 2009, in the throes of the economic crisis, my teaching contract at HBS was not renewed, and I was fortunate in being offered what turned out to be a unique position at Babson College, which has been consistently ranked for over twenty years as having the leading entrepreneurship education programs in the world. After spending six months consulting to an entrepreneurship fostering nongovernmental organization in Saudi Arabia, I began to be fascinated with the question of whether our profession knew enough about how entrepreneurship developed in societies to intentionally create more of it. That led to the Babson Entrepreneurship Ecosystem Project (BEEP), which is an action-learning initiative with projects in Colombia, Mexico, Denmark, Brazil, and Canada.

All of these experiences provided me with the raw material and experiences that make up *Worthless, Impossible, and Stupid.*

Surprise

At a recent conference at MIT on business opportunities in Brazil, one of the speakers summed up: "In a word, Brazil is juicy." He was not referring to the "juice" of electricity, but in Sorocaba, twenty-five miles west of São Paulo, Bento Koike and the venture he founded, Tecsis Wind, have shipped over 12,000 fifty-meter wind turbine blades that operate 24/7 in the wind farms of North America and Europe. Virtually all of Koike's critical raw materials come from the Northern Hemisphere, and all of his customers are there as well. The value—the real "juice"—is created and captured in Brazil.

Six thousand miles away in Reykjavik, Iceland, a few dozen Actavis executives power the activities of the world's fourth-largest generic pharmaceutical maker, selling over one thousand different generic drugs from Boston to Beijing.[1] Between 1999 and 2007, Actavis grew a hundredfold when entrepreneur Robert Wessman and partners took over the small, insolvent drug maker. Investing his life savings, his mortgage, and his reputation, Wessman created an extraordinary amount of value for himself and other shareholders and brought needed, inexpensive drugs to forty world markets.

Another six thousand miles further in a Tokyo hospital, a fifty-year-old patient is swallowing a miniature video pill that will identify the source of gastrointestinal (GI) bleeding in her small intestine. The video pill is a self-guided mini-missile that travels down patients' GI tracts and has created a mini-revolution in health care—it has been used over a million times and has literally saved thousands of lives. The PillCam was invented and commercialized in Israel by two Gabis, Gabi Meron and Gabi Iddan, creating unique benefits for doctors and patients around the globe, and along the way allowing shareholders in the new venture, Given Imaging, to capture hundreds of millions of dollars in gains.

About fifteen hundred miles from Israel, Sandi Češko has built a retail empire in Slovenia based on TV shopping. In all of Studio Moderna's twenty Central and Eastern European markets, where TV shopping had been viewed with deep suspicion, Studio Moderna came along and changed their views. After twenty years of being ignored and then spurned by powerful private-equity groups, Studio Moderna is generating hundreds of millions of dollars in revenues, which have allowed Češko and other shareholders to sell a piece of the company, creating big gains for shareholders as well as valuable products for their customers.

Peter Diamandis, chairman and CEO of the X PRIZE Foundation, a nonprofit that runs competitions to encourage technological development, describes an important aspect of the winning innovations: "All significant breakthroughs have looked crazy the day before they became breakthroughs." With the PillCam, Meron established an entirely new diagnostic category. No one imagined that this was possible, certainly not Given Imaging's arch competitor Olympus. Neither could anyone have anticipated Koike's success in founding a wind turbine blades market leader in Brazil. Češko's foray into selling lower-back pain devices on TV in Slovenia was greeted not just with disbelief, but with derision. And Wessman, the "not most likely to succeed" (according to high school classmates), brought Actavis from nowhere to join an elite team of generics market leaders.

As the strikingly global and diverse cast of characters in *Worthless* (see the conclusion) will illustrate, successful entrepreneurs see and realize value where others think there is none, and act in ways that are contrary to what almost everyone else thinks is worthwhile. Thus, in this book, I present *entrepreneurship as the contrarian perception, creation, and capture of extraordinary value.* And as you'll see in the following pages, to create and capture that extraordinary value, you must see or sense value in things that many other people see as worthless, impossible, or stupid.

Worthless contains the stories of entrepreneurs who have done just that: created and captured extraordinary value by seeing opportunity where it was unnoticed, ignored, downplayed, or disparaged by others. These entrepreneurs are not the high-flying Silicon Valley superstars you see on TV or read about every day. Indeed, I would be surprised if you have heard of any of them, in spite of how successful some of them have been. They are not rock star larger-than-life superheroes, but hardworking, insightful, and fiercely committed men and women, young and old, in all corners of the globe, from Iceland to Israel and from Beirut to Brazil.

They are largely under the public radar; but in addition to flying unnoticed, they are also flying upside down. Like the proverbial bumblebee whose stubby body and short wings shouldn't enable it to get off the ground, defying the laws of physics, these entrepreneurs succeed at something that shouldn't work, yet does. That is what makes them so interesting for us to watch and so important for us to understand.

Entrepreneurship—perceiving, creating, and capturing extraordinary value—is part of the human experience. In this respect, it is similar to art, poetry, music, and storytelling. Every society's people have developed unique ways of expressing themselves; entrepreneurship is also a form of self-expression. It is like art and music in another way as well: Although art and music are ubiquitous, not everyone in a society is a musician or an artist—or an entrepreneur—although from childhood we all have innate abilities to sing and draw. *Extra*ordinary means not ordinary, not usual. Everyone is different, unique; by definition, very few people can be extraordinary. The widely diverse people and stories in this book show that there are countless ways of being successfully entrepreneurial. *Worthless* aims to change and broaden your own perception of what entrepreneurship means; I can tell you that writing it has certainly changed my own beliefs about entrepreneurs and entrepreneurship.

By the end of *Worthless,* I will challenge beliefs many of us have come to hold dear, asking probing questions such as: Do you need to be an innovator to be an entrepreneur? Do you need to be young? Do you need to be an expert? Does entrepreneurship have any negative social impacts? Does value creation need to be "extraordinary" for it to be entrepreneurship? By shedding light on these and many other questions, the above definition of entrepreneurship bears important practical implications not only for entrepreneurs, educators, and policy makers, but also for anyone who has ideas about solving big problems and changing the world for the better.

Preparing to Read *Worthless*

Worthless, Impossible, and Stupid emerged from the ground up from my own thirty-year immersion in the real-life phenomenon of entrepreneurship, as entrepreneur, consultant, partner to entrepreneurs, entrepreneur educator, venture capitalist, and as a private (angel) investor in entrepreneurial ventures. But my thoughts on this complex phenomenon only began to crystallize in 2005 when I went back into the classroom after over two decades of immersion in entrepreneurship. Ironically, it was back in the context of academia that I met and got to know very personally many of these ordinary-extraordinary people while developing the teaching cases for my HBS class.

Before reflecting too much on what all this experience and observation has amounted to, I will first introduce you to a broad range of examples: You'll meet people like Dutchman Bert Twaalfhoven. Eighty-one years old at the time of this writing, he retired at seventy-one from a career spanning forty-five years and over four dozen ventures, from manufacturing jet engine parts to introducing coin-operated washing machines into Europe. Or Hong Kong–based Mary Gadams, a US expatriate who established RacingThePlanet in 2002, a series of grueling 150-mile, six-day races through the world's most hostile deserts. The exotic experience and Gadams's unorthodox financial strategy has resulted in continuing growth and an experience so compelling as to convince thousands of participants to pay their fees hundreds of days in advance to assure a spot in races that are frequently oversubscribed. Or Vinod Kapur of Keggfarms, whose chicken-breeding acumen resulted in the Kuroiler, a disease-resistant bird that lays five times the usual number of eggs, bringing needed food and income to a million poor households in India. Or Carl Bistany, part owner of SABIS, one of the leading educational management organizations in the world, with public and private schools on several continents, tens of thousands of students, and millions of dollars in revenue without any external investment. All the entrepreneurs whom we'll meet on these pages are listed, with a brief summary of their accomplishments, in the book's conclusion (see the sidebar "Cast of Characters" there).

I will be delighted if you "partake" of *Worthless* in its entirety, from start to finish. To me and many of my students the stories are fascinating in and of themselves, but there is cumulative value in the way they build on one another to form a whole. Nevertheless, it is a rich meal, and I think you will also be able to pick and choose, skimming quickly through some parts and diving in more deeply in others.

Worthless has four parts, each one illustrated by several detailed stories. Part 1 calls into question the common stereotype of the entrepreneur as an innovative youngster with deep expertise driving his or her new venture. Part 2 explores why going against the crowd is inherent in the process of entrepreneurship. Part 3 looks at the various types of adversity that entrepreneurs face, showing that whereas certain types of adversity are serious inhibitors of entrepreneurship, others can be surprisingly beneficial. Part 4 and the conclusion use the entrepreneurs' stories as a springboard to spell out some of the important implications of viewing entrepreneurship as the perception, creation, and capture of extraordinary value.

I hope that *Worthless* and some of its arguments will trigger discussion and debate, as it raises many issues related to the ambitions we all have to improve the societies we live in. I will confess up front that many of these issues are weighty and exceedingly complex, and I don't always have satisfactory answers for them as they touch on income inequality, economic development policies, and the role of personal gain.

But let's take a first look at some of the *Worthless* entrepreneurs, especially those who shatter some of our stereotypes about who the typical entrepreneur really is.

PART ONE

WHO IS AN ENTREPRENEUR?
THREE MYTHS

"Think of the best example of an entrepreneur you know of, and I will read your minds."

This is the start of a mind-reading trick I have performed for audiences all around the globe. Perhaps you can already anticipate where this is going. After fifteen seconds or so, I show a slide of Steve Jobs, Bill Gates, Jeff Bezos, Larry Page, and Sergey Brin, to the inevitable smiles of recognition. My trick is over; sadly, it is the only trick I know how to pull off.

For most people, when they conjure up images of entrepreneurs, they invariably compose a picture of a twenty-something, tech-savvy college graduate (or dropout) in Silicon Valley, who after working awhile at Google or Microsoft or Facebook, dons jeans and sneakers to set off to do it better. That is the stereotype—and as appealing as that stereotype is (with its grain of truth, perhaps), it's one that paradoxically can discourage many people from setting off down the entrepreneurial path.

I began to notice this deterrent power of this entrepreneurial stereo-type when not just one MBA student, but a steady stream of them taking my International Entrepreneurship class at Harvard Business School would approach or write me starting around midterm. By that time, we had discussed more than a dozen of the unusual cases I had written on entrepreneurs in places as diverse as Brazil, Slovenia, Iceland, Japan, Hong Kong, and Saudi Arabia. None of the entrepreneurs was particularly famous, certainly not outside their home sphere, but what they had accomplished was by any measure inspiring. I just hadn't realized *how* inspiring until I saw the effect these stories were having on my students.

"Professor Isenberg," many of them would say, "these cases have really opened my mind; when I signed up for the class, I imagined that only those rare individuals with innovative new products or ideas, like Jobs, could succeed as entrepreneurs. Now I see that it *is* possible for entre-preneurs to start out with lots of energy and some skill, and they make it happen. I can do that; entrepreneurship might just be in my career path after all." Not a month goes by without my hearing back from some of these students, many of whom have ventures well on the way to success, and some with money-making exits.

There have been dozens of attempts by experts to re-create the un-deniable magic of Silicon Valley. Paradoxically, I believe that the near-mythical status of the valley can serve to dampen the prospects of people who have it in them to become entrepreneurs, but don't know it yet. As a result of our stereotype of genius whiz kids inventing something spectacular, people have mistakenly assumed that entrepreneurs have to be young, have an amazing new idea, and have deep expertise in their subject matter.

Obvious, right?

I have learned to be careful of that *O* word, at least as far as it applies to entrepreneurs. The director of a documentary film on the future of entrepreneurship asked if I could list the three next hot areas. I declined and told him I thought the question was a bad one for entrepreneurs: *Their* job is to identify hot prospects by themselves; my (and other "expert") opinions are irrelevant and probably wrong. If a group of experts tells you where the hot spots are then it is probably too late. Nothing is obvious in entrepreneurship, as the next chapters will illustrate.

CHAPTER 1

Myth #1

Entrepreneurs Must Be Innovators

The only innovation was to put chili and lime juice
on the popcorn instead of butter.

—Miguel Davila, cofounder, Cinemex

Do entrepreneurs need to be engineers, have a wall of patents, or work in the proverbial garage (or in the fad *du jour,* an accelerator)? The cases in *Worthless* will show that whereas those assets can be useful and important, extraordinary value is often created from gaps in existing markets, from the copying of businesses from one market to another, or in industries that (mistakenly, in my opinion) few consider innovative— real estate, commodity trade, financial services, import agencies, retail, and so forth. Furthermore, much value can be created with what I have called *minnovation*—that unexpected twist on an existing idea, the incessant, often counterintuitive tweaks of the business model, the minor product adaptation, or even "just" the ability to put together and lead a fantastic team that is supremely resourceful in overcoming obstacles and driving the tweaked idea to market, that is, creating extraordinary value.[1]

At the end of the day, even the most innovative idea can end up as only a footnote in the inventor's hall of fame (or much less) if an entrepreneur does not turn that idea into something that creates tangible value—something the market will buy. And an idea is no better than a theory—as Jay Rogers's Local Motors was when his business partner pulled out—until someone uses his or her capabilities, assets, and information to make something real from that idea. Finally, only a small part of the ultimate value is in the idea itself—most value is in the realization, not in the recognition. Even copycat business models completely devoid of innovation can create huge value; copies of Google, Groupon, and Amazon.com crop up and become big in unexpected markets. This is significant for policy makers as well, since many governments around the world mistakenly believe that noninnovative entrepreneurship bears no social benefit and should not be supported.

No products can be less innovative than generic products—they literally copy what someone else created before. Nowhere is that more striking than with generic drugs, because the generics business starts when the patents of the innovative drugs (actually termed *innovatives* by the pharmaceutical industry) go stale and the drugs have inherently no differentiators; the innovation is officially dead. In generic pharmaceuticals, all the products are by definition devoid of innovation. Does that mean that there is less entrepreneurship in creating and capturing value in the field of generic drugs?

Icelander Robert Wessman might disagree. In 1999, he took over the tiny, failing Actavis (under a different name until 2004) and, in eight years, built it into the fifth-largest generic pharmaceuticals company in the world. By 2007, the company boasted eleven thousand employees, a presence in forty countries, 650 products, twenty-one manufacturing plants, twenty-six successful acquisitions, and R&D in five countries and four continents.[2] I personally would never have predicted that a multi-billion dollar generics leader would emerge from tiny Iceland, far from all major markets.

Wessman was just twenty-nine years old when he returned from Germany to his home country of Iceland, where he took over the helm of what was then a small, illiquid, domestic maker of generic pharmaceuticals. His first transition day as CEO was memorable, as he was called into the company cafeteria to be introduced:

> The chairman and the CEO started arguing bitterly in front of everyone. Not having spoken yet, I walked to the middle of the room and asked them to stop the fighting. I introduced myself to the stunned employees . . . After a painfully long silence, one asked, "How old are you?" "Are you married?" asked a second. As there were no further questions, I adjourned the meeting.[3]

The boyish-looking Wessman had spent the early years of his career working for a Icelandic shipping company, ending up running its German operations, and knew nothing whatsoever about the generics business. In fact, apropos of entrepreneurial superstars, Wessman comes from a quintessentially middle-class Icelandic background, worked at odd jobs since he was a kid, but was so unimpressive, almost unnoticeable, that his classmates remember him in this way: "We would never have voted Robert as most likely to succeed; he just did not stand out; he was actually kind of shy."

But in hindsight, Wessman's lack of expertise and knowledge might have been an advantage: "In some ways it was easier for me," he recalls. "Conceptually the generics business is a simple one. The complexity is in the execution. I immediately knew we had to be huge, or die."

The generics business is brutally competitive. The concept is that a company essentially copies successful drugs as soon as they come off patent protection and tries to sell them at a fraction of the price of the on-patent innovatives. Price and speed to market are critical.

Wessman concluded that the only way for Actavis to survive long term as a generics player was to aim not just to be a solid player, but to be a major player, with world-class research and development, a low-cost supply chain, and presence in all major markets. Wessman's confidence was based in large part on his belief in his own capabilities, never doubting that he could accomplish this. He backed his beliefs by mortgaging his house and borrowing funds to buy more stock at every chance he had. He also had to provide personal guarantees for the €10 million bank loan needed to escape impending bankruptcy. So much for motivation; his steadfast self-confidence in his own capabilities to make this happen would be tested right away, as it turned out.

In the early stages of trying to bring the company to markets outside tiny Iceland, Actavis had essentially its only marketable product awaiting German approval at a time when competitors were fast on the company's heels in Denmark with competitive products. If the competitors succeeded in getting Danish approval first, this would also allow the product into Germany, too, because of an agreement between Denmark and Germany about generic drugs. Suffice it to say that tiny Actavis was losing money, was unable to pay salaries, owed money to the banks, and without new revenues would have to close.

In almost every case, only the first generic company to receive a marketing authorization (MA) in any given market goes on to gain sufficient market share to make any profit, because margins are razor thin and you need a large market share to make any money at all. So being first in Germany was do-or-die for Actavis, in particular because without the German MA, Wessman knew that Actavis would be forced to default on its loans—effectively pushing the company, and Wessman, into bankruptcy.

Actavis had been promised approval in writing by a junior clerk from the agency before year's end, but when approval was not forthcoming and the Denmark competitor's approval loomed, Wessman went to the edge. He got hold of the federal agency's director, a very senior and important official, by phone and put a metaphorical gun to his head: "If we don't get approval before year end," he threatened the director, "I will personally sue you and the institute." That is not a tactic that I typically teach my students for how to deal with powerful regulatory authorities.

But Wessman's aggressiveness paid off. A day after he delivered his threat—whether he could have carried it out or not—he received news that the German MA would be forthcoming, ahead of any Danish approval for his competitor, allowing Actavis that first-mover advantage. "Without that approval, there would have been no Actavis," recalls Wessman.

The global market for generic drugs kept climbing, approaching $100 billion, and mostly in the relevant prescription drug segment that Actavis was competing in. But to compete successfully in that large market, Wessman knew that Actavis needed to be much bigger and have much more global reach. So he began an intense stream of acquisitions, making more than thirty successful ones by 2008, including companies in India, Russia, Romania, the United States, Hungary, Bulgaria, the Czech Republic, Poland, and Turkey, and integrating them all into one global Actavis.

Through all that activity, Actavis has poured its resourcefulness into *how* it did business in addition to *what* it sold, simultaneously broadening its product portfolio, globalizing its supply chain, expanding its markets, and deepening its research and development. Perhaps nothing speaks more clearly about how Wessman (who stepped down as CEO in 2008 to run his own investment fund and ultimately to start a new generics venture, Alvogen) values innovation and execution: At Actavis, an employee is given one point for a brilliant idea, ten for planning it, and a hundred for successful implementation—more or less exactly the way Actavis succeeded at putting itself on the global map.

"The only innovation we introduced was putting lime juice and chili sauce on the popcorn instead of butter," is how Miguel Davila sums up the Cinemex founders' approach to building the pioneering multiscreen cinema chain in Mexico.[4] The chain was founded on a tried and proven business model that the three founders imported lock, stock, and barrel (*sans* chili sauce) from the United States and Canada.

Davila and fellow Harvard MBAs Adolfo Fastlicht and Matthew Heyman founded Cinemex just a few weeks after graduating. The idea of multiscreen cinema was already old hat, but not in Mexico, and Davila, Fastlicht, and Heyman saw the possibility of creating huge value in bringing the idea to a market that was still relying on the "brick-and-stick" model: "You bring a brick to sit on and a stick to beat away the rats," jokes Davila. Single-screen theaters, uncomfortable seats, unappetizing concessions, and cheap, government-controlled ticket prices were the norm in Mexico in 1994. The Cinemex theaters transformed entertainment for customers in Mexico, but there was really nothing in their concept, their business model, or the way that they executed it that any of us would consider innovative, no matter how far we stretched that word. They were excellent copycats who sold Cinemex ten years after founding it for $300 million to a private-equity group, having successful acquired the gorilla's share of a high-end market that they themselves had created. Entrepreneurship? *Si!* Innovation? *No!*

The trick for the Cinemex founders was in how well they could turn that idea into reality, mixing small parts of novelty and creativity with huge helpings of flexibility and scrappiness, all with a generous portion of contrarian risk-taking, moving in aggressively when the Mexican financial crisis of 1994 struck and drove more conservative competitors to retrench back to the US market. In fact, it was during the financial crisis that the Cinemex founders accelerated their investments in locking up new locations, despite a double whammy of seeing the peso portion of their newly raised $21.5 million in equity investment lose a big chunk of its value, while being socked simultaneously with a tax bill for the capital gain of the appreciated dollar portion. In fact, the crisis was exactly what gave the Cinemex start-up the window of opportunity to sign agreements with new malls that previously would not give them the time of day.

The three partners had met at business school and began to formulate their thinking while playing poker at night. They opted to use their second year at Harvard to exploit an independent field study, putting together a plan for a business they would try to finance and operate. Their field study came at a price—the academic credit they got was nothing compared with the hundreds of hours and thousands of dollars they spent traveling back and forth between Mexico and the United States. It was so consuming that they, by their own admission, tried to coast through the remainder of their final year at school, doing minimal work while putting in fifty-hour weeks on the start-up concept. Their plan was a carbon copy of the successful North American movie theater chains, but it was certainly ambitious for three students. A ninety-three-page document envisioned a company with sixteen theaters, 158 screens, 32,800 seats, and annual revenues of $71.6 million—all requiring $6 million in venture funding to pay for the rapid construction, leasing, and opening of an initial ten theaters by July 1996.

Davila and his partners spent the final months of their MBA program flying to and from Mexico to pull together the enormous financing they'd need to back their idea. They each exhausted every source of personal funds they could get their hands on—including maxing out credit cards and dipping into rainy-day savings. They had many false starts with possible backers, including heirs to the Johnson & Johnson fortune, Bankers Trust ("Mexico is too risky for an investment"), the CEO of a potential competitor ("We're way ahead of you guys in the Mexican market"), to mention a few. Many potential investors actually seemed very positive, but the entrepreneurs could never quite nail down a deal.

As they got closer to graduation, each of the three had to decide whether to take desirable job offers. They didn't want to lose the sure thing—the kinds of jobs people go to Harvard Business School to achieve—but they were so close to making their new venture a reality.

Money and the pressure to decide got tighter and tighter. By the summer, all three men, having been turned down by everyone, began to have second thoughts about whether they should have hung on to their job offers instead of putting all their chips on the movie theater company.

It wouldn't be until October 1993—five months after graduation—that they finally caught a break. Davila and Fastlicht had been trying to secure an advanced agreement for prime mall real estate in Mexico City, and Heyman had moved to New York to try to find investors. But as hopes began to fade that anyone was ever going to back their venture, Heyman decided to move to the West Coast and settle into a real job after all, bringing with him his few possessions and the pager he used as a lower-cost substitute for a phone. Just as he was leaving New York City for the West Coast, the pager went off. "Get back to New York," came a message from Fastlicht. "We have a meeting with J.P. Morgan."

As it turned out, a chance discussion at a dinner party was finally the luck they needed. J.P. Morgan was going to invest in their plan, enough to trigger a total investment of $21.5 million, the largest private-equity raise in Mexico to date, a bit more than their $6 million target.

The trio raced full speed into creating their chain in Mexico City, but it wasn't long before a second, more unexpected challenge reared its head. In December 1994, before Cinemex had opened even one theater, the Mexican government devalued the peso, cutting its value against the dollar in half. It was the worst economic crisis in Mexico's history. The compensation package the founders had negotiated with investors was suddenly halved. But worse, the devaluation of the cash held in pesos instantly decreased the cash value in dollars from $21.5 million to $13.8 million. For the investors who had pledged their investments in dollars, the devaluation made no difference. But 30 percent of the investment in Cinemex was pledged in pesos by Mexican investors. Construction activity in the area came to a halt. The crisis and its ripple effects persuaded all of Cinemex's competitors that the entertainment market was so risky that they withdrew, stopping their projects midway.

The founders had actually spent only $200,000 setting up offices and making early-stage plans so far—almost all of the work and investment was still to be done. "It would have been very easy for everyone to say, 'It's time to turn the light off. This is a time of crisis, let's walk away,'" says Davila.

From Cinemex's vantage point, however, this was a moment to turn into an advantage the adversity that had deterred everyone else. "We talked to our investors and told them, 'We understand we've lost purchasing power,' but if you look at this, it created a huge opportunity for us," Davila recalls. "Our Mexican competitor would be completely unable to move, and US companies got scared and said, 'This is not the time to go into this market.' Our investors agreed with our assessment and reaffirmed their support." Once the Mexican investors learned this, Davila recalls, they agreed to stick with it, too. "They were almost like, 'They must know something that we don't know . . . we want to stay in!'" The founding group convinced the Mexican investors not only to stick with their agreement, but to essentially double their investment—to come up with the same number in US dollars that their previous peso pledge had amounted to, maintaining the original $21.5 million.

But the peso devaluation would have side effects on the Cinemex strategy, too. Originally the company had planned to launch all over the country at once, trying to create a new national brand, with a ticket price of fifteen pesos. Now, instead, the company decided to focus on dominating just Mexico City, which controlled 40 percent of the box office revenues in Mexico and which was (and is) the single largest Spanish-speaking movie market in the world. Controlling Mexico City, the entrepreneurs hoped, could give Cinemex more effective negotiating power with distributors.

They also decided to strategically price tickets high: Instead of charging fifteen pesos, Cinemex would charge twenty-five pesos, much harder for local customers to afford. For that money, Cinemex would make sure the experience was high quality, unexpected, upscale. In place of "bricks," Cinemex theaters would offer plush, comfortable seating in luxurious theater settings. In place of "sticks," they would offer unexpectedly tasty concessions. Because much of the competition had disappeared overnight, Cinemex was able to negotiate deals in various desirable locations that had previously been unattainable for the start-up.

By August 1995, the venture was ready to open its first multiplex in a new luxury shopping mall. But as luck would have it, just a few days before the doors were scheduled to open, the team would face its final, daunting hurdle prior to launch. The Mexican movie theater union had had a seventy-year grip on the movie industry in Mexico and operated under some laws from those times. (For example, work rules meant that someone who sold soft drinks was not allowed to sell popcorn.) Some 150 men, women, and children protesters turned up in the lobby to "Occupy Cinemex," intent on preventing its opening.

Davila had been in the middle of a media interview when he received word of the protest, so he invited the reporters to accompany him to the theater's lobby. Davila confronted the union organizer in the midst of a speech, accusing the man of being a "thief and a traitor to his people." The organizer lunged at Davila, who is a rather sturdily built guy, and the journalists had a field day reporting on the attack.

Using the public attack to get a court injunction against the union for trespassing, the Cinemex team next bluffed the protesters. Cinemex announced to the public that the theater would open on Friday, but then opened on Wednesday instead, with no protesters in sight. Once the theater was actually in business, the dispute moved to the local labor board, which ultimately sided with the company. It then replaced the seventy-year-old union with a modern, less stringent union for movie workers.

Cinemex was, from its opening weekend, a commercial success that exceeded expectations. The founders may not have brought an original idea to the market, but they did bring a set of skills, knowledge, and capabilities that complemented each other enough to get the show on the road, so to speak. What they accomplished in fact changed the local cinema culture and, in a market of close to twenty million people, dominated that market and made $300 million for their investors and themselves. And I am not sure how much even the one innovation—chili and lime juice—contributed to that.

"When I speak to potential entrepreneurs," Davila reflects now, "I tell them, don't expect that the sky's going to open and a lightning bolt is going to hit you with the next Facebook idea. Those things are Haley's comet—they come by once every hundred years. You don't need to have that as entrepreneur. You just have to figure out something people need and find a way to execute it better than everyone else."

———————

If you had one dollar to invest, would you invest it in an innovator or an entrepreneur?[5] It is a simple little question. After a few seconds of thought, most of us would answer, the latter. Yet we all know that innovation is a good thing. I myself grew up in a scientific family, and my father, a biophysicist, was an inveterate innovator, creating new lab equipment, making meals of fish the locals considered trash, composing his own music, and even inventing new games at home. But my father was no entrepreneur—his self-employed father (my grandfather) inculcated indifference toward, and even distaste of, business in his son at a young age, and my father had a "respectable, salaried job" as a scientist and, later, a professor his entire career.

The question strikes us as strange initially, because we reflexively equate innovation with entrepreneurship. There are institutes for innovation and entrepreneurship and degrees in innovation and entrepreneurship. When I Google "innovation" and "entrepreneur" together, I get about 250 million hits, half again the 150 million I get for entrepreneur by itself. Even if you hear a bad word here and there about entrepreneurs (the financial entrepreneurs on Wall Street have been reviled since the crash of 2008), you never hear anything bad about innovation: it is as close to motherhood and apple pie as you can get.

Deservedly so. Innovation is an important social good, and economic research shows that innovations (especially technical breakthroughs) have been consistent, long-term drivers of economic and social prosperity over the ages. Innovation is crucial to societal advance.

So why does the entrepreneur get our dollar? One reason is that we are not quite sure in whom we are investing when we invest in the innovator; we do not identify a specific economic actor, or if there even is an economic actor. Is it the bench scientist? The engineer in the field? The product development manager in the market? I know exactly who the entrepreneur is, but I am never quite sure who is the innovator. Is it anybody tinkering with a grand idea, or just an elite few? Is it a group of people or a lone inventor? I might invest my buck on an innovator if I could find one; I suspect if I did, then lurking behind the innovation cover would be an entrepreneur.

Most of us would agree that innovation has something to do with the tangible manifestation of novel ideas. But entrepreneurship is about the creation of tangible value. Ideas help, but the *sine qua nons* for entrepreneurs—hard work, ambition, resourcefulness, unconventional thinking, salesmanship, and leadership—will usually trump brilliant ideas. The perception of extraordinary value is just a piece of the picture, which only becomes complete with creation and capture of that value as well.

To be clear, innovation is wonderful because (a) it has an intrinsic aesthetic appeal, and (b) it can frequently lead to extraordinary value creation and capture, that is, entrepreneurship—*if* an entrepreneur comes along and actually utilizes the innovation. But an unintended consequence of the use, or overuse, of this vaunted concept is that it can paradoxically intimidate some potential entrepreneurs who think that without that brilliant idea, they should stay put in their executive or professional positions and not take any risk to strike out on their own.

So let the entrepreneurs rummage through piles of society's innovation assets. As they determine what is valuable from scrap, I invite you to watch with me as they surprise us in their value creation.

CHAPTER 2

Myth #2

Entrepreneurs Must Be Experts

Let's take another quick look at the list of entrepreneurs shown in the sidebar "Cast of Characters" in the conclusion. Who were the experts, and who were fairly ignorant of their industries when they started off? The split is roughly fifty-fifty. Mary Gadams was an experienced ultramarathon competitor when she launched RacingThePlanet, and Carl Bistany had been a teacher in the SABIS schools, but Bert Twaalfhoven knew nothing about aluminum extrusion, jet engine repair, or coin-operated washing machines when he launched those businesses. Ron Zwanziger, today a recognized expert on blood glucose monitoring, recalls how his company got started: "We were wet behind the ears and inexperienced, so we decided to find a topic where inexperience wouldn't matter—we chose genetic engineering." I know, it sounds pretty funny, but that was their reasoning at the time.[1] That first venture led to Medisense, the market's number one blood glucose monitor at the time.

It would be an exaggeration to claim that expertise is a disadvantage or even irrelevant for entrepreneurship; in fact, there is evidence that having a founder launch a venture with a decade or so of industry immersion under his or her belt is a predictor of growth and success.[2] But an argument can be made that looking at a topic with fresh eyes and without the blinders and beliefs about what is "impossible" facilitates being able to see opportunity where others do not. Whether we think it is an advantage or not, *a priori experience in the subject matter is certainly not a prerequisite,* even for highly technical endeavors. Entrepreneur and philanthropist Naveen Jain (who is also on the X PRIZE Foundation board) says, "The real disruptors will be those individuals who are not steeped in one industry of choice . . . but instead, individuals who approach challenges with a clean lens, bringing together diverse experiences, knowledge and opportunities . . . non-expert individuals will drive disruptive innovation."[3] At a minimum, whether we think it is an advantage or not, a priori expertise in the subject matter is certainly not a prerequisite, even for highly technical endeavors. This is important primarily because many would-be entrepreneurs (such as my students) assume that expertise is a sine qua non of entrepreneurship and thus avoid pursuing an apparent opportunity in areas of their own ignorance.

————————

Abhi Shah frequently repeats both to his staff and to my students when he visits my classes: "Thinking small is a crime." In point of fact, Shah is not a lawyer and knows nothing about crime, but the firm he founded and runs, Clutch Group, manages the work of four hundred lawyers in the United States, India, and the United Kingdom.[4] He has never even spent a day in a courtroom. Until he started Clutch Group, Shah's only experience with the legal system was a childhood tour of the US Supreme Court. It was precisely his lack of legal training that helped him listen, with ears unfettered by assumptions, to the pain points that both clients and lawyers were experiencing, and build a business on their frustrations. He himself believes that if he had been a legal expert, he would never have seen a gap in the market.

Clutch Group is a legal process outsourcing company. Just six years after its 2006 launch, Clutch Group has about $25 million in revenues and projects aggressive growth in the years to come. In its brief existence it has already received numerous awards as the top-ranked provider of legal process outsourcing by *The Black Book of Outsourcing,* Dun & Bradstreet, Frost & Sullivan, the International Association of Outsourcing Professionals, and *Chambers Global 2011: A Client's Guide to the World's Leading Lawyers for Business* (an industry-leading researcher and provider of legal directories).

For years lawyers have managed to convince their grumbling clients that only large, well-staffed law partnerships, racking up large bills, could handle sophisticated legal work. But by building a network of offices in a handful of major cities in the United States, including New York, Chicago, and Washington, DC, Clutch Group provides law firms and in-house corporate counsel with sophisticated legal support, including document review, contract management, litigation support, regulatory and legislative compliance, and legal research. In essence, Clutch Group does some of the most complicated, time-consuming, and detailed work traditionally done by expensive law firms for a fraction of the cost—using Clutch's global network and proprietary software systems to optimize the matching of tasks, expertise, accreditation, and cost.

From the beginning, Shah never felt that lacking firsthand legal experience and training would be a handicap. He believed he had the right set of personal assets—a demonstrated ability to sell anything, the drive to persevere against obstacles, and, perhaps most importantly, a burning personal desire to succeed—to launch his business. As is true for many other successful entrepreneurs, Shah's confidence derived more from recognizing what he didn't know, what he needed to learn, and who else he needed on his team, than from expertise.

Shah was born in the US state of Georgia to Indian parents who were temporarily studying and working in the United States before returning to their native Ahmadabad. Shah's parents, from the state of Gujarat, had learned the value of hard work.[5] Whether he was ready for that same lesson or not, they gave it to him when he was just sixteen years old.

When Shah returned to the United States to study as a young admission at Texas A&M University in 1996, his father refused to pay for Shah's $20,000 tuition, even though the father could have afforded to do so. Instead, he "gifted" his son with a lecture on how he and Shah's mother had worked their way through college on their own. The only thing he was willing to give his son, who was scheduled to start school at the end of the summer, was a phone number. If Abhi called that number, his father promised, the older man who would answer could probably figure out how to get a job that would help the younger Shah earn his tuition, room, and board.

Not particularly happy with his father's answer, Shah called the number and learned that it was a company that sold books. "That's easy," Shah remembers saying to the manager he spoke with. "Where is your bookstore?" "There is no bookstore," the manager responded. "We sell books door-to-door." OK, Shah thought. It could be worse. I can probably handle that. "What kind of books?" he asked.

"Bibles."

OK, it *was* worse. Not only had Shah been raised mostly in India, but he had been raised a Hindu.

"Life is a learning experience," the manager quipped, and asked impatiently if Shah wanted the job or not.

In need of money, Shah agreed to try, but again he was surprised. When he turned up in Nashville for a week of training, he was told that salespeople are expected to individually purchase on credit their inventory of books to sell and to be responsible for it during the summer.

At the end of the week, each trainee drew the name of the territory he or she would be assigned. Abhi Shah from India drew Talladega, Alabama. Talladega is nothing like Shah's Ahmadabad: it has a population of 16,000 spread over twenty-three square miles, or 695 people per square mile. Ahmadabad is almost a hundred times denser, with about 60,000 people per square mile. Shah was to share the sparse sales territory with three other students, so off they went to Talladega, bibles in tow. As it dawned on him that he'd have to work his sales beat with forty pounds of books—Shah cuts a very slim figure—he placed another call to his father to borrow money for a used car: "We'd love to help you out, son, but twenty years ago, when your mother and I were making our way through school, our parents couldn't afford such luxuries as used cars . . ." No car.

So Shah convinced his landlord, a teacher on summer break, to drop him off in a different spot every morning, and he would work his beat on foot. "At least in India I was used to one hundred degrees Fahrenheit with high humidity," Shah recalled wryly.

The first morning at the first house, no one came to the door. At the second house, he was waved along. The third house unleashed a dog on him. And at the fourth house, a little kid answered, and seeing Shah standing in front of him, shouted, "Mom, there's a *tan* guy at the door!"

Not surprisingly, it was the most difficult summer Shah can remember. With no alternatives, Shah kept it up for ten weeks, determined not only to earn tuition money, but to make sure he wouldn't have to write a check to the book company. By August, he managed to barely exceed break-even. His net income, after all his expenses, was around $2,000.

When he got to Texas A&M, scholarships, loans, and financial aid allowed him to cobble together what he needed to bridge the gap. You would have thought that eighty-hour weeks lugging bibles door to slamming door in the sweltering heat of Talladega would motivate any Gujarati Hindu to consider alternatives for his next summer. But somehow confronting the challenge made Shah even more determined. "It was absolutely impossible by any measure of sanity," he recalls. "But the fact that I had not met my goal—I wanted to fight and go back." So he returned to Talladega the next summer.

Having learned what didn't work—being a novice in both selling and the bible—Shah got himself a run-down car, ate Happy Meals from McDonald's, and watched every penny. He began to study the bible like a divinity student: "I knew my bible inside and out."

That summer, he sold his self-imposed target of over $10,000 in profit, and it only got better from there. "The third summer was a defining moment for me," Shah recalls, noting that he took away three priceless lessons from pounding his way across hot Alabama pavements summer after summer: "First, I was going to be in business for myself, no matter what. I felt like I was unbreakable. I could do anything. Second, I learned how lucky I was in life: compared to the trailer parks I would visit, I was privileged. And third, I learned the value of hard work. No matter how hard a challenge is, no matter how ridiculous it is, no matter how little you know about it, you can do whatever you set your mind to."

Shah entered Harvard Business School a few years later with the same sense of purpose. His goal was to start a business process outsourcing venture in India. Business process outsourcing, or BPO, had already become a reality of the global economy: Western companies were taking advantage of India's highly educated, English-speaking workforce and outsourced key support functions for significantly less money than it would cost to handle in their home territories. Most Indian BPO companies handled lower-value, labor-intensive administrative work that needed to be done carefully but didn't need particular expertise. Call centers with thousands of English-speaking operators were the classic example.

Shah didn't know what aspect of BPO he would focus on, but for summer break, he targeted getting an internship with a CEO of some BPO company. He was looking for an executive who was prominent and well connected and who would give him 24/7 access so that Shah could learn as much as possible from the CEO personally. Through contacts from his volunteer work organizing the US-India Political Action Committee in Washington, DC, Shah approached Jerry Rao, founder of software company MphasiS, a BPO with over twelve thousand employees. Compared with selling bibles in Talladega, persuading Rao to agree to an internship, along with 24/7 access, must have seemed a piece of cake, and Rao agreed—Shah just had to agree to work 24/7 himself.

But Shah didn't expect the wild ride that awaited him when he showed up for his first day in MphasiS's Bangalore office: rushing in with the news that MphasiS would be put up for sale, Rao turned to Shah in front of the entire executive team: "How would the hotshot Harvard student like to lead this process?" Shah, along with the other MphasiS executives, was stunned. But by the end of the summer, Shah knew the BPO industry intimately, and MphasiS was eventually sold to Ross Perot's EDS. As Rao told me later, Shah had effectively sold himself as well: Rao would personally invest in any venture Shah decided to go into. Shah was "impressive, persuasive, diligent in execution, persistent, and excellent at people relationships; if I introduced him to a friend, within a few weeks he would be closer to the friend than I was," joked Rao. "He was universally liked at MphasiS."[6]

Shah returned for his second year at HBS, entirely focused on identifying a business to start, evaluating numerous ideas suggested by Rao and others. Working with an analytically minded classmate who shot down thirty-six of thirty-eight ideas, Shah did manage to draft two business plans, which died only slightly slower deaths.

Facing graduation with no job in sight—Shah was so committed to his entrepreneurial choice that he had not even prepared a résumé—and with $100,000 of school debt, Shah gave himself six months to figure out what his venture would be before giving up. "Needless to say," he says, "I didn't call my dad for money."

But Shah began to see and connect dots that others had ignored. First, he heard the bitter complaints of many of his friends who had gone to law school and were now working twelve- to fourteen-hour days, six and even seven days a week, at large law firms. At dinner one night with a group of lawyer friends, he was struck by just how miserable they already were. "They had nice salaries, but none of them had a life. I figured if enough people were unhappy, there must be an opportunity somewhere."

It was the spark Shah needed to try to turn big pain into a big new opportunity, because Shah was not interested in anything small. At the same time, Shah had become friendly with Rao's son, who had worked as a paralegal for a prestigious New York law firm. They began to discuss whether some aspects of legal work could be outsourced more efficiently globally. At the time, legal services represented a $500 billion market, dominated by a relatively small number of US and UK law firms, which represented more than half the global market.

Shah decided to talk his way into a position that would actually pay him to do the research he needed to do to understand if his hunch had merit. So he walked over to the Harvard Law School campus one summer day and pitched the idea of doing a research project for a law school research center. The way legal services are being bought and sold, Shah argued, was an enormous pain point for both sides. If the law school wanted to better understand the current state of the market, he, a fresh-eyed HBS graduate, would conduct an in-depth field study. His inexperience in the legal industry, he told the law school, was an advantage. He offered a clean slate, no preconceived notions. He could deconstruct what was off-kilter in the supply and demand of the legal world, and he could do so with the analytical skills of an HBS grad. The law school offered Shah $1,000 per month and travel expenses for the project—but also something more valuable: the Harvard Law School calling card to get into the offices of the general counsels of some of the *Fortune* 100 companies to learn from the world's most significant buyers of legal services.

From the general counsels' perspective, one of their biggest gripes was the fact that they typically had to pay law firms from $300 to $1,000 and up an hour for legal work, work they often commissioned only when they were faced with large litigation cases and were desperate for help. Not only that, but they were also forced to pay for every minute of time chalked up on an assignment by the most junior of lawyers. "Why do I have to pay three hundred dollars an hour for a kid who just walked out of law school to actually learn on my dime?" the general counsels griped. "If anything, law firms should be paying us for training their associates."

Lawyers were unhappy. Clients were unhappy. It was a $500 billion market. In India, recent law graduates were unhappy as well. India produced twice as many English-speaking law school graduates as the United States did every year, all with similar common-law training, but the very large majority of whom could not find jobs as lawyers. So there was a third major pain point.

Shah believed he had finally found the right intersection of his commitment to start a big business, his personal sales and analytical skills, and three large pains to alleviate. The opportunity fueled his natural ambitions—he began to envision turning the provision of legal services on its head.

"Think big! Thinking small is a crime," is one of Shah's favorite sayings. He began to sketch out what he calls his *"Ocean's 11* strategy," named after the George Clooney, Brad Pitt, and Matt Damon movie about pulling off the ultimate heist of a Las Vegas casino by assembling the eleven individuals with the perfect combination of skills needed to accomplish each part of the caper. What skills did he need, and who were the best people—in the world—to provide them?

Shah decided first that he would need to attract investors and advisers who as a group knew all the important facets of the industry but could also make the initial investment in the business, help shape the strategy, and even get into the trenches when execution help was needed. Shah believed he could do no better than to hold Rao to his promise that he'd be a seed investor. "He was the linchpin of my *Ocean's 11* strategy," Shah recalls. Not only had Rao built and sold MphasiS after it reached more than ten thousand staff, but he also had critical financial services contacts as the former head of Citicorp in India, and Citi was one of the world's largest consumers of legal services. Rao's willingness to make a few strategic phone calls and put his personal stamp of approval on Shah and the fledgling start-up would put them in a different league and be essential in recruiting the other *Ocean's 11* players. Rao agreed, and Shah's strategy was in motion.

With each successful recruit, he had more star power to recruit the next dream team name. Their credibility became his credibility. And Shah convinced his advisers to put in at least $100,000 to show skin in the game and have a piece of the future "Microsoft of outsourcing," as Shah put it.

Shah's own youth, highlighted by a youthful appearance, was mitigated by the gray hair on his advisory board. He also used his borrowed credibility and big vision to attract top industry executives to join a top-notch management team and make a key acquisition in the United States to kick-start the new venture's sales.

In the six years since, Shah has opened operations in India, New York, Chicago, and Washington, DC—with plans to open in other major cities in the next few years—but these three US cities alone represent over two-thirds of the revenue potential for Clutch. The company has grown even during the global recession that hit almost immediately after he launched Clutch Group. "Markets go up, and they go down," he says, noting that this is precisely what gave him the opportunity in the first place. Clutch Group now counts *Fortune* 100 companies and leading global law firms among its clients.[7]

But keeping up with changing markets hasn't derailed Shah. "The bottom line is, you have to stick with it," he says, recalling how his sales experience prepared him for running his own company. "That's become our DNA: we are a company of people who don't give up, no matter what." Shah is quick to repeat his favorite quote from Sylvester Stallone's eponymous character in *Rocky:* "It ain't about how hard you can hit; it's about how hard you can get hit and keep moving forward . . . That's how winning is done!"[8]

———————

Abhi Shah's experience illustrates some important implications of defining entrepreneurship as extraordinary value creation and capture. One of these is the drive, aspiration, and ambition, terms related to Shah's thinking big, to envisioning the achievement of something extraordinary. As we see in numerous examples of entrepreneurship, striving to accomplish a big vision is one of the drivers of the creation and capture of extraordinary value, and the opposite belief that something is impossible (or worthless or stupid, as we will see later) is its inhibitor. Throughout *Worthless,* I will ask from time to time where entrepreneurs get their burning ambition, but it is clear that ambition and expertise are intertwined; it is just not clear whether expertise leads to ambition, or the other way around, or both.

That entrepreneurship, even technical entrepreneurship, can thrive without expertise is illustrated in the story of how non-engineer Oliver Kuttner achieved one of Peter Diamandis's "crazy technological breakthroughs" to win $5 million from the X PRIZE Foundation.

The X PRIZE Foundation is about nothing if not about thinking big: the nonprofit's unique mission is to "bring about radical breakthroughs for the benefit of humanity, thereby inspiring the formation of new industries and the revitalization of markets that are currently stuck due to existing failures or a commonly held belief that a solution is not possible."[9] In short, the X PRIZE is challenging people to attempt to achieve what most of us believe to be impossible. As we see throughout *Worthless,* "impossible" can be a lead indicator for entrepreneurial opportunity.

A few years ago, Kuttner, a real estate developer, car hobbyist, and car dealer, heard about an X PRIZE for cars and set for himself the far-fetched goal of winning it. Oliver Kuttner, too, believed that not being the biggest technical expert could actually help him achieve what experts would have told him could not be done. The radical breakthrough objective of the Progressive Corporation X PRIZE for cars was to build a car that had mileage greater than 100 miles per gallon (MPG), carried four adult passengers, had four wheels, had a range of over two hundred miles, went from zero to sixty miles per hour in less than fifteen seconds, met the

Consumers Union's dynamic safety standards and emission requirements, and could be mass manufactured. A "radical breakthrough" indeed!

If he could win the long-shot prize, it would be a manageable hop from there, Kuttner reasoned, to building an innovative (yes, innovative) car business. But of course, he had one small detail to take care of to achieve that big vision: he had to build the "impossible" car to win the prize.

With ambition lit, Kuttner decided to assemble a team that would start by completely reconceptualizing every aspect of how a car moved, was operated, and was built, thus standing automotive engineering wisdom on its head. Although Kuttner had aspired to be an engineer in college, his first job out of college was to run a body shop. He nevertheless recognized that "the best body shop owner only does so much in his life," he recalls. So he next bought a used-car dealership, which in turn led to buying and selling classic Italian cars. He was himself a case study in buying low and selling high, seeing value where others saw junk. "I got into Italian cars when nobody cared about them," he recalls. "I bought a Ferrari convertible for two thousand dollars. Now it's worth millions of dollars." Soon he expanded to become a BMW, Porsche, and Audi dealership.

Apparently not one to sit still, Kuttner started to dabble in weekend automobile racing. For four years, he threw himself into International Motorsport, as driver, team owner, and team manager. Racing was exciting, not only because of the speed per se. "Speed is about efficiency," he says. "Racing compresses time—every decision you make gives you immediate feedback." Every mistake and every improvement get magnified.

Although he had long ago given up all thoughts of becoming an engineer, Kuttner's appreciation for the profession only grew. "Good race car engineers are brilliant people," he says. "They're very serious about doing a good job, building good-quality things, thinking thoroughly about problems. It becomes a work ethic."

When Kuttner read about the X PRIZE, he saw his chance to make a mark, and he decided then and there he was going to win, engineer or not. "I know what I want, and that's what really counts," he recalls. "I can *hire* engineers."

Tapping his contacts in the auto industry, Kuttner, like Shah, assembled his own *Ocean's 11* team of world-class experts, many of them agreeing to moonlight just for the challenge. They were together set on making something that would boggle the judges' minds, not "just" meet the X PRIZE specs.

The team began to take apart the automotive incumbents' assumptions about automobiles. "We looked at all the data [about technology and speed and strength], and we thought, people are just missing this!" Kuttner recalls. The most striking finding was that improving the efficiency of the engine, where most car manufacturers had focused, is not nearly as important to gas mileage as is the efficiency of the car itself. The team focused on making the car "light and slippery."

It took three years of working in rented facilities in Lynchburg, Virginia, an hour from Kuttner's hometown of Charlottesville—and working virtually with team members in Detroit, Salt Lake City, Chicago, Germany, and, eventually, Italy—for Kuttner's new company, Edison2, to accomplish what it set out to do. The team developed a car so lightweight and aerodynamic that you could push it with one thumb, providing eight pounds of pressure (as the crew chief for Edison2 did for the efficiency test at the X PRIZE competition). To demonstrate the impact of the radically new design, they took an engine out of a Smart Car and put it in the Edison2, which led to an immediate increase in mileage from 41 to 89 miles per gallon, compared with the same engine inside the original Smart Car. And because of its "slipperiness," the Edison2 car was also able to sustain crashes: the diamond-shaped car deflects the impact rather than absorbing it, thereby avoiding being crushed.

There were 111 teams from around the world that entered the X PRIZE competition in 2008. But in September 2010, Kuttner's car won half of the $10 million purse, the other $5 million shared with the two runners-up. None of the three winners, by the way, was from one of the established carmakers. Kuttner, the guy who dabbled in cars outside his day job, had beaten automotive engineering experts from all around the world.

Whether this breakthrough can be translated into an entrepreneurial venture is still unclear. But that is Kuttner's intention—he has used Edison2's know-how and track record to license its intellectual property to bigger players, and he has $8 million of his own capital sunk in the venture for skin in the game. The company's current car model, he says, already makes the X PRIZE winner look like a museum piece. One version is an electric vehicle prototype that uses a ten-kilowatt battery (compared with, say, the twenty-four-kilowatt battery used in the Nissan Leaf) and gets the equivalent of 245 miles per gallon.

As the Edison2 technology has evolved, the company has become "energy-source agnostic." The breakthrough, Kuttner reiterates, is in the car itself, not the engine. After looking closely at the relationship between weight, drag, and efficiency, the team realized that the keys to ultimate efficiency were low weight and low aerodynamic drag. Batteries, it turns out, weigh enough to make a negative difference. If the car is light enough, it takes such little energy to accelerate that there is very little available for regeneration; in other words, being light and strong is the key. In the future, Edison2 might even dabble in hybrid, diesel, solar, or natural-gas cars. Kuttner has recognized that different types of cars have different advantages in different situations: highway cruising, stop-and-go traffic, and so on. One completely reimagined car might not be the answer for every kind of driving.

Kuttner has a long road ahead to convince paying customers that his cars are necessary for them. Whereas his original lack of expertise in automobile engineering was probably an advantage rather than a disadvantage, the inertia and skepticism of a traditional industry is a challenge. He'll have to convince investors, customers, and business partners that what he has built has the potential to be enormously valuable. "Whether we become the next Apple or just a footnote in history," he observes, "remains to be seen."

———————————

Entrepreneurs like Shah and Kuttner are able to use their confidence in themselves and their visions to convince others to believe in them, to see the world the way they see it, even if it doesn't make sense at first. Personal expertise in law, engineering, science, or finance is not necessarily the critical variable. Robert Wessman saw the global market leadership potential in the tiny Icelandic generics maker partly because he came from entirely outside the industry. Shah, neither a lawyer nor a software engineer, was trying to build the Microsoft of outsourcing (recently Shah has switched to using "the Apple of Outsourcing"). Nor is Kuttner an engineer; he did not even build the X PRIZE winner himself. He built and led a design team to rethink the basics. The entrepreneurs' lack of expertise in their chosen fields may have helped them develop fresh insights, insights not tainted by years of learning what is impossible to achieve.

Although I believe that ignorance is *not* bliss, entrepreneurs, whether experts or not, do need to view a market or an asset with completely fresh eyes to recognize or create new opportunities. Expertise is not essential as a starting point. Of course, today Wessman knows generics as well as anyone—deep industry knowledge is both cause and effect, as much a by-product of the entrepreneurial choice as its cause. As Shah sees it, "Someday I will at least get an honorary law degree!"

CHAPTER 3

Myth #3

Entrepreneurs Must Be Young

It takes a long time to become young.

—**Pablo Picasso**

The G20 has an affiliate called the G20 Young Entrepreneurs' Alliance "to convene each year in advance of the G20 Summit, with the aim of championing the importance of young entrepreneurs to the G20 member nations."[1] In the United States, there is an organization called the Youth Entrepreneurship Council, whose mission it is to "promote entrepreneurship as a means to overcome youth unemployment and underemployment," and it advocates the Youth Entrepreneurship Act.[2] Beyond the United States, youth entrepreneurship programs in the Middle East and Latin America are commonplace. Googling "youth" and "entrepreneurship" yields eighteen million hits, whereas googling "old age" and "entrepreneurship" yields three million. Perhaps the only consolation is that the definition of youth is rising faster than many of us are getting older: the official definition in some countries is thirty-five and under, and the G20 Young Entrepreneur Summit now defines it as forty and under.

I have held discussions with many of these groups, yet I remain puzzled by the powerful singling-out of youth in conjunction with entrepreneurship, and I have yet to see the terms *old, elderly, senior,* or *geriatric* applied to the equally large population of non-youth, among whose ranks some of the best entrepreneurs are to be found as well. But the strength of the youthful stereotype is evidenced by the policy distinctions between "youth" entrepreneurship and the entrepreneurship of "those others." Many of the entrepreneurs in this book could not be considered young. Gabi Meron was forty-four when he launched his first venture, Given Imaging. Carl Bistany was forty-two when he took over as CEO of SABIS. Michael Dimin was fifty-six. Jay Rogers, at thirty-five, was hardly a youth and was much older than the typical MBA graduate. Nahum Sharfman was forty-four. Laurent Adamowicz, fifty-four. Mo Ibrahim, fifty-two. Oliver Kuttner, forty-five. Vinod Kapur was in his fifties.

One interesting "elderly" entrepreneur is Atsumasa Tochisako. During a 2004 conference on the role of banks for improving economic conditions throughout the world, Tochisako began to draw up a plan for how he could build a big business by creating a concept of financial inclusion among the billions of the world's have-nots. Having spent hours listening to what he saw as action-less rhetoric, Tochisako flipped over a piece of paper and began sketching out a business model for his new venture, Microfinance International Corporation (MFIC).[3] This wasn't a twenty-something, jeans-and-sneakers, Silicon Valley start-up youngster planning a social media iApp in the local venture accelerator. This was a Washington, DC–based, fifty-two-year-old, suit-and-tie senior executive who had, one year before, left a thirty-year career at Bank of Tokyo-Mitsubishi to start MFIC. The business plan may have been on the back of the sheet of paper, but it was hardly a spur-of-the-moment impulse.

It was, rather, the culmination of decades of experience at the bank and Tochisako's analysis of an overlooked and untapped segment of the population that could benefit from better financial services than what traditional banks were either willing or able to provide. It had the potential, Tochisako believed, to be a new multi-billion dollar market.

In our popular (and, I believe, inaccurate and even prejudicial) stereotypes about who can and cannot become an entrepreneur, Tochisako had three strikes against him. He was a top executive in a conservative bank, he was Japanese, and he was over fifty.[4]

Yet Tochisako has built a proprietary software platform for handling the hundreds of billions of dollars of cash remittances around the world which, if he succeeds in scaling, will transform hundreds of millions of lives. Already he has raised over $43 million from some of the other most conservative players in the field—players that are betting a lot on MFIC to succeed.

Tochisako initially saw a viable business opportunity to sell services to a segment of the US population that other financial institutions only saw as not worth their while—a large segment of the immigrant Hispanic populations that had neither bank accounts, credit cards, nor credit histories and that were sending billions of dollars back home every year—$60 billion by some estimates. Because of his decades of experience and intimate familiarity with international funds transfers, Tochisako believed there was untapped potential value in these ignored or rejected customers.

Migrant remittances sent to developing countries are a surprisingly large slice of the world economy—the flow is conservatively estimated to be about $300 billion per year, an amount roughly the size of each of the economies of, for example, Switzerland, Singapore, and Chile. In some countries, in fact, such as Mexico, remittances account for up to 20 to 30 percent of the national gross domestic product (GDP). However, the vast majority of both senders and recipients lack bank accounts—the money is seldom put into, say, a savings account to build assets in the destination countries. It simply floats from one pocket to the next, with the remittance intermediary, such as Western Union, taking a high percentage as its fee along the way.

This situation, Tochisako thought, could be turned into something far more valuable for everyone in the chain—the person sending money, the financial intermediary accepting and distributing the cash, the operator of the remittance platform, and the ultimate recipient. By 2006, Tochisako's sketch on the paper was becoming reality in the form of a financial services company that operated outside the traditional channels. By 2012, his venture, MFIC, had reached annual revenues of almost $10 million, employed seventy people, and was enabling transfers between dozens of countries, with mobile remittance services on the way.

———————

Banking was far away from Tochisako's youthful dreams of being an airline pilot. The son of poor Japanese parents, he worked hard enough at school to earn a place at the prestigious Doshisa University of Kyoto, while focusing all of his spare time and energy on preparing to become a pilot when he graduated and putting himself through flying school to obtain his pilot's license.

But Tochisako's timing was ill-fated. In 1976, the year he graduated, the Japanese economy went into a tailspin, and for three consecutive years, no Japanese airlines were hiring. Disappointed, Tochisako accepted the first good position offered to him: a job with Bank of Tokyo. It was not really a place he had imagined himself long term: Bank of Tokyo was one of Japan's most revered, yet conservative, institutions. He did well in his early years there and the bank saw him as a rising star, but his ambivalence caused him to refuse the bank's repeated offers to send him to do his MBA in order to avoid a long term commitment to his employer.

As a dubious reward for his stubbornness, the bank dispatched Tochisako to Mexico as a Spanish-language intern. When he arrived from

Japan with his young bride, speaking no Spanish at all, he was told by his superiors that he was to find his way to a remote Mexican town to study the language at the local university. Being in that Mexican town would radicalize Tochisako's view of poverty and plant the seed for what would decades later become his new venture.

As he practiced his growing language skills, he was befriended by a local street vendor, who one day invited the young Tochisako to his dirt-floored home for dinner. Warmly welcomed by the vendor, his wife, and their three boys, Tochisako enjoyed the simple meal and conversation. It was the youngest child, José, who asked Tochisako if he would be coming back soon. Thinking that he had just made a new little friend, Tochisako's visit had not meant friendship to the boy. "I hope you will come back so we can have meat again," José explained. "Did we eat meat tonight?" Tochisako asked in bewilderment. José pointed to a small, paper-thin sliver on top of the soup, which Tochisako could still not recognize as meat. It had been the first meat José had had in many months.

The chance comment started a train of thought that would rattle around in Tochisako's head for two decades. The street vendor and his family were hardworking, decent people, honest and trustworthy. But they didn't have access to the kind of financial resources that people in other parts of the world counted as everyday options. "The role of the bank should be to add oxygen to every single corner of society and the economy," Tochisako thought. "But the reality of Mexico and many countries, as I would learn, was that even if you worked really hard, you could not get access" to the kind of resources that could help people improve their lives.

Tochisako's hopes of being a pilot gave way to a silent promise to José and the millions of Josés in the world. "That night in my mind," he recalls, "I committed that although I was then a very junior banking officer, I was going to study and become a professional in all aspects of finance. Someday, once I was prepared, I was going to do something, maybe create a new kind of bank, to give good people opportunity."

Over the next few years, after completing his stint in Mexico, Tochi-sako was rotated to Ecuador and Peru. "Every single chance," he says, "I raised my hand and tried to understand as much as I could to become a financial professional as soon as possible." He climbed step by step up the corporate ladder at Bank of Tokyo, becoming at age twenty-eight a financial adviser to the president of Ecuador, among other roles.

When he was in Peru, Tochisako received a postcard from the street vendor, informing him that José had succumbed to a high fever and died. Tochisako was deeply saddened. "It was a reminder of my promise to José," Tochisako recalls, his voice softening.

But Bank of Tokyo had other plans for Tochisako. Every year, he had a new assignment in Latin America, bringing with it experiences that might have discouraged another person. "Every single Latin American country I lived in was full of disturbances—riots, shootings, demon-strations," he recalls. But he absorbed all the details of the communi-ties around him and saw how money—or lack of access to it—shaped economies and societies.

In 1989 he received his first assignment outside a developing economy: Bank of Tokyo in Atlanta. Ironically, Tochisako felt at home in Atlanta, which was then ranked as the second-most dangerous city in the United States. But he also noticed that the large immigrant population eschewed traditional banks—immigrants who held steady blue-collar jobs, yet who had no choice but to rely on expensive paycheck and money remittance services to send money to their families back home.

After two years, Tochisako was called back to Tokyo and given a series of special assignments to revive ailing parts of the bank or disentangle the problems of failing clients, huge manufacturing and trading con-glomerates that the bank, closely aligned with the government, wanted to save from failure. The bank sent Tochisako in alone to resolve these complex problems, sometimes with the fates of tens of thousands of em-ployees in the balance. Each time he completed an assignment, Tochisako would announce to the bank president his intention to resign so that he could start his new venture, and each time the president would tell him that he had just *one* more important task for him to do before Tochisako could go.

Tochisako wasn't getting any younger, but his passion to solve the problem he had seen was only burning brighter. Perhaps most importantly, he had built an unusually comprehensive set of capabilities for identifying critical issues, for navigating complex systems and webs of relationships, for identifying root causes of problems, and for building trust with a group of people who have every reason for suspicion. Tochisako also had learned international banking operations through and through.

In January 2000, when Tochisako approached the president of the bank for what was his ultimate resignation, as he half-expected the president pulled another assignment for Tochisako out of a drawer. Fortunately, this last assignment got Tochisako even closer to his goal: He was being transferred to the Washington, DC, office as the bank's chief US representative. It was there that he finally began to set his ideas in motion and catch up on lost time. At age forty-eight, Tochisako enrolled in a part-time MBA program at George Washington University as the oldest student in class. "I took every single possible class to expedite my graduation," he recalls, "because I knew I didn't have much time left." He graduated, while still holding down his demanding job at Bank of Tokyo, in fifteen months.

As the bank's US representative in the nation's capital, Tochisako frequently attended international conferences on economic development in emerging economies. Those discussions typically addressed immigration, microfinance, and remittance. However, although there was much focus and practical work on the first two, the dialog on remittance seemed to go nowhere. Established money service businesses, such as Western Union, dominated the remittance market, but they charged fees that could go as high as 20 percent per transaction. Discussions to regulate or incentivize the money service businesses to lower their fees for the good of the world were to no avail. "The agencies in DC were at a loss to improve the behavior of remittance services," Tochisako recalls.

But the agencies, Tochisako felt, were missing the point—financial services companies didn't even see the market in the first place. While there were numerous programs to help poor people in faraway countries, the most advanced country in the world had left more than 20 percent of its population unaddressed right at home. And remittance was just one of many services the immigrants needed. There was a huge mismatch between supply and demand.

Indeed, what to Tochisako seemed to be an opportunity, to the American banks seemed a nuisance: people of low net worth who were high credit risks and who needed low-margin financial services. It was not a problem without demand—it was a problem with *unprofitable* demand. The banks could see the value of microfinance in places like India or Brazil, but they couldn't see microfinance as it related to the United States.

Even for those few Hispanic immigrants with bank accounts, using the banks to wire small amounts of money back home was inconvenient in terms of time and cost: a bank wire transfer of $200 could cost $25–$40 for the wire fee, take three days, and require that the recipient have a bank account and pay currency conversion commissions on top. As a result, both banked and unbanked remitters used the ubiquitous money service businesses and became used to paying the exorbitant fees.

Check cashing was a related service with large potential, thought Tochisako. Accurate information about check-cashing activity by the Hispanic immigrant population was difficult to obtain, but ignoring ethnicity, about 180 million checks worth $55 billion were cashed annually in check-cashing businesses in the United States, disproportionately by low-income earners, generating $1.5 billion in fees. Most check cashing was handled by small corner-store operations. Check-cashing services were in turn closely associated with payday lending, by which small loans were available to people for short periods at rates that could exceed 300 percent per annum.

Tochisako began to formulate a new financial model for this large population—like Oliver Kuttner and Carl Bistany, deconstructing an established industry and completely reconceptualizing it. "I know my chances of success will be less than fifty percent because nobody has ever accomplished this," Tochisako says. "But I'm betting all my expertise and know-how that I can make this work."

With $430,000 from savings, friends, and cofounders, Tochisako established Microfinance International Corporation (MFIC) in 2003—to a resounding chorus of skepticism, which his colleagues expressed in no uncertain terms. At his good-bye party at Bank of Tokyo, his mentor at the bank told him, "I can guarantee you that out of one million bankers, no one could ever think about what you are about to do. We are guaranteeing you a brighter future and income if you stay with us. Why throw everything away? Why stay in a foreign country and do business with the bottom of society?" But Tochisako believed that it was exactly his years of banking experience in Latin America and his fluent Spanish that uniquely equipped him for the successful launch of his new venture.

The idea was to use a money-transfer software platform, developed by an Ecuadorian banking software company owned by a trusted friend and used by dozens of Latin American banks, to offer simple, quick online funds transfer at minimal cost, passing savings on to the United States–based customers, who would repay MFIC with their loyalty and purchase of additional services. Customers would benefit from reduced fees, and MFIC would benefit from a profitable bundle of services, including check cashing, insurance, and microloans, and because all of these services utilized the same underlying platform, MFIC could profitably charge fees of, for example, $10 for a transfer, whereas Western Union would charge four or even five times as much for the same transfer. Tochisako and his staff also went out of their way to make customers feel welcome, respected, and appreciated when they came in for services. Tochisako even located MFIC's first Washington branch, a yellow-and-orange-painted building, adjacent to Western Union's gray office, to emphasize the difference.

But as we will see in subsequent chapters, entrepreneurship that has the potential to create extraordinary value almost always encounters market inertia and resistance, and MFIC was no exception. "Acquiring the first customers was particularly difficult," Tochisako says. "How would we get Hispanic immigrants to trust a new organization set up by a Japanese expatriate?" MFIC's first attempts to draw in customers through ads in local papers were complete failures. So Tochisako and his staff walked through the neighborhoods of Washington, DC, handing out flyers that played up their low fees to El Salvador because of the heavy local El Salvadoran population. The slow trickle of individual customers willing to try out the cheaper remittance services slowly grew into a flow as word of mouth brought in friends and relatives. By the end of 2006, MFIC had fifty thousand customers, prototypically male immigrants with a low but stable income, lacking financial literacy, and uncomfortable interacting with large, impersonal bank branches.

MFIC has since grown significantly, acquiring a few small remittance companies in other states, cutting deals with multinational banks and wireless carriers to allow them to use the MFIC platform for a fee, and raising capital to fund both operational expenses as well as loans. From less than $1 million in revenues in 2006 to nearly $10 million in 2011, the company has seen growth that, Tochisako optimistically believes, is just starting. Transactions are growing almost exponentially.

None of MFIC's capital has come from venture capitalists, who see the new venture as an aberration. In fact, skepticism has come in geographical waves. "New York investors had no idea about the existence of the big demand—they didn't know or didn't want to see it," Tochisako says. Wealthy Latin American investors, who Tochisako hoped would see the opportunity more clearly, were unwilling to back him, he says:

"They said, 'I have climbed up the stairs. Why do I need to help others by investing in you?'" Other investors have signed investment contracts, only to renege at the last moment, leaving Tochisako to again and again bet MFIC's future on his abilities to sell his concept to Japanese investors, who believe in Tochisako, his vision, his reputation, and the capabilities he had honed over his decades at Bank of Tokyo.

Whether that is enough to help Tochisako succeed is not clear: The path for him, as it is for most entrepreneurs, has been rough at times. Epilogue: Surprisingly to me, in 2012 Tochisako resigned from MFIC in response to a fundamental disagreement with the board of directors about future MFIC strategy. But he is undeterred in realizing his original vision. As of late 2012, he was working with a family-owned Midwest-based bank with a common vision to raise $20 million in funds to continue the ideas he initiated at MFIC. He's also in the early stages of expanding a smaller business he founded alongside MFIC in 2003, MicroManos. The company had focused on supporting immigrant job hunters, but Tochisako, now in his late fifties, plans to expand its branch-based financial services and move to a more web- and technology-based services approach, such as by using mobile phones and the internet to launch new types of loan programs that can satisfy most immigrants' financial needs.

As Tochisako illustrates, the process of building any institution designed to ignore all conventional wisdom is a messy, iterative one. Risk is an inescapable part of building any venture that has the potential for great rewards. It might take Tochisako years to do it, but he is intent on keeping the promise he made those decades ago in Mexico.

———————

Entrepreneurship is an equal opportunity employer. It's not just Tochisako who is proving the exception to the supposed rule about entrepreneurship being the province of the young. Joining many of our protagonists in this book, Colonel Harland Sanders was in his sixties when he started the Kentucky Fried Chicken chain, and Ray Kroc was in his fifties when he began building the McDonald's franchise system. Arianna Huffington started the successful website *The Huffington Post* when she was fifty-five.

Still, the powerful stereotype of the young entrepreneur endures. Maybe it's because Bill Gates, Steve Jobs, Michael Dell, and Mark Zuckerberg were so successful in their youth. Yet even most of these iconic young entrepreneurs relied on "adult supervision" in the early growth years, hiring experienced hands to help them navigate the tricky start-up waters. Perhaps it's because television and movies have glamorized the idea that entrepreneurship is best practiced by the young before they are tainted by years of learning the way the world works, rather than how it should work.

But the evidence does not support the stereotype. In 2008, researcher Vivek Wadhwa showed that the number of founders older than 50 was double the number of founders younger than 25.[5] The average age was 40 for men, 41 for women. In fact, Wadhwa's study revealed that the highest rate of entrepreneurial activity had shifted to baby boomers in the 55–64 age group—a trend he predicted would continue for several years to come. A more recent report by the Kauffman Foundation revealed that people aged 55 to 64 starting new businesses were a growing segment, with that age group accounting for nearly 23 percent of new entrepreneurs in 2010, compared with fewer than 15 percent in 1996.[6] Admittedly, because these studies tend to look at company formation and not necessarily at value creation, much of what they are reporting is about small businesses for self-employment only. However, in a study published in the journal *Psychology and Aging,* researchers at the University of Oregon recently concluded that people reach their competitive peak—their willingness to risk their knowledge, skills, and monetary reward in competition—at age 50.[7] Researchers in France and Israel recently surveyed 545 managers and reported that peak vitality and motivation in organizations was reached at 57.[8] And a study of over 200 start-ups in Sweden showed that 10 to 15 years of industry experience in the founding team (that means, not youth) is positively correlated to the growth of the firm.[9]

The more I think about it, the less it makes sense to me that the best age for entrepreneurship is predictable at all, or that the sectors or types of entrepreneurship should be much influenced by how old an entrepreneur is. Figure 3-1 makes the point: when people have the least to lose—the least to risk—they are still relatively young. No mortgages, no kids' college tuitions to pay, no families to support, no expectations of maintaining a comfortable lifestyle. But people are also the least capable at that age—they have less experience in knowing how to build organizations, less leadership experience in motivating teams, less-developed professional networks, less professional credibility, less

FIGURE 3-1

Relationship between age and entrepreneurial capability

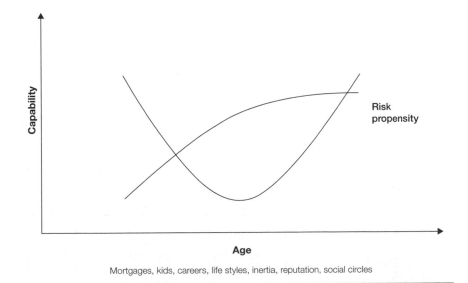

industry knowledge, less capability for judgment, and less understanding of how customers think and behave. A *Wall Street Journal* article in 2005 summarized dozens of studies on aging, concluding that although there is some cognitive deficit associated with advanced age, the elderly use information more effectively, making decisions less tainted by emotion, for example.[10]

The age where we might be better placed to start new, risky ventures is middle age—but that's the time in life when our personal tolerance for risk is lowest—children are entering college, retirement funds need to be built, careers are at a peak—because there is more to lose. As our tolerance for risk increases as those responsibilities are tended to, we are getting older and older.

The ideal time to start a business "should" be at age 70! Indeed, Silicon Valley's *Mercury News* recently described the rampant age discrimination among entrepreneurs and their backers. The legendary venture capitalist, Sequoia's Mike Moritz, described himself as a fan of ". . . 20-somethings starting companies . . . They don't have distractions like families and children and other things that get in the way of business."[11] Very successful serial entrepreneur Sandy Kurtzig, in her sixties, declines to specify her age as she is launching her new venture, raising capital, and recruiting people, explaining, "I don't want to advertise it."[12]

A priori prescriptions about *who* has the ability to be an entrepreneur, *when* the person should make the entrepreneurial choice, or *what* he or she can achieve run counter to the conception of entrepreneurship as contrarian; extraordinary value is created and captured by people doing what other people think is worthless to do. Our stereotypical entrepreneur is one of an innovative youngster with powerful product, preferably supported by novel technology. Yet a large number of real-life entrepreneurs around the world aren't major innovators and aren't necessarily technical experts, and many start their businesses well past their twenties and thirties. Can innovation, youth, and expertise be assets for an aspiring entrepreneur? Perhaps; perhaps not.

Generalizations about who can and cannot become entrepreneurs, and where they can do it, are not only self-limiting, but empirically elusive as well in part because entrepreneurship is about exceptions. So there may not be anything meaningfully typical about entrepreneurs at all. They certainly don't *need* to be young. They don't need to be an expert in something. And they don't need to be innovators. Those are myths.

Judging from my MBA students from Harvard, Babson, Reykjavik, Technion, and Columbia, and hundreds of people in dozens of countries, entrepreneurship that is ambitious, hard driving, and aspiring to create and capture extraordinary value is something that many of us can do if we want to badly enough. But we have to be willing to go against the grain, to look for value where the majority of people do not see it, and to do something that may seem crazy until it is a success, as the next chapter will show.

PART TWO

RUNNING AWAY FROM THE CROWD

If *everyone* tells you it is a good idea, run the other way.

—Jay Rogers, Local Motors

Many of today's most successful companies were launched by entrepreneurs during particularly inauspicious economies (Microsoft is one oft-cited example) or in the most inauspicious markets. One estimate is that half of the *Fortune* 500 and half of the *Inc.* list of fast growing companies started in such circumstances.[1] On the surface, this should seem strange to us because one of the most important skills we want entrepreneurs to have is the ability to assess markets for their attractiveness prior to entering into new business lines or ventures: the more attractive, the better. Obvious, right? Evidently, this lesson does not hold for entrepreneurs, who, failing to listen to the "experts," time and again transform unattractive industries in unattractive times into attractive opportunities. Entrepreneurs thrive in adversity; I guess they didn't get the memo!

There are several possible explanations for the relationship between entrepreneurship and bad times: One is that exiting competitors leave a less crowded market. Another is that as a result, entrants can pick up people, companies, property, and other assets cheaply. A third is that the swelling ranks of the unemployed leave many people no choice but to strike out on their own. And a fourth is that starting a company in a recession allows only the hardiest ventures to succeed based on a particularly compelling value proposition, while at the same time inoculates the venture against future downturns by creating toughness and frugality.

All of the above explanations are good candidates, but regardless of which we prefer, there is a surprisingly ubiquitous relationship between adversity and entrepreneurship. The overarching reason is that the process of entrepreneurship is seeing value where no one else does, and persistently refusing to cave to the naysayers. That means that entrepreneurs are always bucking the current, going against fashion, doing what the rest of us think is not worth doing.

That also implies that even those who make their living backing big "winners" get it wrong a lot by betting on losers or by missing some huge wins because the ventures just seemed too ridiculous or even crazy.

One of the world's oldest and most successful venture capital firms, Bessemer Venture Partners (BVP), has invested in some of the world's biggest winners, such as Staples, Skype, and Celtel, and the partners are justifiably proud of these wins. But with uncharacteristic humor for often dry hard-headed venture capitalists, BVP also wryly publicizes its "anti-portfolio," all of the now wildly successful companies that the firm's partners thought were too ridiculous to invest in.[2] "[BVP's] long and storied history has afforded our firm an unparalleled number of opportunities to completely screw up."[3]

Google was one such huge miss. One of BVP's partners had a friend who rented her garage to founders Sergey Brin and Larry Page for their first year. In 1999 and 2000, she tried to introduce the partner to "these two really smart Stanford students writing a search engine. Students? A new search engine? In the most important moment ever for Bessemer's anti-portfolio, the partner asked her, 'How can I get out of this house without going anywhere near your garage?' Another miss: eBay. 'Stamps? Coins? Comic books? You've *got* to be kidding. No-brainer—pass.' BVP passed on Intel, Apple, FedEx, and PayPal. FedEx's Fred Smith approached BVP seven times and was turned down every time."

It should give us pause that even the most highly trained professionals, with decades of experience in sorting the truly crazy no-brainer passes from the true game changers, frequently miss the boat. This huge difficulty in distinguishing value from folly in early stages is one of the big entrepreneurship puzzles I will try to shed light on in the last chapters of *Worthless, Impossible, and Stupid.*

As BVP's admirably honest anti-portfolio shows, very frequently the bigger the opportunity, the bigger the contrarian element. Entrepreneurs pursue, create, and capture extraordinary value in spite of overwhelming negative feedback from the best professionals, the tops in their fields, not to mention "helpful" friends who know with certainty that the idea will never work. As it turns out, it is exactly those outliers that have the potential to become the most successful (and the least successful as well). And these statistical aberrations are doomed to elude systematic selection processes. Entrepreneurship, and the process of betting on it, may be impossible to systematize, precisely because of its contrarian nature. It requires an enormous leap of faith by the entrepreneur that he or she has seen something that others miss.

This was Jay Rogers's approach when he launched Local Motors (which, by the way, a former BVP partner passed on as well).

CHAPTER 4

Why the Best Entrepreneurs Seem Crazy

Great wits are sure to madness near allied,
and thin partitions do their bounds divide.

—John Dryden, "Absalom and Achitophel"

In December 2008 Toyota's executives, heads hung in shame, gathered to announce the first losses since 1938—almost \$2 billion—of the world's largest auto manufacturer.[1] Across the Pacific, number two General Motors, the symbol of corporate America, had just taken out an emergency federal loan, approved by presidential order. Rumors of impending GM bankruptcy were rife—predictions that were to come true a few months later. These were the darkest few months in all of automotive history. These were also the months during which Jay Rogers was convincing private investors to back his new car company. Not a green electric vehicle or a hybrid, but a gasoline-powered sedan.

Was it an untimely choice to launch a car company at exactly the same moment the global auto industry was on its knees? Many would think

untimely too soft a word; how about foolhardy? When Rogers founded
Local Motors, a car company that uses crowdsourcing to design its cars
and then allows customers to come to the factory to finish the manufacturing of their own car, he was interested in doing what nobody thought
made sense; in part his confidence that he was on the right track was
because nobody thought it made sense.

That's something I repeatedly emphasize to my students. It is the job
of the entrepreneur to sniff out and realize opportunity that is overlooked, undervalued, or even berated by others. One of the times that
this is most evident is when industries, such as the automotive industry,
are falling apart.

The lesson hit home for Rogers, who signed up for my Harvard Business School class in 2007 to help prepare himself to launch his venture.
"If everybody knew it was a good idea, then somebody would already
have tried it," he explains. Don't expect any applause at the start.

As *Worthless*'s protagonists illustrate time and again, very few opportunities excite anyone other than the entrepreneur at first. This is inherent in the process of recognizing and formulating what an opportunity is, and is at the heart of the contrarian perception of extraordinary
value.

In just four years, Local Motors has managed to convince paying customers that Rogers's view of the market was right. Some 140 of them
have ordered their own Rally Fighter at about $75,000 per car, with
five per month (and increasing) regularly rolling out of the Local Motors microfactory in Phoenix and numerous special projects underway to
build special car fleets for companies and license the Local Motors technology to large vehicle makers. Sixty Rally Fighters have already been
released "into the wild," as Rogers puts it. Along the way, Rogers raised
nearly $12 million from private investors. That's not to say it has been
easy; many experienced investors simply shook their heads in disbelief
at Rogers's wrongheadedness. But Local Motors's $15 million sales pipe-

line in December 2012 suggests that those skeptics just might have been wrong.

———————

Jay Rogers had never been interested in taking the easy road. After graduating from Princeton University, he helped his father build a biomedical testing business in China (which failed) and then did a stint in finance. With an offer from Stanford Business School in hand, Rogers asked to defer his admission so that he could first serve as an officer in the US Marine Corps. When Stanford denied his request, he joined the marines anyway and spent most of the next five years in Iraq, Afghanistan, and other areas of the Middle East.

The impression it made on him was formative: "I saw the roots of major geopolitical conflicts coming down to oil," he recalls, and oil had a lot to do with cars—how they were used and how they were made. Rogers had long been interested in the auto industry. His grandfather invested in and ran the Indian Motorcycle Company in the 1940s and, then, according to Rogers, lost every cent he put into it. Rogers's family was used to putting its own views of opportunities to the acid test and understood that it is easy to get burned.

When he finished his tour of duty, in 2005 Rogers entered Harvard Business School with the idea that it was the way cars were made, not how they were designed, that could be revolutionized. Unlike some of his classmates who used business school to get the basics of business and create useful contacts among students, Rogers designed his time there as his own personal entrepreneurship boot camp. Every class he took, the summer job in a consulting firm's automotive practice, and his field study projects prepared him to start his own car business. "You can make business school as hard as you want it to be," he recalls. "I wanted to steel myself for launching a successful business when I graduated."

In his second year Rogers and a classmate with auto industry experience were awarded a $25,000 grant from the Social Enterprise Initiative at HBS for a study to reinvent how automobiles were made. Rather than making increasingly large plants and assembly lines more efficient through scale and industrial engineering, Rogers and his partner wanted to break down automobile manufacturing into small-batch cells in localized manufacturing facilities that would profitably produce a small number—a few thousand—of any particular design. Furthermore, the local microfactory would involve a global community of designers with the local community of customers, to give customers a unique connection with their cars, even to the point of being involved in making the car that they had ordered and would drive and take care of.

Rogers and his partner visited Ford and the other incumbents, as well as tech-oriented start-ups such as Tesla, to learn as much as possible about the status quo and pain points. "The thing I saw missing," Rogers recalls, "was that none of them really knew exactly who their customers were." One noteworthy exception was Factory Five, a profitable Wareham, Massachusetts–based venture that specialized in manufacturing car kits that customers could assemble themselves. Factory Five had built an online customer community by actively mining digital forums for ideas; at any given time, you could count on seven hundred to a thousand people participating in a discussion. This level of engagement surpassed what any major auto company had been able to achieve, and it fed Factory Five's novel business model, which was based on the community having significant input into the company's decisions about which cars they should be putting on the road. Factory Five's success in building this user community was eye-opening to Rogers and his cofounder, and as graduation neared, the partners modified their business plan to make user and customer involvement the core of their company.

But as the countdown to turning their idea to reality ticked away, doubts began to gnaw at Rogers: Were they really onto something new and worthy? Were they both equally committed to the uncertainty and sacrifices awaiting them? Or would it be wiser to relegate their business plan to the ranks of filed documents, an interesting idea backed by the kind of numbers that every second-year MBA knows how to pull out of thin air? After all, they were two students challenging a century-old industry. Were they naive, audacious, or prescient? Were they on the path to throwing away their expensive degrees?

"As a marine officer," Rogers says, "I believed that you needed supreme commitment before going into combat, especially against an unclear threat." So he and his partner agreed to take twenty-one days for soul-searching and talks with their spouses before deciding if they were ready to commit to each other and start off down a one-way street.

Those were difficult days for Rogers. He had six-figure job offers in consulting and venture capital in hand; the steady income would earn him the chance to pay off his business school bills, as well as the respect of his classmates. At the same time, "I didn't have any 'go to hell' money," Rogers recalls; not to mention that he and his wife had two small children. At thirty-five and older than most MBAs, he realized that all the arrows were pointing away from taking a serious entrepreneurial risk. But having a talented partner as committed as he was would tip the balance in his decision.

Or so he thought.

At 9 a.m. on commitment day, his partner knocked on Rogers's door in tears. "I'm not going to do this. It's just a hard and risky idea on a piece of paper," his partner said, having stayed up all night with his wife in discussion. "I have to decide whether to launch a business with no funding and no cofounder," he told every person he could get hold of for advice. "Is this a dumb thing to do?"

"Without exception, everyone told me I was nuts. Nobody was going to say this was smart," Rogers says. "Not even my wife."

But the warnings made Rogers want it even more. Although I take neither responsibility nor credit, Rogers tells me now that he heard *my* voice, in the back of his mind, telling him something I've said to all my students: "If everyone tells you it's a good idea, run the other way." Which is *not* to say that the converse is true: "If everyone tells you it's a bad idea, then it must be good." If everyone at a party says that you have had too much to drink, don't argue, just hand over the car keys.

Many potential entrepreneurs find themselves with the same agonizing dilemma as Rogers did that day; in fact, the most talented of them, those whom society and investors and customers would want to become entrepreneurs, are often the ones who have the most enticing alternatives to setting off down the risky entrepreneurial path. These are the successful, highly paid future executives whose talents are in high demand and whose phones ring with headhunters' inquiries. They are the best MBA graduates being wooed by world-famous investment banks and consulting firms, the experienced and innovative engineers, scientists, and consultants with offers of nice compensation packages to pay off their school debt and give security to their young families. Of course, there is no right answer for any of them: The choice to become an entrepreneur is difficult and personal, and sometimes problematic to justify rationally.

––––––––––

Rogers called the consulting firm and the venture capital firm and declined their offers, and the jilted employers were not gracious in rejection, particularly the venture capitalists. "They told me I was being absurd," Rogers says. "It was hard enough without that."

Rogers was just beginning to experience for himself what most successful entrepreneurs also experience, repeatedly: they and their opportunities are greeted not with open arms and smiles, but with doors slamming in their faces, sometimes by their closest friends, allies, and mentors. Those slammed doors should not be mistaken as signs that there is no opportunity there; in fact, a slammed door can be impetus for the entrepreneur to look for a new door to discover, one with an opportunity behind it.

Rogers was able to ignore the plethora of doubters because he believed in his own ability not only to see value, but also to create it—to turn his "preposterous" plans of teaching a lesson to the automotive industry and making a new car in a new way, so compelling a car that people would not just buy it, but would make it with pride and fall in love with it. Rogers was sure that his own experience and skills could help him bring together the resources to deliver to car owners a product and an experience that the large automobile companies simply couldn't.

Rogers had a glass of wine to celebrate his decision, expecting to feel liberated in the morning. Instead, he felt like hell: "I just made the most ridiculous choice in the world," with neither savings nor partner nor job options.

Luckily, along the way, Rogers had discovered one lifeline: a New York investor believed enough in Rogers's leadership and concept that he offered to invest $1 million. But disappointment in the form of a huge expectation gap was quick to replace comfort: the investor was asking for a 90 percent stake, a non-starter for Rogers's anticipation of blood, sweat, and tears, who would also need stock options in order to entice other talent to join him later. Swallowing hard, Rogers declined. "I didn't sleep that night," he recalls. "I just wanted to throw up."

His wife, having eventually agreed to throw herself completely behind Rogers and Local Motors, announced cheerily, "Well, we'll just have to find the money from someone else!"

Rogers turned to Mark Smith, founder of Factory Five. Fulfilling the role of the now-commonplace term *angel* (someone who invests in an early-stage entrepreneurial venture, but more importantly offers guidance and support), Smith offered to provide office and shop space adjacent to his own facility and give Rogers design and engineering support, as well as the advice of his entire management team. And within weeks, a $1 million investment followed.

With his well-researched B-school business plan and the confidence of capital behind him, Rogers began to refine his vision for Local Motors. "Big car companies take a lot of time, have multiple masters to please, have huge fixed costs and capital sunk into factories, and require lots of money for operations," Rogers reasoned. That business model also made it very difficult for them to cope with energy efficiency mandates. Local Motors would do it all backward. Rather than making cars greener themselves, he would make cars in a greener way, cutting down on the resources wasted by large-scale, centralized mass production; long-distance shipping; and huge and wasteful inventories of vehicles then sitting in dealers' lots. A bonus to the emotional connection that Local Motors would give to its customers would be a more sustainable manufacturing process.

Impressed by Factory Five's engaged community, Rogers began to harness the power of community for Local Motors and formed a plan to involve boundary-less digital communities in the global design of producing vehicles locally at on-demand microfactories.

Local Motors was also tapping into a strengthening trend: "The do-it-yourself nation is upon us," Rogers says. If people are engaged in complex weekend projects on their homes or hobbies, he reasoned, why wouldn't they be engaged in the idea of helping to design a dream car—and then showing up at a small, local factory to actually help build it?

Although Local Motors would start small in one location, Rogers planned to scale one microfactory into a national and, later, global chain of community-based microfactories dotting the landscape. There, customers would show up to help build their own cars not too far from where they lived. In manufacturing small numbers of cars instead of massive production lines, Local Motors would design its cars to federal standards, but the small quantity and individual assembly would allow the company to avoid the expensive and lengthy crash-test procedures. Consequently, it could get cars into the market much faster and cheaper, thus requiring less capital.

To launch a virtual car-design community, Rogers connected with the Art Center College of Design in Pasadena. In 2008 the auto industry recession had left an unemployed mass of the best and most creative Art Center designer graduates to tap into. Rogers reached out to them, asking the designers to upload their portfolios to the Local Motors website and to participate in the company's interactive community with fellow car enthusiasts. But when Local Motors' first offer of $500 to uploaders produced underwhelming results, Rogers hired a graduate of the automotive marketing program at Northwood University in Midland, Michigan, to design a site that would encourage the community he sought from die-hard designers.

Apparently the message got across, because serious designers started to join, and within a year, Local Motors had fourteen hundred actively engaged. By April 2008, his first design competition had attracted twenty-two submissions, seven of which came from designers with respected reputations. That first $2,000 prize was awarded to a thirty-year-old transportation designer from Australia, who submitted an off-road performance vehicle dubbed the PanTerra. Within the next few months, Local Motors staged three more contests in other regions, with the designers themselves deciding who would win the prize money.

By the summer of 2008, Rogers upped the ante and engaged the now-enthusiastic community in voting on which design Local Motors would actually build; ideas and opinions flew fast and furious, and online debates were heated. The last thing Rogers wanted was apathy to his first car; he saw the safe consensual choice as the most risky one. He wanted Local Motors' first car to be risqué, daring, something that the Detroit auto industry would never conceive of backing—something some people would even hate. "If some people don't hate it passionately, no one will love it passionately either," Rogers reasoned. This wasn't going to be just a souped-up soccer-parent suburban SUV. The car had to be a high-speed vehicle able to go off-road in desert terrain and operate in intense heat; it had to have a built-in fire extinguisher and boast a sleek body style. Rogers and his team made the final call, which included considerations of manufacturability in Local Motors facilities, ease of compliance with federal safety standards, as well as economics.

The winner was named the Rally Fighter, a fighter-plane-influenced design based on the input of twenty-nine hundred community members from over one hundred countries and looking like something out of a superhero comic strip. Love it or hate it, you certainly couldn't ignore it. "We got the controversy we were looking for," Rogers recalls; some thought the choice was terrible. The winning designer, a graduate of the Art Center, won $10,000.

The venture would sell the cars with the promise and requirement that the owner would spend a couple of three-day weekends in a Local Motors factory. Only two thousand of every design—each car numbered—would be made. If you make your own car, Local Motors told customers, you'll understand your car. And if you understand your car, you'll be a better—and safer—driver in a car that you helped build. And your car will be something to be proud of.

Now all Rogers had to do was convince people to shell out a hefty $59,000—a price that would leave a decent profit for Local Motors—while the auto industry was slashing prices as it continued its tailspin.[2] But that's where Rogers's capabilities, and his own concept of what at least one big segment of car buyers wanted, are helping him turn the perception of an opportunity into the real creation of value. With an inspiring sales pitch replete with novel features for the buyers, and good word of mouth in the auto-enthusiast community, Local Motors has become a reality. The Rally Fighter design and the build-your-own concept are growing in their appeal, and the trickle of orders in the spring of 2009 has turned into a growing flow.

The car-enthusiast community has embraced Local Motors' offbeat approach. One review described the Rally Fighter as "unique in every sense of the word," noting that "even better than that is the fact that this machine is completely street legal and is actually 50-state-emissions compliant."[3] And as planned, the Rally Fighter is more gas efficient than its peers—it gets as much as 20 MPG, compared with, say, 5 or 6 MPG for a military-type vehicle.

In addition, the company has created a new capability along the way: Local Motors has figured out how to design, make, and deliver high-performance cars far more quickly than its competitors. The capability has led to some high-profile wins, such as with the US Department of Defense, from which Local Motors won a challenge bid to design and deliver a prototype combat support vehicle in under four months. Not only was the short time an unprecedented challenge, but Local Motors delivered under the deadline, causing President Barack Obama to single out Local Motors in a televised speech as the promise of America's future in manufacturing:

> "Not only could this change the way the government uses your tax dollars because . . . instead of having a ten-year lead time to develop a piece of [military] equipment, . . . if we were able to collapse the pace at which that manufacturing takes place, that could save taxpayers billions of dollars. But it also could get products out to theater faster, which could save lives more quickly and could then be used to transfer into the private sector more rapidly, which means we could get better . . . products and services that we can sell and export around the world. So it's good for American companies, it's good for American jobs, it's good for taxpayers, and it may save some lives in places like Afghanistan for our soldiers.[4]

"GM, Ford, and Chrysler didn't do that for President Obama," Rogers says. "Local Motors is real."

How has Rogers come this far? He has done so, in part because he combined his view of how things could be made—a view others did not share—with his view of opportunity in an industry that the market was down on. Rogers' unusual leadership capabilities and experiences were part of the equation, too, in converting his seemingly stupid idea into something that would pass the acid test of the marketplace. Through the novelty of his concept and his battle-hardened style, Rogers keeps navigating around roadblocks to pull together the cash, the staff, and the customers to keep his car company on the road.

But let's be honest. Whereas Local Motors is building cars that customers want and the signs are positive that sales will continue to accelerate, as of this writing, Rogers has not yet built what we would call extraordinary value. I personally am optimistic, but Rogers himself knows well that he has hard miles to put in before he can crown his venture a success, before Local Motors is more than a novel idea and a valiant effort.[5] Every month, he and his team work hard to bring in more customers and more investment. He still has the naysayers' skepticism ringing in his ears. Nothing would please Rogers more than proving them all wrong.

———————

Like Jay Rogers but worlds away, Carl Bistany has been battling skeptics, too. While Jay Rogers is creating a significant business by eschewing the traditional automotive assembly line to give a novel consumer experience, the CEO of SABIS has been working in the opposite direction. He is challenging a different traditional model—that of the classroom—by making the process of public education so that it is *more* like the assembly line, not less.[6] Toyota's efficiency and quality are Bistany's benchmark to emulate, not a conservative incumbent to out-innovate. Unlike Rogers's critics, Bistany's aren't would-be investors (his company is privately held). Instead, they are community-based skeptics, including many local leaders, who can air their opinions in highly influential public forums, such as school committees and mainstream newspaper articles, about how we should educate our children.[7] While Local Motors has just started deconstructing car manufacturing, SABIS has taken several generations to prove its contrarian view, and just under Bistany's leadership, SABIS has expanded fifteen-fold into large global markets.

Like Jay Rogers, Carl Bistany and his predecessors have taken a contrarian look at a mature industry—education—to make its impact on society. Building a business opportunity on a novel view of how to educate children, SABIS systematizes the entire educational process so that it can be monitored, measured, resource efficient, and profitable. Indeed, Bistany is determined to have a revolutionary global impact on public and private schools and already manages some notoriously challenging US inner city charter schools, such as in Brooklyn, New York; Springfield, Massachusetts; Flint, Michigan; and New Orleans, to name a few. And SABIS has ambitions to have five million students by 2020.

Not surprisingly, the philosophy and methodology of SABIS Educational Systems arouse fierce debate among those who encounter it, including my own students. To its critics, SABIS seems to bring improbable logic to one of the most important—and polarizing—public policy questions in the world: how do we best educate our children?

Fortunately for Bistany, the facts are favorable. Today, SABIS has 74 schools in fifteen countries; 3,150 teachers and another 1,500 or so staff; 1,600 textbooks in six languages; and 62,000 students. A point of comparison is KIPP (the Knowledge Is Power Program) Academy, much praised as the gold standard for raising the educational performance of students in disadvantaged schools in the United States. SABIS, although much less known than KIPP in the United States, reaches far more students (KIPP has about 39,000), with far fewer schools (KIPP has about 125).[8] Whereas KIPP is a nonprofit originally founded and currently bolstered through charitable donations (about 15 percent of the current total KIPP budget), SABIS is completely self-sustaining and profitable. Although the privately owned company does not reveal its figures, revenues for its charter schools in Springfield are $18.6 million, with net profits of over $1.4 million.[9] Per-school revenues in the United States appear to be in the range of $3 million to $5 million. SABIS schools are typically in the upper percentiles on all outcome measures, including standard test scores and college acceptance rates. And the student and faculty morale are particularly high.[10]

In its United States schools, SABIS serves primarily disadvantaged communities, and none of its students is selected on ability, but instead are chosen for their willingness to learn. Similar to the students at KIPP, the large majority of SABIS students are low-income and minorities, eligible for free or reduced-price meals. But whatever its successes, SABIS's results are not based on outstanding teaching: It is the design and operation of the SABIS *system,* honed over decades, and not the teacher, that drives effectiveness and scale. "We achieve high standards of learning, regardless of whether we are lucky enough to recruit the best teacher," Bistany explains. It's a system comparable, he says, to a well-run Toyota plant. "We all expect every car out of a production line to meet a certain quality standard," regardless of whether the supervisor running that shift is "exceptional . . . So why would we bet the future of our students on the existence of a great teacher? That's why we have created a *system of learning,* where teachers are actors within that system [and] are there to motivate and engage students to help them reach their utmost potential. Like Toyota, it's the system driving the process, not the individual."

It's an uncomfortable assertion for those of us who have gone through, and sent our kids to, an education system that depends on inspiring teachers. In Bistany's view of the world, the individual teachers do not, and should not, matter as much as the system.

SABIS performance speaks for itself, but what really surprised me when I first read about SABIS was where it is based. Not Silicon Valley, New York City, Los Angeles, or Bangalore; SABIS is based in Adma, Lebanon, a small village in the northern periphery of Beirut.

Like modern-day Phoenician traders, the Lebanon-based SABIS has built an education management company with presence in the Middle East and Europe, as well as in the United States, a company for which being profitable is an essential characteristic, not a "nice to have." In fact, when I last spoke to him, Bistany was on his way to Microsoft's headquarters to lay out the case that solving the global educational crisis is one of the big business opportunities in the world. "Today, China graduates about six hundred thousand engineers a year," he explains. "India, about four hundred thousand; the US about seventy thousand. You can see very quickly that the competitiveness of nations is dependent on how well they are able to educate—and not just an elite few, as the US has always done."

SABIS has its roots in the nineteenth century, when a young Lebanese reverend, Tanios Saad, persuaded a middle-aged missionary who was providing relief aid to poor Lebanese women to join him in building a school for girls. Located near Beirut in Choueifat, the school was so successful that the girls surpassed the local boys academically, causing parents to persuade the founders to enroll boys there, too. After a trip to the United Kingdom inspired Saad to emulate the British educational system, the school's performance and reputation grew further, with families throughout the Middle East sending their children to receive what had become a world-class foundation in math, science, and English (the language of instruction).

The Choueifat School stayed in the hands of subsequent generations of the Saad family until 1954, when Charles Saad invited Ralph Bistany, a young physicist, to come for what was supposed to be a short stint to help Saad with both the teaching and, no less important, getting the school's financial house in order. Bistany never left, and he became Saad's business partner as well.

It was Ralph Bistany who laid the groundwork for what has become SABIS's trademark approach to education. As Carl Bistany, Ralph's son, who became CEO in 1996, recalls, it was a combination of the desire to improve society through education and the need to compete against other, better-funded educational institutions (such as Lebanese schools supported by religious organizations, the British Embassy, and the US State Department) that led to SABIS's business model.

Ralph Bistany, the father, spelled out his philosophy when I met the seventy-seven-year-old man in Cairo in 2009:

The business of education is to transfer knowledge from the teacher's head and the textbooks into the kids' heads in the most effective way in the shortest time and at the lowest cost. Treating education as a business creates accountability, quality, and thus continual improvement. In order to transfer knowledge into students' heads, you have to understand what is and is not there before you start. So in 1954, before I taught even my first class, I spent a lot of time finding out exactly what each child did and did not know. It would have been futile to teach advanced concepts if the basic ones were missing. This ultimately led to a very systematic and structured curriculum that was always preceded by checking each student's level of understanding before he or she joined us.

SABIS challenges four widely held beliefs ("myths," according to the Bistanys) about what education could and could not be. When my students, including executives with school-age kids, discuss this case, I am surprised at the level of controversy, even occasional animosity, which the SABIS system generates. It is equaled perhaps only by admiration, by many, for its results and a disbelief, by others, that it in reality generates the results it does.

One belief is that individualized instruction in small classes is best. "Individualized instruction is a misconception," says Carl Bistany. "Even in a small, twenty-student class, a teacher has just a couple of minutes per student in a period, in addition to lecturing and other activities. The only way to really customize instruction so that it precisely addresses the specific concepts that any student has to learn is by dividing the students into small groups to practice and check." The key factor in the learning process is not individual instruction, Bistany argues, but is to teach each very specific concept, have students practice the concept, and then check actual evidence that each student had in fact learned the concept.

Small classes do not allow teachers to do this any more effectively than large classes.

A second belief is that quality education can only be achieved if it is not for profit, because, ostensibly, the profit motive would cause educators to cut corners and sacrifice quality in order to make money. Bistany demurs: "You, the educator and administrator, must have skin in the game to continually improve yourself and enhance your product. Can you imagine if Microsoft or Apple were nonprofits? You would never see the level of creativity, quality, or competitiveness that you see today in those companies. The discipline of profit makes you build better products, and invest in research and development."

The third belief is that the more money governments invest in education and schools, the better; the higher the education budget as a percentage of the overall local or national budget, presumably, the better education policy is. But Bistany believes that less is more: "We want to measure how the kids' reading skills are developing by looking at how many books kids are reading, not how many books have been bought and put in the library."

And finally, memorization is universally disparaged as an important learning strategy. Not so simple, according to Bistany. "Memorization without understanding—yes, that is bad," Bistany says. But memorization is essential for children to build their knowledge bases and understanding.

At the heart of SABIS's teaching methodology is the decomposition of every concept to be learned into numerous fine-grained learning points, the understanding of each one of which can be definitively assessed by the teacher in every classroom session; an example would be "The student is able to define an improper fraction." Bistany explains that the cause of the vast majority of students' bad experiences in our schools—demotivation, boredom, dropping out, bad grades, discipline, and the like—is the result of students being taught more advanced concepts without having *really* learned the more basic ones. For this reason, it is essential that each teacher always knows exactly what each student does and doesn't understand at the resolution of every learning point. The uncompromising emphasis on ongoing fine-grained assessment, using proprietary and uniform software tools across all SABIS schools, means that no teacher is allowed to deviate from the systematically constructed curriculum that SABIS has honed over many years of educating thousands of students from widely varied backgrounds and aptitudes. And SABIS's control system allows Bistany "to pick up the phone [from Lebanon] and ask the school director [in New Orleans], 'Catherine, what's happening in grade two? You have so many kids who are failing, who failed last week and are still failing. What are you doing about it?'"[11]

Anticipating the vocal critics who claim that the SABIS system prevents teachers and students alike from developing their creativity, Bistany does not shy away from viewing teachers as acting out a script SABIS has written for them: "You usually wouldn't want your actors writing the script as they were performing the play; neither do we want our teachers writing the educational script as they are performing in the classroom." Do any of us believe that good acting precludes creativity? Bistany would argue that SABIS teachers are able to exercise as much creativity in the classroom as can any movie actor or opera singer or concert pianist, all of whom follow scripts created by others.

Although he lived in a part of the world that few would consider a launching pad for global winners, early on Ralph Bistany had come to look beyond Lebanon and the rest of the Middle East as markets for SABIS. There were two reasons for this. One was his experience of the tenuousness of SABIS's economic sustainability: SABIS's fragility was lastingly imprinted in his mind during the Lebanese Civil War of 1975, when he had to evacuate the school to Sharjah in the United Arab Emirates.[12] Diversification would be one antidote to this vulnerability. Almost immediately, as Choueifat proved itself in Sharjah, Ralph Bistany opened up additional Choueifat schools in other UAE locations.

Second, Ralph Bistany viewed his mission as no less than to reform the entire process of public education, regardless of location and geography, and over time, Ralph Bistany and Leila Saad had come to view Lebanon and the UAE as just a testing ground for what they would build out to be a much more general concept and methodology for the school, by now renamed SABIS. And there was one more related reason for taking SABIS global: achieving leadership on a world scale would be evidence that the SABIS model was not just some idiosyncrasy, but a generalized system that could be replicated and thus grow to have a global impact. Bistany's vision exemplified the view of private equity pioneer Sir Ronald Cohen: "Your business will grow to the size of your vision."[13]

So driven by a big vision, but having neither a concrete plan nor financial resources to achieve it, Ralph Bistany was very responsive to the suggestion of a Lebanese friend who knew of the Choueifat schools' reputation and success. An expatriate married to a British woman, the friend suggested that Bistany look for a location in England for the first school outside the Middle East.

Like most ventures, as we will continue to see in *Worthless*, SABIS was not an immediate global success, and Ralph Bistany and Leila Saad, the latter of whom continues to serve as chairperson of the SABIS board, experienced numerous difficulties in moving into new regions. One was the fact that the school, with its stellar reputation among the Middle East cosmopolitan elite, became a magnet for expatriate Lebanese families and, instead of opening up to the local market, turned into an enclave for well-to-do refugees. On their side, British families, relying on the renowned brand of the English education system, shunned the school SABIS had established despite its home in a beautiful old Victorian manor in Bath. SABIS's Bath school was not a success, and the school was closed in 2001, although it is set to reopen soon.

But the lesson of coping with adversity, manifested in local fears that a foreign company—worse, a Middle Eastern one—could not be trusted to educate their students, did not dampened Ralph Bistany's resolve. In

1985, SABIS extended its sights beyond Europe to the New World in the United States. Although it was the biggest single educational market in the world, crime- and drug-infested schools and high dropout rates were the subject of daily media coverage in virtually every major United States city. But instead of heading first to the inner cities of New York and Los Angeles where pain was greatest, SABIS made its beachhead in Minnesota, the heart of the American Midwest, a counterintuitive choice Ralph Bistany made after reading a *Fortune* article that ranked Minnesota as the best secondary school system in the country. If SABIS could compete with local schools for top performance in Minnesota, he reasoned, SABIS would then be able to crack any other market. And so with a mission to exceed even the highest local standards, Lebanon-based SABIS built what was to become an acclaimed private school in Eden Prairie, Minnesota.

In the 1990s, Bistany's son Carl, then forty-two, became the CEO of SABIS. The younger Bistany brought with him business and technical experience in IT, experience teaching at SABIS, and a huge ambition to turn SABIS into a profitable engine for revolutionizing public education throughout the world.

One of the first things Bistany did was to lead the company into the mainstream public school system via the then-new charter school legislation. Since their inception in Minnesota in 1991, charter schools have been the subject of controversy in the educational community and often garner headlines due to the impassioned community debates they ignite. The schools were conceived as an attempt to radically improve the quality of education by freeing public school systems from many of the restrictions and policies that governed them (such as union membership, curriculum requirements, and lack of teacher accountability) while simultaneously holding them strictly accountable for results and financial discipline. Though the issue was fraught with potential political and community minefields, many entrepreneurs then believed that there was a lucrative business opportunity at hand, and the charter movement saw the emergence of both for-profit and not-for-profit educational management organizations, some of which even listed their shares on NASDAQ.

According to the charter system, US schools operating under charter are funded by the local school district, which is funded through state or federal money, typically allocating between $5,000 and $10,000 per pupil. As Bistany saw it, SABIS could break even with around six hundred to seven hundred students in all thirteen grades (kindergarten through twelfth grade), meaning that profitability could be attained with a moderate-size school.

SABIS was chartered in 1995 by the Springfield, Massachusetts, school system to open and run SABIS's first charter school and to be one of thirteen charter schools to open in the state's first year of charters.[14] It was another test for the SABIS system because Springfield's inner city schools had been the poorest-performing in the entire district. Within five years of opening and with virtually the same student population from pre-charter days, SABIS students' test scores were from the beginning the best in the district. Eventually, the first SABIS graduating senior class was also the first to have 100 percent of its students accepted to college—a perfect record that has since been sustained by every SABIS graduating class.

Recently, the Springfield school has also been named by both *Newsweek* and *U.S. News & World Report* as one of the country's best public schools. In the 2011 MCAS (the annual achievement tests administered in Massachusetts), SABIS students in Springfield performed ahead of their peers in comparable district schools: 30 percent more SABIS students scored "advanced" or "proficient" on 2011 English MCAS tests than did students in the surrounding district. The difference was 31 percent in math. In 2011, Springfield's graduating class received in excess of $9 million in scholarships, Bistany reports. "Many of those kids are the first in their families to graduate high school. This has totally changed their futures. There's a whole new wide world of opportunity for them."

Lest you conclude that these results speak for themselves and rapid spread is inevitable, there have been setbacks. SABIS lost its charter in Chicago in 1999, an event that resulted in litigation and a mea culpa from the City of Chicago, which was forced to acknowledge publicly that indeed SABIS had successfully opened on time and on budget and that the SABIS educational approach was sound. But the loss of the Chicago contract is trotted out as ammunition by SABIS opponents in other cities, including a *New York Times* article that same year about a decision to implement the SABIS system in Queens.[15]

"Education is a very challenging business," Carl Bistany says. "It's not something that is solved by money or just putting brains around the table. If this were the solution, governments like Germany, the US, and the UK, who have access to a lot of both, would be successfully increasing the standards of public education. Yet this is still a major societal problem." Bistany is certain that a completely new approach is necessary.

As for SABIS's future as a business? The company is responding to proposals all over the world—including from India and Brazil. "Being a for-profit venture, you have to worry that if you are not doing well, you will be losing your shirt," Bistany says. "That is what continuously forces us to ensure that learning is actually happening and that we are adding measurable value. We worry about how much information is learned per unit time. Can we do it more efficiently, at a lower cost? You need incentive and fear of losing your shirt. If you don't have that fear, you're not being driven to enhance yourself on an ongoing basis."

Bistany, of course, intends to continue to push against the boundaries of common beliefs about what actually works in putting knowledge into our children's heads.

———————

Local Motors is a three-year-old upstart, with strong indications but still unproven in the marketplace, and SABIS is a century-old family business with a legacy of demonstrable accomplishments. Local Motors is a manufacturing company with a service strategy, and SABIS is a service company with a manufacturing strategy. Local Motors is Jay Rogers's first venture out of school, and SABIS is the family's venture in schools that Carl Bistany took over as a mature businessman. Local Motors is as local as it gets, in the heart of the American Southwest, aspiring to be your friendly neighborhood factory and revolutionize car making. SABIS is as global as it gets, off in the Middle East managing far-flung schools and aspiring to revolutionize education. And the entrepreneurs themselves are about as dissimilar as you can imagine, separated by time, geography, culture, age, industry, technology, educational background, and language.

Yet it is difficult not to be impressed by the entrepreneurs' commonalities, namely, seeing value in a situation that others disparage as worthless, impossible, or stupid and, contrary to what is expected, realizing an opportunity that creates extraordinary value for customer, society, and entrepreneur alike. They have a common contrarian mind-set that allows them to create opportunity where others see nothing.

CHAPTER 5

Why the Best Ventures
Seem Worthless
(or Impossible, or Stupid)

Almost every successful entrepreneur can recant many examples of how people thought his or her idea was ridiculous. History is replete with famous rejections by people who didn't share the entrepreneur's complete confidence in the value of an idea, just as the "anti-portfolio" of Bessemer Venture Partners testifies. To paraphrase Nobel laureate Albert Szent-Gyorgyi, entrepreneurship consists of seeing what everybody has seen, and doing what nobody has done.[1]

That's what's so important about those who build value from an idea that either no one sees or dismisses as worthless, impossible, or stupid. Who would see value in sending a package from New York to Newark by way of Atlanta? FedEx founder Fred Smith. But there are just as many examples of people who successfully defied conventional wisdom without earning Smith's fame. Those who will end up succeeding don't automatically censor themselves because certain problems are supposedly too difficult to solve or too complex to navigate or because opportunities are too remote to ever turn into something of value.

Value from worm poop? That sounds like a topic of some kind of late-night adolescent conversation. But while a freshman at Princeton University, Tom Szaky came up with a novel method of manufacturing fertilizer from the feces of red worms: he fed Princeton cafeteria waste to millions of the minuscule worms and then packaged their then-liquefied waste in used plastic bottles donated by schoolchildren. Terracycle is now a fast-growing "greentech" company, successfully diverting billions of units of various wastes and using them to create over fifteen hundred products available at major retailers, ranging from Walmart to Whole Foods. With offices in twenty countries, Terracycle distributes its fertilizer through The Home Depot and other major retailers.

Entrepreneurs see and create value in situations that other people view as worthless, impossible, or stupid. That's the job of the entrepreneur. Of course, no one, including the entrepreneur, can know with certainty if a new product or service will end up being valued—or be relegated to the huge scrap heap of "surefire" ideas that didn't pan out—until the product or service has actually been tried and proven valuable in the real world, usually because someone buys it. Only in retrospect can we judge how ideas that seemed devoid of value were actually worthwhile.

That is another of the big puzzles of entrepreneurship—we only *really* know that the value exists after the fact, a conundrum I will elaborate on in the last chapters of *Worthless:* Until they are converted into actual value, entrepreneurs' ideas might truly be worthless, impossible, or stupid—in fact, many are. As FedEx's Smith put it, "in retrospect it was ridiculous to try to put this system together, which required so much up front money, and required changing a lot of government regulations, but I didn't know that at the time."[2] Where would the field of logistics be today if Smith had given up?

In hindsight, of course, ideas that work seem obvious to most of us—"I could have thought of that!" But none of us *did* think of that. And even if we did, we didn't go out and do it. Entrepreneurship is about seeing, not imagining, value where no one else does, acting on that perception, and then turning it into value for both customers and entrepreneur alike. And because the entrepreneur converts worthless ideas into worthy services or products, often driven by the prospect of making a financial (and sometimes social) impact that is unexpectedly big, entrepreneurship is not only about the perception of value—in many ways, the perception is the easiest part—but also about its creation and capture. But curiously, as we will see in later chapters, many beliefs about entrepreneurship, including those of experts, focus primarily on the perception of opportunity and not its realization.

Worthless

Little in this world might be considered more worthless than the ill-cared-for, cheap, sun-rottened fish brought in by the Tobago fishermen just as local market prices are plummeting from the daily glut. But one venture is figuring out how to get those fish within twenty-four hours, unfrozen, as "amazingly fresh fish" portions onto the tables of the best restaurants in Manhattan and Chicago, making more money for everyone along the way, from sea to table.

Indeed, a decade after its founding, Sea to Table works with sixteen docks, representing many hundreds of fishing boats sustainably fishing from Tobago to the Aleutian Islands of Alaska to the Gulf of Mexico to the Gulf of Maine. The company generates annual revenues of almost $10 million and 60 percent per-annum revenue growth, with strong profit margins as the company rapidly scales up its market coverage.

––––––––––

In 1996, when Sean Dimin was thirteen years old, his family took a vacation in the most distant place their frequent-flier points would take all seven of them—the island of Trinidad, just a few miles off the Atlantic north coast of Venezuela. The American family then took a short flight

to the less touristy island of Tobago, packed into a four-wheel drive Su-
zuki Samurai, and drove across to the relatively unspoiled east coast of
the twenty-five-by-five-mile island that juts out into the Atlantic, sixteen
hundred miles southeast of Miami, and twenty-five hundred miles due
west from the Cape Verde Islands of Africa.

There Dimin and his family made their own entertainment by convincing some local fishermen to take them along on their daily trips. For
a family that loved fishing already, going twenty or thirty miles offshore
in open, wooden and bamboo skiffs with small outboard engines was the
adventure they had sought. It was like stepping back in time: far out to
sea with the local fishermen with little boats and hand lines, the Dimins
encountered a plethora of impressive types of fish. "The currents come
off Africa, flow down to Antarctica, then then come back up the coast
of South America to the area we fished in," Dimin recalls. "We found a
vibrant fishing community."

Each day on that 1996 vacation, some combination of the Dimin clan
would go out to sea with a different local fisherman, taking turns in boats
run by men nicknamed Rat Face, Boogie Man, or Double D. Dimin recalls, "We would come back every day with a boatload of fish, which we
caught pulling in the lines hand over hand."

For Rat Face and his peers, there was only one problem with each
great haul they brought to shore. *All* of the local fishermen had their
hauls at the same time, and by midday, when they got back to the island,
the local market was flooded with fresh fish, with prices dropping by the
minute. So each day Rat Face had to load the fish into a pickup truck and
drive it to the other side of the island, hoping to get it to market there fast
enough before it spoiled and prices plummeted further.

Watching that senseless waste of some of the finest fish was painful for Dimin's father, Michael. He began to conjure a minirevolution
in the seafood distribution business by getting the otherwise worthless
fish, doomed to become garbage or chum within hours of being caught,
directly and immediately into some of the world's top restaurants, at

a premium as "amazingly fresh fish." Twenty-four hours from the lines of some of the poorest fishermen to the plates of the best-heeled diners in the United States would create a new win-win-win-win game—for fishermen, chefs, diners, and their new venture that was forming in Michael Dimin's mind. There would be a fifth win for the environment: an integral part of his business vision would be to support fishermen who were sustainably fishing smaller catches in a way that allowed fish stocks to replenish themselves.

The idea percolated for four years after that family vacation, but then Michael Dimin was ready to jump in. He replaced the famous advice of *The Graduate*'s Mr. Robinson—"plastics"—with "fresh fish" and left his job as director of a New Jersey plastics company. He rented an apartment in Tobago, bought a purple pickup truck, and got to work.

———————

Typically, fresh fish to be shipped from the Caribbean was iced once it was brought in to the dock and then traveled a circuitous route to faraway distribution ports like Miami, where it was frozen, before taking days, sometimes weeks, to eventually wind its way to a restaurant, with a chain of middlemen taking their margins and upping the prices along the way. In contrast, Dimin would establish his supply chain on the island and cut out all the middlemen. If he succeeded, he could pay more to the fishermen, charge the restaurants a premium for "amazingly fresh fish," and make a profit. The fish would get from dinghy to diner within a day.

You might assume that the local fishermen would jump at the chance to get more for their daily catch—but it was an uphill battle for Michael Dimin to convince any of them that this was not, well, nuts. Despite the fact that the Dimins' new company, Tobago Wild, offered to pay even 10 to 20 percent above local rates, the Tobago fishermen weren't taking the bait, and with their survival instincts honed over generations, they suspected a trick. "Skepticism would be an understatement," Sean

Dimin recalls. The objections included protecting their current channel ("If I sell to you, I won't be able to sell to my usual guy, and what if you don't work out?"), failure to understand their value proposition ("Why should I ice my fish when I don't have to worry about that now?"), fear of not getting paid, and some community undertones about fishermen who dealt with foreigners.

"I remember holding a meeting on the far east end of the island try-ing to get steadier fish deliveries from the fishermen there," Sean Dimin recalls. "As I was beginning my rational and eloquent pitch, one year out of college, a fisherman named Iron offered to sell me all his fish for twice market price. When I asked why, he said it was because rich, white boys should pay that much for his fish. I quipped that I would offer him half market price because he was so ugly, and we got along just fine af-ter that."

It would take the Dimins two years to convince the local fishermen to change their ways because few of them realized that this deal was legiti-mate. And the extra work Tobago Wild required—immediately gutting the fish at sea, packing it in ice, and texting the catch details—didn't seem right away to be worth the extra money. Why couldn't they just catch fish and throw it into the bow of the boat, the way their fathers, and their fathers' fathers, had done it?

Michael Dimin logged hours and miles driving his purple pickup truck around the island with all kinds of enticements. He helped finance boats, bought fishing gear, provided better hooks, and even brought copies of *National Fisherman*. "My brother would bring sneakers from New York to give to the fishermen," Sean recalls. The fishermen, from their end, were accustomed to rudimentary, even unsafe, conditions. Some would go out to sea with no radio. If they were lucky, they might have a cell phone. Others simply painted a big *X* on the side or deck of their boat if they got into danger so that they could be spotted from the sky. "We gave a GPS as a prize one year," says Sean. Another year they distributed coolers to

120 local fishermen and set up ice bins in each village, always explaining how to use the new equipment.

With time and persistence the fishermen began to cooperate. Selling the concept in New York's top restaurants was a bit easier. Chefs were eager to get a steady stream of "amazingly fresh fish." The Dimins would charge the restaurants a modest premium, and the restaurant had a sustainability story to sell to an increasingly socially conscious clientele. Chefs could also tell curious customers the details of every portion: who caught it and where, when, and how it was caught. This was the opposite of how the traditional fish industry had been getting fish to even high-end restaurants, in which dealers would find out what fish the chefs wanted for their restaurant and then find a wholesaler that could supply it, anonymously.

Expanding the distribution throughout the island, along with the processing, packing, and shipping, was still the hard part. Michael Dimin had to figure out how to make ice drops in each village every night and how to build and run the company's own local fish processing plant to prepare the fish swiftly for packing in special boxes with cold packs. That required capital, which came out of Dimin's pocket. "We did not *want* to own a processing plant," Sean recalls. "But we had no choice if we wanted this to work."

Every day, when it found out the catch on each boat, Tobago Wild logged the fish into the computer and then instantaneously informed the chefs. Orders needed to be placed by the next morning, and the portioned fish were delivered from Tobago to Trinidad to New York, under special arrangements with the airlines. Once the fish reached New York, Tobago Wild's refrigerated truck dropped off each restaurant's order.

It wasn't always easy to keep its promise of "amazingly fresh fish." Flights got grounded because of weather, trucks would break down, and power would go out. Because they were bootstrapping their operation with their own savings, the Dimins were exhausted trying to make it all work. When Sean graduated college, he moved to Tobago to run the processing plant, giving his father his first break in years, eventually to take over the entire operation from sea to table. "We worked from before the sun came up to the night shift. And then back up at five," Sean says. Seven days a week.

Eventually, the Dimins built a large-enough volume and enough credibility on the island to turn their fish processing plant over to local management and became, instead, its customer. With the operation spun out, and with most local fishermen in Tobago working with Tobago Wild, the Dimins began to look beyond Tobago for supply. They developed the same idea of sourcing fish in Alaska and eventually all around coastal United States, including Louisiana in the Gulf of Mexico and into the Gulf of Maine.

Reflecting its increasing reach, in 2009 the company changed its name to Sea to Table. Around the same time, Sean, now running the business with his dad, began to see an opportunity to diversify the company's business model and to add to its unusually long supply chain an unusually short one: Sea to Table began to supply local chefs local fish from local fisherman. "People like to eat from their own local seas," Sean says. "This is a general trend because it supports local businesses, and it cuts out distribution costs. If I'm in a restaurant in New York, I want the option of eating fluke from Rhode Island and tuna from Montauk." So Sea to Table has been building a ground-delivery business that takes the expense of FedEx air shipping out of the formula.

By 2012, Sea to Table had relationships with docks around the entire coastal United States and Tobago. The docks coordinate the work of anywhere from one to twenty fishing vessels each and six hundred restaurants, including some of the most famous in Manhattan, Chicago, Boston, and Los Angeles. The Dimins work closely with various government and nongovernment agencies to support sustainable fishing. The company shuns work with any of the large commercial fleets that fish questionable international waters or under inadequate fishery management regulations with no clear traceability back to the harvest location, method, or fishing vessel. Each fish that Sea to Table sells is identified by its sustainability rating.

As Sean Dimin sees it, the traditional fishing industry is stuck in its expensive structure, whereas Sea to Table has reconceived every element of the business to maximize flexibility: "I don't know if they see the threat yet. But *we* get it. We can see where this goes. And it's good."

But he is most proud of something else. "I like it when we get that aha! from a fisherman. When he says, 'Business is going really well; keep sending us orders,'" Dimin says. "Now I get calls from fishermen who say, 'How did chef so-and-so like my fish?' That's great."

Impossible

Imagine if your doctor told you that you needed some routine tests inside your digestive tract. That would cause most of us to squirm: we might immediately react to the anticipated discomfort and indignity (albeit largely only imagined, for those of us who have been through it).

Now imagine, on the other hand, that instead of an intrusive colonoscopy or worse, your doctor gave you a small capsule to swallow that contained a fully ingestible camera and transmitter rolled into one. The capsule's radio transmitter would send video images to a portable data recorder worn on your waist as peristalsis pushed the capsule past your stomach and through your bowels. No sedation. You just would go about your normal day.

Who wouldn't choose the digestible capsule? One quarter-million people a year now make that choice, and growing every year.

Alas, such a technology was the stuff of science fiction—like something out of the cult classic *Fantastic Voyage*—until just over a decade ago, when Gavriel "Gabi" Meron envisioned what might be possible. The first video pill does not yet completely replace colonoscopy, but it does take the place of much more onerous procedures to image the small bowel, and the large-bowel product is in advanced stages of FDA approval.[3]

When Meron, CEO and founder of Given Imaging Ltd., introduced the world's first video pill, called the PillCam, to the market in 2000, it was heralded as "truly astonishing technology" that "changes the face of medicine." Given Imaging earned "you'll never believe this!" widespread media coverage on *Oprah, The Today Show, CBS Evening News,* CNBC— and even Ripley's *Believe It or Not.* Jim Cramer on CNBC's *Mad Money* said Given Imaging could "revolutionize the health care industry." But as impossible as creating a successful video pill seemed to everyone but Meron and inventor Gabi Iddan, the ability to pull off all the other aspects of bringing the product to all the world's major markets, with regulatory approval, in just three years may have seemed even more daunting. So many things, each one of which seemed undoable, had to happen at the same time. Technologies involving chemistry, electronics, materials, communications, and dozens of patent applications would have to be developed, integrated, miniaturized, and then manufactured, scalable to the millions. Dozens of clinical studies by medical industry leaders were required for the medical community to give its acceptance. The FDA had to approve the PillCam as safe to digest. Special manufacturing processes had to be developed.

All of that had to be done in record time so that Meron and Iddan could stay ahead of competitors, the Japanese market leaders Olympus, Fujinon, and Pentax, three 500-pound gorillas with 90 percent of the large-bowel endoscopy market. These three were certain to accelerate their own R&D the minute they learned of the feasibility of making a functional video pill for the small bowel. Even though the PillCam had the potential to revolutionize endoscopic medicine of the small intestine, it would also require convincing and training thousands of gastroenterologists around the world to use the technology, equipment, and software required to run and interpret the diagnostic tests. It was nothing short of a moon shot—one being led by someone who was neither a scientist nor an engineer.

Despite his lack of degrees, Meron had had excellent preparation. That's because the first years of his career were spent in senior administrative positions in the Israeli army, including managing several army-wide industrial development projects involving thousands of people, budgets of hundreds of millions of dollars, and complex contract negotiations with civilian suppliers. He earned his MBA during his service in the army and, after he left, spent years in executive positions in a variety of technology companies in both Israel and the United States. He finally earned the CEO title at Applitec, a manufacturer of endoscopy cameras, after first setting a different flailing start-up in video imaging technology on its feet as general manager.

It was then that Meron met the inventor of the video pill concept. Gabi Iddan, who later became the chief scientist of Given Imaging, approached Applitec and Meron with his notion. Iddan was a military scientist with experience in developing remote-guided missiles. On a physician neighbor's challenge, Iddan had begun to wonder whether a video pill could also be tracked and guided in the human GI tract with similar technology. As Meron then began to study the problem, he learned that GI problems send scores of millions of people around the world to the hospital—thirty million every year in the United States alone, at a cost of $120 billion to the healthcare system.

A portion of those diseases would have been much easier to treat had they been detected in their early stages. Until the PillCam, medical practice had been extremely limited in its ability to diagnose pathologies in the small intestine, because of its being a narrow, seven-meter-long organ that folds in on itself many times inside the abdomen. Doctors had been limited to using various types of flexible endoscopes that had to be painstakingly forced through a patient's small bowel or an inflatable balloon to open up the intestine so that a fiberscope could penetrate without perforating the soft intestinal wall. X-rays with radioactive agents were also common at the time, but highly inaccurate as well as toxic in high doses.

The accepted procedures had numerous drawbacks, such as the risk of tearing the intestinal wall, severe patient discomfort, exposure to X-rays, the need for sedation, and the possibility of cross-contamination from using the same endoscopy equipment on different patients. Even the best endoscopes could only reach about one-third of the way into the small intestine from either direction. And the equipment and procedures were expensive. All of these factors meant that doctors prescribed them only when symptoms, such as intestinal bleeding, were clearly emanating from the small bowel, and by that time, it was often too late: about 80 percent of small-bowel cancers, for example, resulted in death, often because of their late-stage diagnosis.

Iddan's concept consisted of a miniature camera, a battery, a light, and a radio transmitter packed into a capsule that could be swallowed by anyone, even the elderly and the young. Swallowing and gravity would move the capsule through the esophagus and stomach, and then the natural peristaltic action of the GI tract would take over, moving the capsule through the small and large intestines, all the while transmitting images to a data recorder worn in an external belt around the patient's hip. External sensors stuck on the patient's abdomen (like those used for an electrocardiogram) would keep track of exactly where each image came from in case a symptom were observed there and would require further treatment. The patient could move around unsedated, and within a few hours the Given system would generate a complete image of the small bowel. (I know what you are wondering: no, the PillCam is not reused with other patients. In fact, it is flushed down the toilet during the patient's normal bowel movement.)

After the data is recorded, a gastroenterologist would review the images on a computer work station. If a problem were detected, the physician would know exactly where it was—information that would facilitate treatment or further diagnosis.

When Iddan first presented the video pill to Meron, it was just an idea—it was far from the actual PillCam that Given Imaging would develop. It was just a concept of what Iddan imagined *might* be possible. Meron's first reaction was a skeptical "It sounds too good to be true."

But Meron also understood that if it did work, it would create a new category of diagnosis, with major potential to create a new field, what would become capsule endoscopy. When Applitec's board rejected the idea in favor of focusing on other priorities, Meron left Applitec to pursue the video pill on his own. He persuaded the owner of Iddan's patents, a private technology incubator established by Israel's leading technology investment group and the Israeli military R&D authority, RAFAEL, to give him a small office and a modest salary to develop a business plan. After a few months of market research, Meron was confident that he could overcome the daunting technological challenges, and that he had a fighting chance at bringing the novel product through the regulatory process and into the market, all in roughly three years. With his experience, Meron felt ready for managing a complexity greater than I myself can fathom.

Meron believed that the leading endoscopy manufacturers—Olympus, Pentax, and Fujinon—were likely to eventually mount fierce, well-resourced competition not only because the start-up would enter the GI segment (sorry for the pun) of the medical market, but more particularly because he might ultimately be able to pull off, well, an end-run attack on their core business of large-colon endoscopy. As a result, Meron did not feel he had the luxury of launching a small operation to incrementally test his product in a few hospitals and then slowly build from there. He had to go directly from obscure incubated start-up to major market presence, with a full-fledged global strategy, one that would allow him to open up and maintain a big distance from the likely competitors. Such a launch would require teams of experts (Meron assembled a respected board of advisers and initially hired twenty full-time staff) and more than $16 million just for his initial efforts. Much more would eventually be needed to take the company public and grow it.

"There was so much to get right," he recalls. "There were numerous diverse and cutting-edge technologies we'd have to pull together." He assembled several teams, each with the expertise for a particular piece of the project, with all the team leaders completely confident that they could develop the complex technology for their particular segment of work. Meron recalls, "The piece I had no idea about was—assuming that you've created all this—are the images you are getting relevant? Could we actually see something useful?" When tests of a very rough prototype used on a pig showed Meron that they could see clearly inside the small bowel, the race began in earnest.

Introducing a product that was ingestible required Meron to conform to stringent product specifications that would meet regulatory approvals in the three major markets he had targeted: the United States, Japan, and Europe. Each of those markets has a different regulatory authority—in the United States, the Food and Drug Administration (FDA); in Europe, the Conformité Européenne (CE); and in Japan, the Ministry of Health, Labor, and Welfare—each with different requirements for obtaining approval.

Several of Given Imaging's board members wanted the company to proceed more cautiously, with a first launch in Europe, to stage the risk and investment. Europe was the easiest and least costly place to obtain regulatory approval, and Given Imaging could see how the market responded and course-correct if needed. Meron, however, believed that the really safe approach would be to take what appeared to be the risky one; he argued that a slower, single-market start could reduce the company's chances in the other markets as competitors raced in. Meron prevailed on his board, and he hired CEOs for newly formed regional subsidiaries to simultaneously develop target penetration strategies. As it turned out, none of the regulatory approvals went exactly as Meron had anticipated, and Given's all-out global expansion saved the company a full year of sales and market momentum with normally conservative doctors. The FDA approval took one full year longer than anticipated, so Given Imaging did launch in Europe first, which in turn helped Meron raise the money he needed to keep the company growing: investors saw how ambitious Given Imaging's plans were in three separate markets, and he was able to raise a further $25 million in capital. In Japan, perhaps the riskiest market of all, Meron worked with partners who put in the capital needed and who helped with the regulatory approval process.

In 2000, the world financial markets had gone into deep freeze. In 2001, immediately after receiving FDA approval, Given Imaging undertook the first NASDAQ IPO since the markets crashed after 9/11. The company immediately forged ahead in all three markets, in Japan putting together a partnership in just eight months in the form of a three-way joint venture to obtain Japanese health authority approval and begin marketing the PillCam there.

In the end, it was Meron's willingness to pursue the most high-risk three-market strategy that gave the company the speed, lift, and altitude to reach the highest strata of the medical device markets. If he hadn't sought simultaneous approval, the delay in the United States and Japan might have proved fatal to the whole business, but with European approval in hand and investors aware of the global opportunity, Meron was able to keep the company growing—and ward off the anticipated competition.

Just a decade later, Given Imaging generates annual revenues approaching $200 million, performs a quarter of a million PillCam procedures annually, and has a 77 percent gross profit. Its PillCam has from launch been considered the gold standard in medical diagnostic devices for the small intestine in patients of all ages and is sold all over the world, and capsule endoscopy has become a recognized treatment category, the topic of dedicated medical conferences worldwide.

In hindsight, "it *was* a moon shot," Meron concedes. But it was one that he believed was possible because of who he was. "I came to that position with ten years of specific experience," he says. "I was able to understand the market because I was in it, and I knew the competitors because I was dealing with them. I knew the engineers because I was dealing with engineers in the field. Every day was planned ahead of time, knowing where we wanted to go and what we wanted to achieve." If you do find yourself needing a diagnostic procedure in your small intestine sometime in the future, and the doctor hands you just a small pill, you'll be glad that Gavriel Meron and Given Imaging dared to attempt what others deemed undoable.

Stupid

Will Dean recalls that his professors at Harvard Business School told him that his idea was dumb. When he tells people what he does for a living now, "ninety-nine percent of the people conclude that I'm wasting the best years of my life doing precisely what a business school MBA should not be doing," he concedes.

Whereas Meron reduced suffering with a revolution in small-bowel imaging, it takes a different kind of guts to suffer through a Tough Mudder event. Dean and his cofounder, Guy Livingstone, created a company for people who will pay good money for the adrenalin rush of prolonged fear and pain.

Dean describes Tough Mudder as the organizer of "the toughest event on the planet." Participants in Tough Mudder's ten- to twelve-mile obstacle courses run, crawl, and slide through thick mud. To complete the course, they also need to dash through fire, hurl their bodies into an icy bath, and subject themselves to 10,000-volt shocks from hanging wires (until recently, while being sprayed with a high-pressure hose). (Yes, it is apparently quite safe—though as one recent participant blogged to future participants that they would "feel it in your nuts.") The courses incorporate some of the elements that are experienced in British Special Forces training, which Livingstone actually had lived through.

Every obstacle is named for its particularly sadistic qualities. Consider some examples from past or present Tough Mudder events: "Kiss of Mud: Eat dirt as you crawl on your belly under wire set only 8 inches from the ground." "Bale Bonds: Hurl yourself over enormous bales of hay, rumored at times to be loaded with pitch forks." "Shake and Bake: Get hosed down by local fire department before crawling through sand." "Fire Walker: Run through four-foot-high flames soaking wet." I will leave it to the reader to imagine what "Arctic Enema," "Electroshock Therapy," and "Ball Shrinker" are. Pretty puerile-sounding stuff to most of us. Juvenile. Silly. The Jacuzzi company did not think it so funny; Jacuzzi threatened Tough Mudder with a lawsuit for naming "Arctic Enema" the "Chernobyl Jacuzzi."

By design, it is impossible for any one participant to finish without help. There are no winners, no official times, no inducements to be competitive with anyone except yourself. Surviving the course is the victory. One participant blogged: "It's hard to pick which obstacles made our highlights list as many of those we conquered had their own sadistic charm to them. From walking the plank into frigid water to climbing a mud mountain only achievable via a human chain, each obstacle gave us 'mudders' a shot of adrenaline with a bad-ass chaser. My personal fave, the mystery obstacle of live electrical wires dangling overhead while you surge (pun very much intended) your way through some mud. A word of caution, wet winter hats and live electrical wires don't mix, as I found myself on the end of a zap that left me feeling like I took a Pacquiao left hook."

It sounds to many of us like a harebrained premise, but Dean and Livingstone have managed to turn that premise into a thriving business: for the privilege of ignoble suffering, approximately 140,000 people in 2011 paid Tough Mudder more or less $150 each, in advance. That amounts to over $20 million from Tough Mudder events in 2011 alone, with "healthy" pretax profit margins of around 20 percent.[4]

———————————

Dean attended business school after spending five years working in counterterrorism for the British government. With a love of outdoor athletics one of his drivers, he started working on his Tough Mudder business plan with a couple of fellow students, entering it in the school's annual business plan competition. The judges dragged their plan, well, through the mud. "They unanimously thought this wasn't a good idea," he recalls. "It was very 'niche,' very 'difficult to scale.' It has an 'unclear value proposition.'"

That is judge-ese for "We think it sucks."

Even Dean's own student team didn't take the idea terribly seriously. "I don't think it ever crossed their mind to really start Tough Mudder," he says. It was just a fun way to get some easy course credit.

As he approached graduation and became more intent than ever on starting the company, Dean's peers felt sorry for him that he had no backup job lined up and no outside financial backers. "They'd keep telling me it would be good to pitch it to some investors 'if only to validate your idea,'" Dean recalls. "That's like someone saying, 'Your girlfriend is great, but you really should get a second opinion by having her date one of your friends . . .' Who *cares* what they think? You think she's great!"

So what's so great about Tough Mudder? "We're trying to create an event that tests endurance, but tests it in a way that is genuinely fun," Dean says. "The biggest problem with marathons is that they take themselves so bloody seriously."

Many people didn't even think of marathons and triathlons as businesses—they saw them as charitable events. As Dean saw it, marathons were boring, and even the famous Ironman Triathlon was too predictable. And they were solitary sports. "In many people's minds," Dean says, "the word *endurance* is equated with boring." But in reality, Dean knew, these events could be highly profitable. The New York Marathon, for example, generates an estimated $350 million in fees and sponsorships, according to New York Road Runners, which organizes and runs the race.[5]

In addition to the swelling spending on personal fitness (all over the world), Dean observed the convergence of several cultural trends that could help Tough Mudder be a winner. In particular was the rise of social media and people's increasing willingness to pay for unusual experiences. Participating in interesting experiences, Dean noted, had almost become the new status symbol of a generation of twenty- and thirty-year-olds. "Ask anyone under age thirty-three what they did on the weekend, and they'll either say they did something mind-blowingly fantastic or they'll say, 'I just chilled,'" Dean says. "Somehow to say, 'We had a quiet weekend,' is to say 'I'm boring.'" People pay for extreme experiences like bungee jumping or hang gliding. All of those things, he noted, get reported to friends on Facebook, in what he calls the "humble brag"— something that purports to be a humble mention, but is really intended to make the person look good to his or her friends. "Memories are the new luxury good," Dean says.

Dean believed that he could connect those dots in a way no one else had: "You've got to be able to spot a trend before people are compiling statistics." So in late 2009, with $20,000 of personal savings between them, Dean and Livingstone, a former high school buddy who was a bored corporate attorney with a similar passion for challenging sports, launched Tough Mudder.

The idea was simple: the stupider and crazier the event, the better. They could keep the costs of putting on the events low by using Facebook and other social media, and they could choose cheap, rural locations that were a bit outlandish, instead of major metropolitan areas that would require special permits and police arrangements. Participants would pay the fee in advance so there would be no chasing to pay bills, and Dean and Livingstone could use the down payments to finance the operation.

Dean scheduled Tough Mudder's pilot event in Pennsylvania in May 2010. He and Livingstone were hoping beyond hope that five hundred people would agree to pay $70 each. They attracted five thousand.

Turns out, getting participants ("Mudders") was not that tough. The logistics of running such an unusual business with a tiny staff was the challenging part. "People thought of us as two silly schoolboys running around after not getting jobs at Goldman Sachs," he recalls. Even the most basic of office management issues was difficult. "We'd get a call from the post office saying, 'I'm not going to ship your boxes because this one has a label on the side.' No one wants to rent you office space, because you don't have a credit history. We had to put down a thousand-dollar deposit to get a phone just because we were British nationals. Can we have a mobile phone? 'No.' Can we have a bank account? 'No. Our computer system says no.'"

One company delivering four thousand heat sheets to keep participants warm at the event's end brought a package labeled to the attention of "Mr. Tough Mudder." The delivery man insisted on seeing ID. When Dean explained he was the CEO of a *company* called Tough Mudder, not Mr. Mudder, the delivery guy drove two hours back down the mountain to get his manager's approval.

But Dean chose to view all of those obstacles as good things. "You have to start seeing these not as another bloody pain you have to deal with, but as an opportunity. These are things that will make our competitors quit."

It was harder to be upbeat about the hardship of staging insane one-time events in different places. Dean and Livingstone had to find counties or rural resorts that would agree to allow them to stage such messy, large-scale events in an area where participants could also have fun staying.

Dean and Livingstone had to pitch themselves—and their stupid idea—over and over to completely new listeners, most of whom didn't quite see the appeal. One manager of a ski resort sent back an email full of expletives: "Your idea is stupid, stupid, stupid. It's a liability nightmare."

Then, each location came with its own quirks. In Mount Snow, Vermont, for example, Tough Mudder had to post security guards in a forest to protect a rare grass. In others, the company had to get permission to bring in new dirt to make the right kind of sludgy mud.

In the final weeks before an event in Georgia recently, local clergy got up in arms about the fact that Tough Mudder would be serving beer to the thousands of participants at the end of the event. "We had our permits in place, the events lined up, and then they started protesting with signs, 'Tough Mudder is the devil.' 'We don't want you metrosexuals here,'" Dean recalls. Despite the likelihood that the event would, Dean estimates, be bringing at least $4 million into the local economy through hotel, restaurant, and gas station customers, Tough Mudder was unable to persuade the local authorities that this would be a peaceful crowd, well worth the work for the local region. (Dean points out that at the end of running twelve miles, no one drinks beer to get drunk—they are all exhausted. They drink one or two just to celebrate.) Tough Mudder finally relented and held its first-ever beer-less event.

In California, bears broke into the aid stations that had been set up along the course the night before the event and ate all fourteen thousand bananas. In Florida, the company had to chase alligators out of a pond that participants would be swimming in. (For the record, the way you do that, Dean says, is to capture a baby alligator first. The baby will squeal, and all the other alligators will follow to rescue it. Author's note: I am not sure I will try that.)

By the end of 2010, Tough Mudder had staged its second event in California and its third event, which had 10,000 participants, at a raceway park in New Jersey. By the end of 2011, the company had outstripped Dean's original business plan exaggerations. Whereas Dean's business school plan had anticipated four events by the end of 2011, with 5,000 participants, Tough Mudder had fourteen events, with about 140,000 participants. The company had hoped for $500,000 in revenues by its second year; forty times that was the reality. "My fiancée told me she'd expected to have to support me for my first five years," Dean says. "Not only have I paid off my business school debt, I've paid off her law school debt as well." The average attendance in 2011 was just under 20,000 participants, with some of the events selling out months in advance. In 2012, Tough Mudder is forecasting revenues of $70 million from thirty-five events, staged not just in the United States, but also in the United Kingdom, Australia, and Canada—and with just one hundred employees to make the events happen.

Tough Mudder breaks some rules about serious sporting events. The participants take a prechallenge oath not to whine. At any given event, there are all kinds of crazy costumes—on YouTube, you can see dress-ups from Elvis, to Jesus, to Borat in his green sling, to Kiss's Gene Simmons, garnering some of the official prizes: "Best Costume—Most Bad-Ass; Worst Costume—Most Dumb-Ass; Least Clothing—Most Ass." There's a tribal, war-chant quality to the pre-event warm-ups. People wear the inevitable small scrapes and bruises like badges of honor as they drag across the finish line. Tough Mudder tattoos are offered onsite. As one blogger described, "Camaraderie is the name of the game. If you don't feel like helping others while doing this, then you must be dead inside." When participants cross the finish line, they are rushed over to the beer table, and the party continues off the course.

Though the participants clearly will have noticed Tough Mudder's success—there has been a notable uptick in the number of other "mud runs"—typically tamer three- to five-mile runs—Tough Mudder is recognized as the wildest, craziest challenge, with sponsorships coming in from Dos Equis beer, Under Armour, Degree deodorant, and Bic razors. Tough Mudder is particularly popular among university students. (I guess it is a wholesome alternative to the infamous bacchanalian spring breaks in Florida.) The Tough Mudder website has a vibrant community, called Mudder Nation.

Even Dean himself has started to become part of the brand's identity. "I was recognized on the subway a couple of weeks ago," he recalls. Perhaps the sweetest revenge of all, Dean says, is that people no longer think his idea is bizarre. Although his professors thought Tough Mudders was worthless, impossible, and stupid all rolled up into one, no one is smirking now. "Now people say, 'I knew it all along.'"

PART THREE

WHEN ADVERSITY MEETS REWARD

If entrepreneurship is so good, then why is it so difficult?

Seeing value where no one else does is usually the first step on the path of entrepreneurship. But plenty of ideas have died on the vine when a would-be entrepreneur couldn't figure out how to turn a vision or a plan into a service or a product that people were willing to pay for. As Sam Walton once put it, "if everybody else is doing it one way, there's a good chance you can find your niche by going in exactly the opposite direction." Seeing value in something worthless, viewing the impossible as an opportunity if it can be made possible, taking something seemingly stupid and turning it into something smart—that's the contrarian nature of entrepreneurship.

On the other hand, no idea, including one that looks absurd, is good just because you believe passionately in it in the face of all the opposition. Entrepreneurship is not just a matter of developing an irrational commitment to a course of action that everyone else thinks is unwise. It is just that the adverse reactions of others—investors, customers, partners—who view ultimately smart ideas as harebrained is a normal aspect of being an entrepreneur, as we will see. In due course, the proof of the pudding will be in the eating, and the process of making the pudding, so to speak, has tested some of the most enthusiastic and self-committed entrepreneurs in the world—and many don't succeed in making a pudding that others want to eat.

And that, it turns out, can be a good thing. Surviving the gauntlet of starting a business against the odds and overcoming all the accompanying challenges acts as an imperfect Darwinian test of which businesses actually deserve to live—and which aren't strong enough to survive. As veteran venture capitalist Todd Dagres, who has seen his share of both extraordinary successes and resounding failures, put it at the Xconomy entrepreneurship summit at Babson College last June 2011, "it *should* be difficult to start a new venture." A degree of adversity strengthens the entrepreneur and weeds out those without the required mettle.

The next three chapters will dissect entrepreneurial adversity into three components: (1) the *intrinsic* difficulty in creating and capturing extraordinary value from any contrarian idea, (2) the *extrinsic* adversity faced by most entrepreneurs because of imperfect environments, and (3) the *opportunistic* adversity that can be found in the large pile of the world's big social problems. As we'll discuss, adversity is an integral part of entrepreneurship. It *is* hard. But as we'll also see, differentiating the three components of adversity has important implications for the long-term success of any entrepreneurial venture.

CHAPTER 6

If You Can't Stand the Heat

Why Every Entrepreneur Faces Adversity

This is tough bloody sh*t.

—Jorge Rodríguez-Gonzales, CEO and founder of PACIV

If entrepreneurship is such a good thing for entrepreneurs, investors, customers, and society, why is it always so arduous?

Every entrepreneur I have met has experienced intense difficulty getting his or her venture off the ground and growing it to scale. Jay Rogers met with skeptical investors and a partner who couldn't stomach the uncertainty. Carl Bistany encounters scorn for SABIS's assumptions and methods. The Cinemex founders got funded on their way to shutting down their venture, only to run into the currency crisis and militant unions. For Actavis's Robert Wessman, the future of the company hung by a thread and a threat (I did not mention the time a violent mob of workers in Bulgaria waylaid him). Atsumasa Tochisako almost lost MFIC to disappearing investors. And so on. It is unclear to me whether a successful entrepreneurial venture is a necklace made of pearls of victory or a choke collar studded with tears of frustration—or maybe both. Some of the ventures in *Worthless* will no doubt encounter difficulties, and maybe even fail, by the time you are reading these words.

How the East Was Won

For Sandi Češko, launching and growing Studio Moderna in Slovenia wasn't any easier than for any other entrepreneur I have seen. It all started in 1992 with a little strip of plastic, which Češko has grown into a major retail force throughout Central and Eastern Europe.[1] The plastic strip came with two ideas that struck him at first as pretty outlandish: he was going to try to sell the flexible strip of molded plastic that was strapped to a person's back as a relief for lower back pain. No one was more skeptical of the device his partner Branimir Brkljač brought him than Češko himself.

The other preposterous notion was for him and his partner to sell the new Kosmodisk on Slovenian TV, the "same way that in the US you had been selling slicers and dicers for decades—it is a multibillion-dollar business there," laughs Češko. The only problem: "Slovenians viewed the guy on TV as a snake-oil salesman, just a notch above criminal," Češko recalls.

In Slovenia at the time, people clearly weren't rushing to buy products from late-night TV like their US counterparts. Anyone buying something from a sleazy late-night TV advertisement was naive and gullible and deserved to be saying good-bye to his or her money.

Fast-forward to two decades later, and no one thinks that anymore. Today Češko sells almost a billion dollars of Kosmodisks and dozens of other products, from high-end mattresses to fold-up bicycles in twenty-one countries in Central and Eastern Europe, Russia, and Turkey. Studio

Moderna has become number one in television shopping in all of its markets and a respected name in e-commerce and in-store retail as well.

Češko's parents had raised him to look for new and better ways of doing everything, even life's mundane chores, a characteristic that occasionally got him into trouble with teachers who did not take lightly to his "improvements." Nor did his incessant questioning of conventional business practices help him, many years later, persuade any of the Western venture capitalists or private-equity investors to back a venture run by a Slovenian who happened to think he knew how to build a retail business better than the Western giants did. They all turned him down, commenting that the successes were temporary and the model surely was not sustainable.

Nevertheless, rather than shrinking during the 2008 financial crash like most of its more famous competitors, Studio Moderna has grown by over 30 percent a year.[2] All of the growth has been achieved the hard way, that is, from increasing the company's sales in its existing markets, existing channels, and without acquisitions. Finally, in mid-2011 General Atlantic, one of the private-equity giants, bought a minority chunk of the company at a twelve-month share price increase of "several times," just after a syndication of professional investors had made the first investment, itself twenty years after Studio Moderna's founding.

In the early days, neither did the Slovenian consumers believe that what they saw was real. And even if Češko and his attractive infomercials could have enticed customers to pick up the phone and ask about the product, these consumers still would not spend money on something they couldn't see with their eyes and touch with their hands. Using credit cards over the phone was completely out of the question.

To overcome the customers' resistance, Studio Moderna set up its own store, the first of many dozens, for customers to come in, see, and try the products themselves and then pay in cash. This was another step in the exact opposite direction then taken by Western direct-response TV

(DRTV) companies, which eschewed in-store sales channels. "We did not have an explicit strategy or intention to open our own stores," Češko recalls, "but this evolved quite naturally from us trying to solve a marketing problem." Owning its stores turned out to be an effective testing ground to get customer feedback on new products before Studio Moderna spent money advertising them on television. Customers were coming along, but banks and investors remained far behind, forcing Češko to survive for twenty years bootstrapping everything.

"When we started," Češko recalls, "there were no reliable call centers, no reliable delivery companies, no third-party service companies. We decided to do everything in-house, or as in the case of delivery companies, we devised very stringent training programs and systems for precisely monitoring their performance." This was in direct contrast to the way the Western DRTV companies had become dominant forces in their own markets in the United States and, increasingly, in Europe.

Češko explains: "We had to train the delivery people to wipe their feet at the door, carefully bring the product inside, and politely answer questions. Previously you could count on them to dump the product outside in the rain, often at the wrong address."

Češko did everything backward, at least from the perspective of the market leaders, the Western DRTV companies with their centralized decision-making and outsourced suppliers. "That is why they failed when they tried to come to Eastern Europe." he explains. "We gave authority to the country managers. They sent American executives to set up and manage operations; we use local talent in every country."

Češko also turned the impoverished infrastructure in all Central and Eastern European countries, one of the venture's major stumbling blocks, into a major advantage: ultimately Studio Moderna developed its own infrastructure—from deliveries to management of its supply chain across borders within the company itself—to consistently offer customers service that assuaged the market's fears and skepticism. It took years of guaranteeing and delivering superior service, but Studio Moderna eventually won the confidence, loyalty, and trust of the market.

The former Soviet-controlled countries to which Češko would expand were no exceptions: residents of these countries were in the habit of getting around the system for everything. "In former Soviet countries and in Russia you are considered gullible if you trust the system," Češko says. That had turned into a kind of Wild West of business conditions, making it doubly important to build a reputation of reliability. "The system was built on complete *mistrust*," recalls Češko. "If the government said, 'Do A,' then automatically people would do B. We built Studio Moderna by earning the trust of consumers who were as cynical as they come." In fact, Češko made a point of using the Western level of service just as a point of departure to be exceeded, and not a standard to be achieved. Studio Moderna would set the bar, not follow it.

You might expect that, in light of that distinguishing track record in market after market, investors would be lining up. No such thing. Češko was reduced to borrowing money at exorbitant rates—30 and 40 percent per year—on the so-called gray market to keep the business growing. Some years he paid more in interest than he did on staff salaries. It was a kind of Darwinian test, a test that is common of all of our entrepreneurs' experience, forcing Studio Moderna to find ways to grow through its internally generated cash.

In addition to the type of adversity that is an innate aspect of entrepreneurship experienced everywhere, as we will see, Češko also had to survive wars in the Balkans, government collapses, and the global economic meltdown of 2008 as well. "You constantly have to adjust and adapt," Češko says. "We were on the precipice in everything we did—we had to earn everything; nothing came for free."

Even when Studio Moderna's sales were nearing $100 million annually, Češko was still battling market perceptions about the value of what he had created. When he approached private-equity groups for funding to help him penetrate further into existing markets and expand into new ones, he was summarily rejected. The mental gulf between what investors thought was possible—and what Češko had actually created—was still too big for them to see across. "No one could believe that we, a Slovenian company operating in Eastern Europe, could possibly be doing what we are in fact doing on a sustainable basis," Češko recalls. "Our existence was outside of their ability to conceive." It would take another few years, as global perceptions of opportunity in emerging markets improved and the "pack" of investors began to flow into untraditional markets, for Češko to successfully convince investors to back his expansion plans.

Češko's unconventional strategy seems to be paying off. Along the way, the company's vision has evolved from a seller of its own brands to a platform for identifying and serving customers' needs—selling whatever it is that meets the company's quality standards and customers' needs at the same time.

Studio Moderna now has offices in twenty-one countries and employs more than six thousand people, with its integrated platform allowing it to efficiently use direct-to-consumer sales through home shopping and DRTV, local websites, direct-mail catalog sales, its own retail stores, call center operations, and a network of thousands of retail and wholesale locations. And Češko is making his first forays into Western European and North American markets: "We are actually selling our mattresses, which are manufactured in Italy, to Italian customers."

———————

With the benefit of hindsight, Studio Moderna looks like just the right venture at the just the right place and right time, but of course, that's not how it looked while it was unfolding. Although it even took Češko himself time and experimentation to see it, early on he realized he had an attractive product and a significant opportunity emerging from his Kosmodisk when everyone else saw, well, a strip of molded plastic. Češko then molded his own perception of opportunity into reality, converting what might have easily turned out to have been a truly bad business concept into the thriving venture that it is today.

This success has required Česko to overcome adversity at every level, starting with his own doubts. In Česko's case, his partner's persistence caused Česko to experiment with the disdained marketing approach: "I wanted to find out if that hurdle, that resistance, could be turned into an advantage for us and a barrier to larger competitors with deeper pockets. If we could use television, backed by surprisingly excellent service, to create a reliable image for Kosmodisk, we could stay on top of the competition. The keys would be information, product reliability, and a trustworthy product-return policy, which in Eastern Europe didn't exist at all."

Having overcome his own resistance, Česko then had to face the skepticism and preconceived notions of, first, customers and, then, bankers, investors, partners, regulators, and media companies. Customers weren't queuing up for a little plastic device to aid back pain. TV broadcasters weren't knocking down the door trying to sell Studio Moderna prime media time. Investors weren't clamoring to invest in companies somewhere near war-ravaged Bosnia-Herzegovina and Kosovo. *The natural adversity to something new, in particular to a product or service that seemed rather unattractive at first, was part and parcel of the Studio Moderna opportunity.*

Jorge Rodríguez-Gonzales, whose story will be detailed in chapter 11, is the founder of a Puerto Rico–based global venture, PACIV. His blunt words—"This is tough bloody sh*t" and "at the beginning it is just sickening"—reflect what almost every entrepreneur experiences. Adversity goes hand in hand with creating extraordinary value from a contrarian idea. Adversity is not the special province of emerging economies, with their challenges of infrastructure and governance. It is found inside the DNA of every endeavor we call entrepreneurship, and overcoming those challenges is the proof of the mettle of the entrepreneur, even in the best of situations. In Česko's case, it required years of iterating, perfecting, and adjusting his business model before Studio Moderna began to take off. If it were easy to create and capture value from such an idea, everyone would be doing it.

The Necessity of Heat

In the past thirty years, I have listened to, and observed firsthand, hundreds of entrepreneurs dealing with the challenges of entrepreneurship, its difficulty, and the many hardships that need to be met and overcome. In hearing their stories, I have realized that experiencing significant amounts of hardship on the way to success is embedded in the experience of entrepreneurship itself. It is the proverbial heat in the kitchen; if you cannot stand the heat, you need to just get out.

In fact, this intrinsic adversity is a logical implication of entrepreneurial opportunity's being founded on the entrepreneur's contrarian perception of value when the market (customers, investors, and prospective staff, not to mention friends, spouses, and professors) sees otherwise. As a result, rarely is the entrepreneur's new product, service, or business model welcomed into the world with smiles, open arms, champagne, and congratulatory speeches; quite the opposite, it is more often greeted with apathy, bewilderment, disbelief, and sometimes even scorn—not to mention the occasional lawsuit by an incumbent.

So it should be no surprise that the next step of garnering sufficient resources from a skeptical environment is almost always an uphill battle. Hiring the best key executives away from prestigious high-income jobs, beating the odds to secure venture capital investment, and fighting better-heeled and more-experienced competitors to make the first sale are always more difficult for the entrepreneur than for the existing player.

Making the entrepreneurial choice means that you have to be willing to push the envelope and then deal with the implications of that choice, including surviving a gauntlet of hurdles. And when you do that, you must understand that you will remain for a significant period on the cusp of that envelope, with the risk of bursting outside of it, falling off the edge, going too far, or creating a product or service that is too complex, too difficult, or too prescient for people to accept.

"Critics have predicted our death three times," recounts Scott Heiferman, founding CEO of Meetup, an online platform for facilitating the local meetings of groups of people with common interests. Today, Meetup boasts eleven million members; holds 340,000 monthly meetings of 105,000 local groups; and is active in forty-five thousand cities.[3] "If no one is predicting your company's death," Heiferman says, "then you're probably not taking enough risks in what you are doing."[4] In case you are wondering, it is not fun when everyone is predicting your death and that makes it even more difficult to collect the resources you will need in order to succeed.

Any new venture has a wide gulf to cross before it becomes robust— the gulf between an entrepreneur's perception of the value of his or her idea and the market's willingness to recognize that value too. As illustrated by Heiferman's experience in getting his venture off the ground in New York City, even the most developed markets are not immune to that adversity, because it is a feature of the entrepreneurial landscape (even though emerging markets do have their own versions of adversity, which I will discuss in the next chapters).

JetBlue is a great American example of how extraordinary success can follow on the heels of extraordinary resistance. It is not a piece of cake even if, as JetBlue's founder, David Neeleman, learned, you have a proven track record of performance as an airline entrepreneur, and even in the United States, the paragon of free-market capitalism and rule of law, with well-developed and regulated capital markets.

"If we don't make it look different from any other airline, we've failed," says Neeleman. But competitors, regulators, politicians, prospective key executives—even airplane makers—all either actively blocked or shook their heads at Neeleman's upstart airline that was trying, as others had tried before and failed, to change the airline game. I have selected a few illustrative quotes from Barbara Peterson's fascinating chronicle of the JetBlue start-up:[5]

- "A few of the Port Authority officials present [at the opening] . . . seemed ready to deliver the inevitable eulogy. One . . . manager even began his remarks by admitting, 'A year ago I thought your idea could never be a reality.'"

- Requesting seventy-five instead of the typical eleven slots at JFK Airport "got the expected reaction from his would-be competitors . . . scorn."

- "The Airbus people were skeptical; they had heard this before . . . Here again . . . a start-up was at a distinct disadvantage. 'A lot of it was convincing Boeing and Airbus that we were a real business,' [Neeleman said]."

- "It had been much harder to get a new entrant past the safety-minded regime in Washington ever since 1997 . . . in the wake of the ValueJet [sic] crash [in which 110 were killed] . . . having the unintended effect of throwing up new barriers to entry, making it much more expensive . . . for a newcomer to break in . . . there could be . . . one hundred government watchdogs assigned to a specific contender."

- "There was no shortage of skeptics when it came to JetBlue; many . . . were openly dismissive of the airline's odds of surviving . . . 'They basically laughed at us,' Neeleman said. 'As they saw it, there were so many things that could doom us.'"

Even the very best, the elite, the proven winners, experience the resistance of the market to ideas that seem, at first, worthless, impossible, or stupid.

The "kitchen of entrepreneurship" is risky and hot and is not meant for everyone. Cooking up something new always encounters detractors who are afraid that you, or they, will get burned. This view of adversity being intrinsic to entrepreneurship has important practical implications, for both the entrepreneur and the policy maker. Ask any forward-thinking policy maker these days about the entrepreneur's "valley of death," and the policy maker won't refer to the deadliest part of the Mojave Desert. They will tell you about the term that refers to the high probability that a new venture will dry up and die because it cannot raise enough money to get from the idea stage to customers. The typical entrepreneur may have what it takes to write an impressive business plan; raise some initial financing from savings, family, and maybe a few angels; and be able to set up a frugal office, hire a couple of people, and develop a proof of concept. But the survival rate from proof of concept to real revenues is so low that most ventures will run out of money and hope and will wither and die.

I myself have witnessed this happen numerous times, and it is a painful process. But the start-up world has a prevalent belief that this valley of death causes otherwise great companies, almost sure successes, to fail because somehow the marketplace denies them sufficient resources to get their "surefire" idea across the burning desert. If only these many "deserving ventures," the story goes, had access to more money, they could have become truly great. Even in Boston—one of the world's highest concentrations of entrepreneurship and the second- or third-richest center of venture capital in the world—the most highly selected winners of the Mass Challenge start-up competition recently listed access to seed capital as their number one problem.

But isn't it a strange coincidence that entrepreneurs across the globe, from Saudi Arabia to Silicon Valley, in their extremely different environments, complain about almost identical challenges? With minor nuances, they all grumble about their struggles with securing early-stage capital, followed by lack of access to talent, unwillingness of customers to engage with start-ups, and oppressive government bureaucracy. Yes, even in the United States. Even in Massachusetts. It doesn't seem to matter if they are high-tech start-ups in Beirut or Brazil or Bahrain. It's difficult to start a new venture, no matter where.

Government policy makers have in recent years found hope in opening the public reservoirs to irrigate the valley of death with funding, on the assumption that this particular valley represents what economists refer to as a market failure and, like all failures, requires fixing. But a market failure exists when free markets are not efficient, when buyers and sellers for some reason don't exchange goods and services with each other, despite a potential overlap between what the price sellers find acceptable and what the cost buyers are willing to bear. The market-failure mantra is thus used by governments as a reason for intervening to modify the economics of exchange so that a market will exist.

But they forget that it is not a market failure if a seller cannot sell something because the price is too high or because the product is not attractive enough or is not what the buyer needs. Is the ubiquitous scarcity of seed capital the sign of a market failure, or could it be something else, even something necessary, in the creation and capture of extraordinary value? Is it possible that the so-called valley of death is functional, that it may be either necessary or even beneficial for entrepreneurship?

A degree of adversity strengthens the entrepreneur and weeds out those without the required pluck. Adversity is also a sign that the entrepreneur is trying something new, counterintuitive, contrarian. Both deserving and undeserving ventures feel the intrinsic stress of adversity.

Every aspiring entrepreneur will face challenges—and therefore risk of failure—in bringing an idea to market. Just because anybody can start a company doesn't mean he or she should. Or that all ventures deserve a priori an equal chance to survive. Resources to support fledgling companies are scarce. It *is* hard to get financial support. It *is* hard to find the right staff to help build a company and its vision in the early stages. From a business point of view, getting a venture from drawing board to marketplace should be a weeding-out process. If the better ventures tend to attract the resources needed to bring their idea to the marketplace, this prevents a lot of resources from being wasted by low-quality ventures that might never survive in the long run anyway.

So the reviled valley of death may actually reflect the "value of death," an effective mechanism to select only the best, for the very reason that it is so inherently hard to survive and prosper with a contrarian new idea. That's the nature of being an entrepreneur: to see the world differently from everyone else, but then to be able to persuade the markets—financial, product, and labor markets—that you are right.

But even when an entrepreneur has successfully crossed that initial gulf, there is still a rocky path ahead, filled with other kinds of challenges. Adversity goes hand in hand with entrepreneurship. And as we'll see in the next two chapters, it comes in other forms.

CHAPTER 7

Some Kitchens Are Hotter Than Others

Succeeding When the Environment *Is* the Enemy

Every entrepreneur aspiring to create and capture extraordinary value will encounter adversity with his or her new product or idea—that is just a fact of entrepreneurial life; it goes with the territory. Nevertheless, in some places, the difficulty is exacerbated by objective shortcomings in the external environment as the entrepreneur moves from concept to creation. In other words, not only is it hot in the kitchen, but it is often hot outdoors as well. It is important for entrepreneur and policy maker alike to understand these different sources of adversity and not get confused between them, because they have different implications for action and policy, which I will explain at the end of this chapter.

As I have described in another publication, we can characterize any entrepreneurship environment in terms of six major domains: (1) policy and leadership, (2) capital availability and capital markets, (3) human capital and formal education, (4) customers and markets that are entrepreneur-friendly, (5) social norms and success stories, and (6) organizations that specifically support entrepreneurship.[1] I have called these environments *entrepreneurship ecosystems,* and many are, to put it mildly, less than ideal. I have studied and worked with entrepreneurship ecosystems in dozens of settings, and they are very complex and entirely idiosyncratic to each country, region, and city and sometimes even to districts within cities. One study of entrepreneurship in different states in Germany showed dramatic differences in entrepreneurship ecosystems, even in contiguous states.[2]

Knowing where you are in the entrepreneurship ecosystem is like having a good map. At the very least, it helps you know what aspects of the environment you are dealing with and enables you to identify your own strengths and weaknesses. And in reality, most environments in the world are seriously deficient in one or more of these domains.

The entrepreneurship ecosystem in Pakistan, perhaps not surprisingly, is deficient in *all* of the six domains. As a result, Khalid Awan grew his Pakistan-based shipping and logistics company, TCS, in a place that provided the company with more than its share of near-death experiences—too many to count—since he founded it in 1991. But as far as he was concerned, that was to be expected. "I never had time to be nervous," Awan recalls. "I knew that failure was not an option. It's like when circus performers are on high wires—they never even look down: *That* [down] is not an option. I always looked up." Awan explains that Pakistani business culture is not very forgiving of failure, not now, and certainly not then.

Awan decided in midcareer to create a business opportunity for himself, something that was rare to do in Pakistan at that time. TCS was founded specifically because Pakistan's policy, not unusual for emerging or challenged economies, was to protect domestic businesses from foreign competition. In Awan's case, until TCS was launched, the government of Pakistan had prohibited foreign express courier companies—FedEx, TNT, UPS, DHL—the right to independently operate, requiring local majority ownership. But to build on that opportunity, Awan had to navigate hurdles that entrepreneurs in other parts of the world couldn't even begin to imagine. Some bosses have to worry about employees turning up to work on time; Awan had to worry about whether his drivers would be safe driving through gang-controlled territories. Some entrepreneurs worry about how to reduce taxes on the business; Awan had to cope with a spur-of-the-moment government decision to declare his business illegal. Some businesses worry about upstart competitors; Awan had to cope with attempts by Pakistan's national post office to put his start-up out of business.

Today, thirty years after its founding, TCS has over two thousand offices in Pakistan, serves five continents, and has a growing presence throughout the Middle East and North America. "My business not only held on, but despite all the storms—political, economic, and social—has grown significantly. We have diversified geographically and into related businesses, and we have developed innovative new products," Awan told me recently. In part, TCS grew despite the obstacles, but also because of them. Finding solutions to every conceivable challenge (and some inconceivable ones) forced him to build a resilient operation. TCS now employs seventy-five hundred people and handles ninety million shipments annually, and in 2011, TCS generated $70 million in revenues.

Awan began his entrepreneurial career when his older brother was offered the chance to establish a joint venture with international courier DHL. At the time, back in 1982, Khalid was working as a flight engineer, a job he loved. But he'd grasped that the rapidly improving aviation technology would likely mean that the third person in the cockpit—the flight engineer—would soon be unnecessary. Wanting to get ahead of the inevitable, Awan began searching for career alternatives just as his brother was given a tip from a former colleague that DHL was looking for a local partner in Karachi.

Getting permission from the Pakistan government to open a DHL branch was complicated from the start. The Pakistani postal service had a monopoly over all country-wide deliveries and wasn't eager to have competition. DHL was able to get permission to launch a joint venture with Awan's brother, as long as DHL remained the minority owner and also limited itself to transporting packages into and out of, but not within, the country.

The brothers quickly realized that they were at a disadvantage if they couldn't offer customers internal Pakistan deliveries as well. Government regulations in those days were designed to protect the domestic monopoly of the Pakistani post office. An 1898 law had made it illegal for the delivery of letters by any entity other than the post office. The definition of a letter was vague, and Awan and his brother seized the ambiguity to argue that there was strong market demand for a domestic courier service. The government relented and gave the brothers approval to start a courier business limited to "business-related documents," though for years to come, this arrangement also left the business vulnerable to the changing interpretations of what constituted a letter.

At the time, there were virtually no private banks in Pakistan; all local bank branches were run centrally by the Pakistan Banking Council. The country's finance minister, who had been educated in the United States and was very forward-looking, Awan recalls, wanted to increase the service standards in sixty-five hundred of Pakistan's banks. At the time, it would take two to three weeks for any check deposited in any bank account to clear—meaning business would often be affected by cash-flow challenges. The minister wanted to improve the standard to two to three *days* instead—and that required a courier service that could move documents all over the country. He was seeking bidders for the work.

So in 1985, out of the blue, the council gave TCS its first big break—and challenge—to handle all interbank check distribution. There was a catch: the government could only afford to pay eight rupees—at that time less than $1—per shipment of each bundle of checks. Prospective bidders were asked to cost out the work and come back to the minister with their proposal. TCS was still a small operation then, with few facilities across the country. But Khalid Awan saw the chance to make it work by copying the hub-and-spoke strategy that FedEx founder Fred Smith had pioneered—a system that Awan thought could work well in Pakistan, too.

After a week of sweating over how to get its costs low enough to make a profit, TCS, which was established specifically to handle the domestic-delivery side of its courier joint venture, submitted the winning bid. Awan wouldn't connect all the branches immediately, but he would start with the major cities and then spread the coverage from there. That was good enough for the council. It turned out, no one else had wanted the work and TCS was the only bidder.

As soon as Awan was awarded the government contract, he returned to his office knowing he needed vehicles, offices, and staff—quickly. He figured he could creatively use the company's existing offices, at least as a stopgap, but there was no apparent way around the need for capital to buy the delivery vehicles. For funding, he turned to some of the very banks that he would soon be servicing, but he was summarily rejected because he had no collateral (TCS had been established by leaving all of the assets in the DHL joint venture). The foreign banks were no more interested. As his assistant watched Awan grow increasingly frustrated, the assistant mentioned to his boss that the man who repaired TCS's few cars had told him that if Awan ever needed vehicles for the business, Awan should come and see him.

Awan gave the man a call, telling him he needed fifty or sixty vehicles immediately. The man said he'd like to bring a couple of people to Awan's offices to discuss the matter further. When the group turned up, Awan wasn't exactly sure what to think. "They were *very* rough-looking," he recalls. The mechanic said the group was considering supplying Awan with up to one hundred vehicles, right away. Awan was eyeing the ragtag band suspiciously, wondering if he could trust them with his largest contract, when he was called away to a sudden international call from a large customer. Returning fifteen minutes later, he found his guests getting up to leave. "We have seen what we wanted to see," they said. "We decided that you can have sixty vehicles next week."

Awan, unknowingly, had just struck his first deal with Pakistan's informal economy—the huge underground gray-market economy that operates outside the boundaries of Pakistan's official economy, as it does in most emerging markets. The informal economy can be part of a supply chain critical to the success—or failure—of entrepreneurs in such emerging markets.

What his visitors that day had wanted to see was whether Awan's still-fledgling domestic business was real, kind of a gray-market due diligence. "They saw me, they saw I had an office, they some me doing some work and talking to some important people on the phone, they saw my employees—and the due diligence was over." The deal for the vehicles and drivers was based on honoring the spoken word—there was nothing in writing. Awan promised he'd pay them, and the vehicles and drivers appeared. And thus TCS's national presence was born.

Unfortunately, on the formal side of the equation, the more successful TCS became, the bigger the threat it represented to the postal service. "They needed to protect their revenues," Awan says. "So they went to the press and announced that no one should give us business, because we are not legal." Worse, the postal service threatened customers of TCS business with prosecution as well, and it worked, although not completely, because the threat was more implied than stated.

Awan soldiered on, constantly worried that the postal service's campaign would turn into something more menacing. One day, it did. Pakistan's ruling political party was upended and an interim government was set up. One night in 1988, Awan got an alarming call at nine o'clock from a government friend in a key cabinet committee. "In two days from tomorrow we will hold a cabinet meeting," the friend informed Awan. "One of the items on the agenda is to ban TCS."

Awan booked himself on the first morning flight to Islamabad. He didn't have a plan, but he knew he had to try to see as many people as possible to plead his case. He wrote out a half-page note explaining that it had been with great difficulty that he'd set up the infrastructure—one that helped the whole country—and he made copies to hand out to anyone who would listen.

Because he'd booked his ticket so late, he had to pay for first-class. As he sat down, nervously pondering whom he should see and how he'd make his way around the crowded capital with so little time, he recognized in the seat in front of him the finance minister who had given TCS the bank contract in the first place.

As Awan's luck would have it, the moment the flight began to taxi down the runway, the minister promptly fell asleep. Awan watched him like a hawk for the whole flight, waiting for the moment he could politely speak to him about his dilemma. But the minister was a sound sleeper, and only when the flight was landing did he rouse from sleep.

"I took my seat belt off while we were still moving," he recalls, in spite of flight attendant admonitions. "I said, 'Sir, you do not know me, but I know you are attending a cabinet meeting tomorrow. I have a small note for you to read.'" The minister grumpily replied, "I do not know about any meeting; I'm just coming back from New York. But give me the note."

As Awan sat back in his chair, he had no idea if he'd done anything to help his case at all. But as the aircraft door opened, he saw the minister reading the note. The minister then turned to Awan and said, "I don't remember what you did [in the past], but I remember that whatever it was you did, you did it well. You are going to have my support." And off he went.

By the end of his day, Awan had managed to meet with five ministers and left his note with virtually all the others. And then there was nothing to do but wait.

His friend, who was in the cabinet meeting the next day taking notes, got in contact immediately after the meeting, reporting that things had gone in Awan's favor. It had been a rather dull meeting, with the TCS item seventh on the agenda. But when the item came up, suddenly, from across the table, four or five voices perked up and said, "No! This should not happen!" TCS would survive.

By that time, Khalid and brother Sadiq had successfully built and run two companies side-by-side—the DHL joint venture and TCS—growing to fifteen hundred employees and thousands of customers. But in 1991 the brothers decided they needed to split their partnership. Under Pakistani law, Sadiq's son was legal heir to his father's assets. But Sadiq's son was estranged from the family and living in Abu Dhabi at the time, uninvolved in the business; it didn't seem right to Khalid to allow the son to control the eventual destiny of half the company. So in 1991 the two brothers agreed that Sadiq would retain the DHL joint venture and the younger Khalid would take TCS. DHL was far more profitable at the time, but Khalid felt that he had time to grow TCS into something significant.

But although almost overnight Khalid became 100 percent owner of TCS, he had inherited a balance sheet with no tangible assets: There was no money in the bank, the offices and all the vehicles were rented, and the employees could walk out the door at any time. Indeed, less than a year later, that nearly happened. Awan got wind of a group of TCS staff who were secretly planning to walk out and take all of TCS's clients with them. The employees felt that they had built TCS into what it was while Khalid was time-sharing his attention with DHL, and they thought they could do better now as a competitor. Awan called a surprise staff meeting. "I have heard that some of you have planned to go off and compete with us," he told the group. "Are any of you man enough to tell me if there is really such a plan?" The hushed silence was broken by one man who stepped forward. "Yes. You have taken us for granted."

Awan asked anyone who was part of the group to step forward. And one by one, they did—his head of marketing, the head of administration, and the heads of both the Lahore and Islamabad offices. They told Khalid that they had contacted rival UPS and offered to be the Pakistan partners and that UPS was going to back them. And they expected key clients to come with them.

Awan fired them on the spot, and they were ushered straight out of the building. Awan and his remaining top staff immediately got into planes and cars and began visiting key customers to tell them what had happened and reassure them that TCS would continue to operate smoothly.

In spite of Awan's swift reaction, TCS suffered defections of both customers and additional staff in the weeks ahead, as UPS signs suddenly popped up in locations all over the country. But all was not as it seemed. The defectors were not, it turned out, actually backed by UPS. One morning his wife handed him the newspaper with a big smile. A front-page notice from UPS announced that any uses of the UPS name across Pakistan were unauthorized and that UPS had given offenders seven days to remove the signs or be taken to court. Seven days later, the upstart mutineers were finished and TCS could regain its footing.

Ironically, what could have been the most devastating challenge to TCS in recent years—the aftermath of 9/11—turned out to be a catalyst for diversification and growth instead. As a country, Pakistan was deeply affected by post-9/11 world attention, and after the tragedy, there was increased scrutiny of the movement of money into and out of the country. What made this situation complex was that for decades, Pakistan had millions of blue-collar and low-level service workers who had found jobs overseas and remitted huge amounts of cash from wealthier economies back to their families at home. Now that the government was carefully monitoring all of that movement of cash, it became clear for the first time just how much money was flowing into Pakistan.

Once again, the challenges of Pakistan's environment provided Awan with the idea for a new chance to create value. The government now wanted to be able to track the movement of money, even very small sums. Banks were not set up to deal with the huge volume of small remittances, but TCS could do it. It already had infrastructure in place to handle small transactions and already delivered cash all over the country. So when Pakistan's Central Bank finally came out in 2007 with legislation called Guidelines for Bankless Banking, TCS was ready. Since then the company's money-transfer business has grown steadily, and Awan sees opportunities to add insurance, savings products, and small loans for business—a bit similar to the services MFIC provides.

The future looks promising in new ways. Awan is now based primarily in Dubai, where he is setting up the structure for a larger operation throughout the Middle East. Just a few years ago a private-equity fund valued TCS at $125 million. Although it is not for the fainthearted, it is possible to overcome the pitfalls and potholes and succeed as an entrepreneur in any environment, even the most unreceptive.

Statistically, the odds are stacked against entrepreneurial success, that is, of creating and capturing extraordinary value. Just how much depends a lot on how you define and measure success, but rules of thumb on the odds range from one in two to one in ten. That means that most aspiring entrepreneurs will experience some form of failure with their enterprise, and of the minority who do succeed, most will have close calls. Either way, at some point in almost every entrepreneurial venture, it is going to feel pretty bad to the entrepreneur. Unfortunately, it is extremely difficult to predict, even in the midst of the crises, if the entrepreneur will pull out of it.

Imagine what it is like facing the prospect that the endeavor you have poured so much of your time and energy into will simply die. It is not pleasant. I have experienced that myself in a venture I helped launched in 1999. We raised over $10 million in equity capital for the venture, and we were forced to close it abruptly in March 2001 during the dot.com crash of the telecommunications and internet markets. And even as the founder of a different company that did survive and prosper, I saw it come very close to going out of business several times during our first five years.

Two of my students won the prestigious Harvard Business School business plan competition, but had to write this letter just a year later:

Dear Supporters:

After more than a year of work, we have decided to close . . . This is a difficult decision but we believe it is the right one, and we are glad we reached it prior to taking in any third-party capital . . . While this has been one of the most difficult decisions . . . we feel fortunate to be able to shut down . . . early. Many startups realize their business isn't viable at a point when . . . too much money has been invested and too many lives have been affected. We could have ended up in this position. "Failing fast" and learning as much as possible from the experience is the second best thing an entrepreneur can do.

So, adversity and entrepreneurship go hand in hand. But there are different sources of adversity, and it is important for entrepreneurs to understand exactly what the origin of adversity is and whether the adversity is intrinsic or extrinsic, even though the phenomenology may be identical. Is the pain and frustration just the normal ante for aspiring to create something big? Or is it the result of being in the wrong place at the wrong time?

If it is the former, then changing scenery won't help too much. Jay Rogers might not be helping Local Motors at all by moving to Boston (where he started) or Detroit or San Jose.

If it is the latter—extrinsic—adversity, then some, but not all, of the pain can be mitigated by relocating to a more conducive environment, where, for example, it is easier to hire the best talent, find the angel investors, or engage with open-minded customers. Scenery can make a big difference: Silicon Valley is what it is to a significant extent because it is a magnet for entrepreneurs who believe the environment is rich with the resources needed to launch and grow a company, not because the "native" Siliconians may somehow be better entrepreneurs.

And if, like Khalid Awan, the entrepreneur decides to tough it out at home, he or she does so with open eyes or, like Sandi Češko, decides to turn the adversity into an advantage. But expecting the process to be painless is always a mistake.

Entrepreneurship ecosystems are very important, but tricky. To some extent, entrepreneurs in difficult environments succeed by creating their own mini-environments that buffer them from their "real world." The World Bank is famous, among other things, for its annual Ease of Doing Business Survey, which collects thousands of local experts' assessments of various aspects of the local business environment and rolls them up into national rankings. Countries covet top spots, and moving up in the Ease of Doing Business Survey rankings is celebrated as a major achievement by government ministers: in fact, some countries are known to invest many millions in trying to clean up their acts to change the rankings, sometimes by impacting the experts' perceptions as much as the reality itself.

But a little-reported internal study in 2011 by The World Bank itself flies in the face of the validity of the bank's own, oft-cited gold standard rankings. I didn't know it, but The World Bank conducts a parallel survey of how business executives themselves, many of them entrepreneurs, see the ease of doing business in their own environments.

When a team of researchers compared the expert surveys with the executive surveys, they found, lo and behold, that there was no correlation at all between the two views of the same "objective" environment.[3] The experts could see the process of getting business permits, for example, as being very convoluted and difficult, whereas business executives might view the process as being straightforward and simple.

How to explain the fact that two groups of people could view the identical environment with such variance? The researchers conclude, using the metaphor of the local climate, that whereas it may be objectively very hot outside, companies have adapted their own ways of coping with the heat, for example, by having office air-conditioning, traveling between meetings in air-conditioned cars, and going out only in the early morning or late evening. In other words, *they create their own environments*. They learn ways of navigating bureaucracy, legitimately or in some cases, illegitimately. They have staff who become expert in understanding and getting approval for the required forms and reports. They use consultants or professional service companies that specialize in interpreting complicated regulations and laws.

This viewpoint is testimony to the resolve, persistence, and flexible problem-solving that many people discover in themselves when faced with external adversity. In fact, like Češko and Awan, many entrepreneurs learn that their ability to overcome extrinsic adversity and to successfully create value in extremely adverse environments can be a competitive strategy and a barrier to entry.

Mary Gadams's RacingThePlanet is an interesting example of how external adversity can be converted into strength.[4] Gadams started her Hong Kong–based business in 2002 with the idea that people would pay to run 250 kilometers across the Gobi Desert. On the surface it may seem like a predecessor to Tough Mudder, but there is very little underlying commonality as a business. RacingThePlanet is about building a valuable brand (think North Face and Ironman) and a high-end adventure sporting goods commerce site (think REI and Patagonia) from the sweat of thousands of people who run hundreds of miles across deserts. The company stages ultra-marathons in the four harshest deserts in the world—the Gobi (the Gobi March), Atacama (the Atacama Crossing), Sahara (the Sahara Race), and Antarctica (the Last Desert). (The Antarctic is considered a desert because precipitation is so low.) Each event is staged over seven days. The more remote, challenging, and culturally interesting the location of the desert, the better.

By 2012 RacingThePlanet had staged dozens of events for close to five thousand participants and is rumored to have generated just under $10 million in annual revenues in 2012. In 2012 participant applications, which run about two for each race slot available, grew by 37 percent over 2011. RacingThePlanet's online store is doubling its sales annually, and the company built Expedition Foods to provide specialty freeze-dried foods for sports people. Gadams believes that the brand equity is becoming valuable and remarks that Ironman is thought to have made $150 million per year with just one customer, and since Ironman has come under new management, its profits have only gotten bigger. The unconfirmed number is certainly inspiring!

The operational complexities of staging large events in such remote and hostile environments are daunting, but have become a source of advantage. Gadams has to provide everything from lodging and medical services to internet connectivity to runners in places not accustomed to tourists, let alone runners. Gadams and her staff have to meticulously plot out each leg of each course so that the participants do not dangerously wander off the trail and so that every one of the hundreds of runners makes it to a campsite, staffed by dozens of volunteers, every night. Courses often cross private lands (in one case, she actually bought a farmer's wheat crop and had it harvested before race time to provide adequate camping space for racers). Gadams has to ensure that local translators are available to overcome language communication challenges. She has to make sure a team of doctors—all volunteers except one—is present in case of dehydration or accidents. RacingThePlanet must coordinate the activities of TV crews from National Geographic or the BBC. Sometimes the company needs to negotiate federal, regional, local, and even tribal permits to cross protected lands.

Gadams has not been immune to the resource-scarcity challenges common in starting any business, especially one that people might dismiss offhand as a whimsical hobby. But baking adversity into every aspect of her business has proven to be a real competitive advantage. No one can match her events at this point, and that feeds RacingThePlanet's acclerating retail sales. Industry experts close to the business estimated that online merchandise sales topped $5 million in 2011—and the company is just rolling out its Chinese-language online store (to add to its Italian, French, Spanish, and English sites), supported by distribution centers in Europe and Asia.

But like the deserts in which she stages her events, the obstacles that will turn up along the way are not predictable. "Everything's changing so fast," she acknowledges. "You just have to try things and see what works. Try to pave your way." Like her racers, she believes that her ambition is one of endurance. "My goal," she explains, "is to set RacingThePlanet up to outlast me." Using the hostility of the environment is an integral element to that sustainability. And, by the way, an integral part of RacingThePlanet's mission is to give back to the environments that support it: the venture has raised over $1 million in charitable donations for the communities near their courses.

In addition to coping with a bad environment, entrepreneurs must also learn how solving the problems of adversity can, in and of itself, lead to large opportunities. This lesson is the topic of the next chapter.

CHAPTER 8

Solving Burning Problems

When Adversity *Is* the Opportunity

I have been to three dozen countries to work on something related to entrepreneurship, whether it has been advising policy makers or private-sector leaders, consulting to entrepreneurs, writing cases, teaching entrepreneurship, or looking at investments. To make a point, I will oversimplify:

Entrepreneurship = adversity + human capital

Of course reality is much more complex, but when I see unusual concentrations of entrepreneurship blossoming in places like Israel, Taiwan, Iceland, and Ireland, it seems to boil down to a simple formula: put smart, educated people in places with few resources where they have no choice but to solve tough problems, and you get lots of surprising value-creating solutions to those problems. In New Zealand, they call this resourceful spunk *number 8 wire,* referring to the time in the country's history when there were few finished products and settlers adapted the prevalent wire used to fence in pastures to solve just about any problem that came up, kind of a predecessor to duct tape.

By now I am used to seeing people solve problems in surprising ways. But one of the biggest wonders I experienced was during my first visit to India in 2006 when an acquaintance invited me on the spur of the moment to attend the first Innovations for India Award in Mumbai.[1] There I watched the silver-haired, elegantly suited Vinod Kapur receive the award for his Kuroiler "super chicken."[2] India, to be sure, has more than its share of adversity—poverty, illiteracy, social conflict, geopolitical tension, terrorism, and corruption. Kapur, a septuagenarian from Gurgaon (near Delhi), took the high level of poverty that wracks India as a chance to create a unique, for-profit venture that would use chickens to tangibly increase the income of some of India's poorest people.

After ten years of tinkering with both genetics and business concepts, Kapur's venture, Keggfarms, was producing a disease-resistant, bioconverting, fast-growing chicken for the villagers to grow and sell. A single Kuroiler rooster produced—no exaggeration—twice as much meat and the hen five times as many eggs as did the typical backyard broiler. Although the following attributes are not relevant to the business itself, the Keggfarms Kuroiler is a majestic bird, with bold, vibrant colors and a firm, penetrating gaze, as well as by far the tastiest poultry meat and eggs I have ever had. Kapur discovered, or invented, a business opportunity along the way. Kapur's feat seems almost as far-fetched as Meron's PillCam.

Kapur developed the Kuroiler for its ability to thrive in rural parts of India, where a dozen or so productive chickens can provide a source of income to villagers, and some extra nutrition to boot. The birds grow to marketable size about twice as fast as traditional broilers. Kuroilers are environmentally friendly "bioconverters" because they scavenge on household waste, insects, weeds, and even ground-up seashells, so they are also cheaper to raise because no extra feed is required. The dual-purpose Kuroilers are useful for both egg production and chicken meat—something that isn't typical in industrial poultry production, where separate gene stocks are optimized for either eggs or meat, but not both.

The big, colorful chicken is the most obvious element of Keggfarms when you first see one. But the most significant innovation in my opinion is not the chicken per se, but the business model, in particular the distribution system, used to get the one-day-old chicks out of Keggfarms' hatcheries and into the hands of Indian villagers quickly and safely. To put that in context, Kapur faces the most horrendous product distribution problem imaginable. He is selling a live, perishable product (newly hatched chicks) often in extremely hot weather. By definition, rural villagers live far from dense urban centers, so it is impossible to increase distribution efficiencies over a geographically concentrated market. In addition, the customer is reachable in the "last mile" only by dirt road or even footpath. Finally, his customers are poor, so individual sales are small and excess distribution costs cannot be absorbed by higher prices or mitigated by large purchases. How much more adverse can a market be?!

By simultaneously cracking both the genetic and the distribution codes, Keggfarms and its Kuroiler have doubled the income of a million households in India, and there are major contracts on the table with several of India's poorest states as well as Bangladesh, Ethiopia, and Uganda, and a newly launched Bill & Melinda Gates Foundation project.[3] And by cracking those codes, Kapur is addressing a potentially enormous social and business opportunity: significant poverty alleviation of the rural poor. But though Kapur's innovation has won widespread praise for its positive effect on the country, including recognition by the United Nations, Keggfarms isn't a charity or even a non-profit. It's a growing, for-profit business solving a burning social problem, a phenomenon which I have observed elsewhere and which led me a few years ago to coin the acronym FOPSE, for for-profit social enterprise (pronounced *foop-see*).[4]

Adversity, both intrinsic and extrinsic, is not just a set of obstacles for entrepreneurs to navigate around and for societies to remove: adversity is a driver of entrepreneurship—of perceived, created, and captured extraordinary value. Adversity itself is the source of some of the biggest opportunities to solve major social problems—war, disease, water shortage, pollution, global warming, hunger, and access to education and basic services. This has always been fertile territory for some significant business breakthroughs. Microfinance, for example, started out as a social innovation that won Muhammad Yunus the Nobel Prize for establishing the nonprofit Grameen Bank. But when for-profit entrepreneurs latched on to the business model, they drove microfinance from a small-scale enabler of a limited segment of microenterprises to a mainstream asset class affecting hundreds of millions of people. Atsumasa Tochisako is attempting a similar-magnitude revolution in bringing more sophisticated banking services to the bottom of the pyramid while addressing a multi-billion-dollar market for MFIC's services.

For entrepreneurs with an eye for counterintuitive solutions, intractable problems and insurmountable adversity can be a crucible for creating and capturing a lot of value. In founding Keggfarms, Kapur had set out to realize his life dream of building a company that would first and foremost bring income and nutrition to India's huge population of poor, rural villagers, but at a profit, not just for Kapur, but for all the intermediaries and the end customers as well.

Vinod Kapur was born in 1934 in Lahore, India, where his father was a government engineer, before the city subsequently became part of Pakistan during the partitioning of India. After Pakistan was formed, the parents and their four boys moved to Simla in the north of India, where Kapur went to high school and college. Kapur recalls his formative years:

My father was nationalistic, with strong family, cultural, and religious values, and he instilled in me a sense of pride in being Indian, as well as a desire to prove that we can accomplish great things by ourselves. Because of that, as a young man I was seriously bothered by the gross income disparities in Indian society, and although I did not have the view that everything could be equal, I believed that lifting the poor from poverty must be our direction. At college I became the head of the communist-influenced Students Union, which was a great embarrassment to my father, so he sent me to the UK to an engineering college to abort my political involvement. However, I remained committed to communist ideology during my earlier years in the UK. My great disillusionment with communism came when Stalinism was exposed for what it was, but although I moved away from communism as a political ideology, my concern for those at the bottom of the ladder stayed with me.

Kapur's first job was at Western Indian Match Company (WIMCO), where at the age of thirty he was the head of a large factory. There he accrued experience trying out various management innovations and confronting old-fashioned labor and union practices, in one crisis settling a 365-hour strike by cutting a deal that would lead to the recovery of lost wages for workers and lost income for the factory. The government of the state of Uttra Pradesh passed a special law to allow the deal to be ratified.

In 1963, Kapur started dreaming about establishing a chicken farm when it was a nascent industry being promoted by the Indian government. Four years later, he established Keggfarms with a loan from his wife, who came from an established family, moonlighting while keeping his WIMCO job. In 1973, he left WIMCO to create India's first poultry breeding farm, using gene stock he purchased from the United States. Keggfarms' successful experience eventually led the still-protectionist Indian government to mandate that all chickens be bred in India.

That opened the door for Keggfarms' growth, but giving up his lucrative job at WIMCO to concentrate on building Keggfarms added new pressures on Kapur. He had a serious personal stake in the success—or failure—of his venture. "I was heavily weighed down by the pressures of having to look after my wife and three children and the need to sustain the standard of living we were accustomed to, in the face of uncertain income."

By 1991, when India dramatically opened its previously protected economy to foreign competition, Keggfarms was one of the leaders in India's relatively small poultry market, a large percentage of the population being vegetarian. Exposed for the first time to market forces, Kapur realized that he could either join with one of the large international players and thereby lose his identity; compete directly, which he considered foolhardy; or identify an opportunity that the large players could not address. Kapur recognized that the large chicken producers, with their environmentally insulated and controlled production facilities, ultrasensitive poultry stocks, and technology-intensive husbandry, would be able to serve the urban centers, which were huge in absolute terms, but they could never serve the 75 percent of Indians who lived in semirural or rural regions.

Per-capita poultry meat and egg consumption in India had been on the rise for years, both in absolute terms as well as relative to other comparable foods, for several reasons. First, with the increased efficiency of industrial production, the prices of eggs and chickens rose the least compared with prices of other products, like mutton, beef, and pork. Second, the mass production of these products; their ready availability in large, urban markets; and decreasing vegetarianism encouraged poultry consumption, particularly in urban areas.

Despite these factors, rural India experienced no comparable rise either in the production of poultry products or in the consumption of meat or eggs, and production in villages remained stagnant, entirely dependent on nondescript, low-yielding birds. Consumption of industrial poultry products remained low because transportation costs rendered them far more expensive than in the urban areas. Over 70 percent of India's population and nearly 150 million rural households thus represented a potential consumption market that could not be efficiently addressed by the industrial poultry production and distribution network.

Kapur saw an opportunity with the very poorest of these villagers, the more than 30 million households (150 million to 200 million people) that traditionally raised backyard chickens for eggs and meat. These poor villagers lived too remotely to travel to the urban centers to shop. Nor could they afford any purchases even if they could get there, since almost all of these villagers were below the poverty line, making about $400 or less annually per household. Conversely, the large, urban-oriented industrial producers did not have the distribution wherewithal or the financial incentive to bring their products to these rural villagers, with poor or no road access, no refrigerators, and no money.

To survive, rural households grew much of their own food, selling any surplus in local markets, and for cash they depended on limited opportunities for manual labor, with the men often leaving home for weeks or months to work. Most rural households were run by the women, who kept a few farm animals in their backyards for personal consumption, such as goats (for milk products and meat) and ducks (for meat and eggs), while the more affluent normally kept cows and buffalos (for milk and work).

Despite the fact that poor households raised chickens for meat and eggs, Kapur estimated that the traditional consumption of eggs in the rural villages was fewer than five per person per year, compared with a national average of about thirty-five, and the annual consumption of meat was just a few grams per person, compared with a national average of almost 1.6 kg. Yield and production were low, and the villagers sacrificed their own nutrition for the extra income of selling the meat and eggs.

Of the 200 million households in India, approximately 170 to 180 million urban or rural households had enough income to purchase eggs and meat. The remaining 20 to 30 million households were those targeted by Keggfarms. This segment included a disproportionate number of Muslims who had no religiously mandated vegetarianism, so Keggfarms at least did not have to face ethnic barriers to raising chickens for this group, who would welcome the opportunity to consume some extra protein while making some money as well.

It took Kapur ten years of experimental breeding and market testing to finally develop a chicken uniquely tailored to Indian rural villages: the brand name was "Kuroiler," derived from the words *Keggfarms, curry,* and *broiler.* Every detail of the breeding had been thought through carefully: the bird was multicolored for camouflage and because Indian consumers believed that white chickens were intrinsically inferior. It thrived on household waste and therefore did not compete with the villagers themselves for expensive grain for food. It required no special animal husbandry methods, protection, medicines, or expensive sheltering. Chicken shelters could be cheaply provided from readily available scrap materials. The chicken was big, aggressive, and wily enough to fend for itself against dogs and hawks in the open backyard environment. It was genetically resistant to disease.

The Kuroiler was meatier and more productive than conventional rural chickens. Hens attained 2.5 kg within twelve months, began laying eggs at five to six months of age (compared to 12 months for conventional hens), and then laid 150 to 200 eggs during their twelve- to sixteen-month egg-laying period (compared to 35 to 40 by conventional hens), initially more than 20 eggs per month. The Kuroiler rooster reached 4 kg in twelve months and a weight of at least 1 kg at around three months, at which weight it could be sold for meat if the owner so chose.

Kapur's near-perfect chicken is an accomplishment that speaks for itself. But perhaps the more intriguing of Kapur's accomplishments are the unconventional methods he uses to get the chickens into rural villagers' hands—with all the participants along the value chain making money for their roles. Keggfarms owns only the hatchery, and all the other links to the rural villagers are independent. The first link is the dealers, who take one-day-old chicks from the hatchery in their vans. Dealers then sell to the mother units that take, typically, a thousand or so chicks and grow the chicks for twenty-one days, giving them early-life supplements to help make them hardy. The chicks will not be delivered to prospective customers until they attain a weight of about 300 grams, by which time they can fend for themselves in villagers' backyards.

Once the chicks are big enough, independent bicycle vendors collect them and make their rounds of villages on their bikes. They'll put one hundred chirping chicks in a basket and hawk them to households that take the birds and grow them to maturity and productivity.

In a way, the Kuroilers are piggy banks for the households. With a capital investment of about $0.60 per chick, the households have high-quality, nutritious food that costs nothing more to produce and that they could either consume or sell to their wealthier neighbors or in the ubiquitous local markets.

In pondering how Keggfarms could diversify into more profitable businesses with sustainable advantages, Kapur also conceived of a branded egg for the high end of the urban market. I did not know this before tasting them, but I, and everyone I have subsequently talked to, believe that eggs from barnyard hens are tastier than industrial eggs. The barnyard eggs also have colorful shells and bright yellow yolks, a result of the hen's eating green vegetation in the backyard. But in India, backyard eggs produced in small quantities in rural villages cannot make it to market—the distance is too far, the transportation and handling are too expensive, and the availability of the eggs is very low and dispersed. So in the large urban centers, most eggs sold are white and bland, and competition with the undifferentiated commodity is on price alone.

And as it turns out, consumers usually don't know much at all about the eggs they are buying in the local stores. They may be stale and dirty and may have been kept in the hot sun during distribution, or even come from flocks that are diseased or are on antibiotics.

So in 2002, believing that city dwellers would pay a premium for a very different egg, Kapur took up the challenge of developing a tasty egg with a bright yellow yolk and no contaminants or antibiotics and that would reach retail stores within forty-eight continuously refrigerated hours. The eggs would be shipped in small enough batches so that within three to four days from production they would be on the store's refrigerated shelves. He would develop the eggs to be a distinct shade of brown (tan) so that they could be readily identified with Keggfarms. Finally, Kapur would pack them in windowed boxes so that a buyer could be certain of the eggs' appearance. Keggfarms would charge a 100 percent premium for its KEGGs.

Keggfarms test-marketed KEGGS in South Delhi for two years, and satisfied with the results, Kapur began to develop a model for ramping up sales. "We sell a carton of six KEGGs to consumers for 30 rupees, *double* the price of regular eggs," Kapur says. "Our price to the store is 25.75 rupees, and our direct production costs are around 13 rupees. So our margins are excellent, and we offer no credit. Using only two three-wheelers with the Keggfarms sign on them, we currently deliver a few thousand cartons per day to four hundred high-end stores, including sending daily batches to Mumbai by train; consumers flock to the stores, and we cannot supply all the demand."

The success of the Kuroiler and Keggfarms has been noticed in other developing markets. In July 2011, Jagdeev Sharma, a researcher from the Center for Infectious Diseases and Vaccinology at Arizona State University's Biodesign Institute, concluded that the Kuroiler had "an important role to play in the fight to improve global health, alleviate hunger, raise living standards and empower women in the developing world."[5] At a recent American Veterinary Medical Association Meeting in Saint Louis, Missouri, Sharma reported: "The success of the Kuroiler chicken in India, where it was first introduced, makes us hopeful for similar improvements in rural Africa, particularly, in Uganda, where our initial results show the Kuroiler significantly outperforming native chickens."[6] Arizona State University and the Ugandan government are now joining forces to study the feasibility of introducing the Kuroiler to small farms in Uganda.

Similar efforts are under way in Ethiopia and Bangladesh. In the past decade, Kapur has won several awards for his persistent and innovative efforts to contribute toward rural economic development. Now in his late seventies, Kapur is still focusing on growing the business, but handing over the day-to-day operations to a full-time CEO.

The key for Kapur was how and where he saw a chance to create value from what others have seen as problems so extensive that they are unchallengeable. The adversity he found fundamentally unacceptable to his value system ended up being the source of his opportunity. But the perception of the problem to be solved, and the belief that his expertise as a poultry breeder was the key, was just the starting point. "We are a business after all," Kapur says, "and we need to think about our profits as well as doing good for the poor."

––––––––––

Kapur is one of many entrepreneurs who are creating extraordinary opportunity from adversity. Every week, we read about interesting ventures that are achieving international scale and generating exceptional value by starting in lower-income, even bottom-of-the-pyramid markets. Few entrepreneurs have accomplished that on a more global magnitude than Mo Ibrahim, who founded the African cell phone company Celtel in 1998, to become one of the trailblazing successes in bottom-of-the-pyramid markets. Ibrahim saw the potential in Africa's widespread, poor infrastructure and communications networks; less daring investors only felt what he referred to as "Africa fright." In just seven years, Celtel's revenues went from zero to close to half a billion dollars, and its value was over $3 billion when it was sold.

A native of Sudan and a former senior engineer at British Telecom, Ibrahim founded Celtel when he couldn't quite understand how all the major telecommunications companies were ignoring what he saw as a market ready to boom. Sub-Saharan Africa, where most people had never used a phone, let alone owned one, had been shunned by the big players, who deemed it too poor, corrupt, and risky.

"All my career I have been in this industry," he recalls. "Then here is a situation where you have huge unsatisfied demand for a service that doesn't exist. You don't have competition with fixed lines as you do in Europe. It was a no-brainer that the cellular route would be a great success in Africa." But other people saw only obstacles where Ibrahim saw possibility.

Ibrahim had been working as a consultant to top names in telecoms, such as Verizon, Bell South, and Vodafone. "I asked them all, 'Why are you not going to Africa? You are paying millions of dollars to get licenses other places. You could do that for free in Africa.'" Ibrahim continued to press his clients as to why they preferred to invest in mature markets where competition and the cost of entry were high.

One day a very senior executive at a US telecommunications carrier stunned Ibrahim: "'Mo, I thought you were smarter than this. You want me to go to my board and say I want to start a business in a country run by this crazy guy, Idi Amin?' I said, 'Africa is not a country, and Idi Amin left Uganda fifteen years ago.'"

Ibrahim saw an untapped market; the traditional telecom players saw corruption, wars, and famines. "That was the biggest challenge," Ibrahim says. "Everybody said Africa is a basket case. And that was, I think, the reason for reluctance of many established operators in going there, because it had that image of a dangerous place full of dictators and crazy people, who are going to steal your lunch, and they're going to do this to you and that, and they're all corrupt; it was very superficial."

Ibrahim was undeterred. "The purpose of any business is to make money; otherwise, it's not a business," he says. "But, I think there's also the element of excitement and challenge." So Ibrahim set out to realize the opportunity of adversity, which involved huge effort on virtually every conceivable front. Based in Amsterdam and funding Celtel initially with the gains from selling his consulting company, Ibrahim began to simultaneously raise capital and bid on licenses. When Celtel won a bid, it would have to design, build, and operate mobile-phone systems in areas that were an eight-hour flight away from its Netherlands headquarters and then days of Jeep rides. The venture had to navigate everything, from the use of traditional tribal lands to mobile coverage across borders of neighboring African countries in conflict, to internal African wars, to explaining to investors how even genocide would not kill their business as well. All the while, Ibrahim had to convince banks that Celtel had enough potential so that they would lend him money with which to build the infrastructure.

Celtel's coping with the difficult logistics (the venture learned that warring tribes would protect cell towers because the structures facilitated communication during the wars) and with the consumers' poverty (Celtel pioneered prepaid cards) fueled Celtel's growth. In 2005, that risk and hard work paid off. Celtel was sold for $3.4 billion to a Kuwaiti mobile telecom company, now called Zain. Celtel had succeeded despite (or because of) operating in the poorest continent on earth, in the segment of the market that was the most adverse, not the least. Today over half a billion Africans have mobile phones, partly because of Ibrahim and his contrarian vision. And Ibrahim and his investors became very wealthy. Today Ibrahim divides his time between two new endeavors: a venture capital fund he established to invest in Africa, and the Mo Ibrahim Foundation, which recognizes and rewards transparency and governance in African leadership with a $5 million prize.

Seeing opportunity in adversity—a problem that seems overwhelming to others to solve—leaves room for entrepreneurs who aren't daunted by extraordinary challenges. "Whenever you have this gap between perception and reality, you have a big business opportunity," Ibrahim says. Fortunately for Ibrahim, as well as for Africa, he saw it when no one else did. In fact, Ibrahim's success story is top of mind for many aspiring African entrepreneurs as they now have a precedent for what is achievable and a role model to emulate.

Iqbal Quadir, whom we will meet in the next chapter, had a similar epiphany for wireless telephony in Bangladesh, but his story, as we will see, was very different.

CHAPTER 9

Personal Gain

How the Chimpanzee Got His
Bananas Back from the Gorillas

A chimpanzee discovers a banana bush but cannot reach the bananas. He calls over a big gorilla who can reach the bananas, but instead of giving them to the chimpanzee, the gorilla starts eating all of the bananas himself. The chimpanzee tries to convince the gorilla to give him some bananas. Hearing this conversation, a second gorilla shows up and attempts to take some bananas. As the two gorillas begin to fight, a few bananas fall on the ground, and the chimpanzee runs to grab a few for himself.

"That was one of my son's favorite bedtime stories when he was young," Iqbal Quadir recalled nostalgically, but as he told me the story, it seemed to me that the allegory reflected Quadir's own experience launching Grameenphone in the mid-1990s. From his conception of what would become Grameenphone, to the moment of the venture's launch, and then for years thereafter, Quadir tried persistently to wrench back bananas from the two "gorillas" he had persuaded to help him pick the bananas he himself had discovered. The two, Bangladesh-based Grameen Bank and the Norwegian telecommunications giant, Telenor, weren't ever exactly best friends with each other, either, and to this day they publicly spat at nearly every chance they get. Yet Quadir himself still speaks with respect rather than rancor about the two partners that helped make his dream a reality and left an indelible positive impact on Bangladeshi society and economy.

Indeed, today, fifteen years from the venture's actual launch, rapidly growing Grameenphone is itself a gorilla in the Bangladesh communications market with about $1 billion in annual revenues and stock worth almost $3 billion. Like Celtel, the venture Quadir took from dream to reality has been a juggernaut for economic inclusion, while also being the jewel in the crown of the Dhaka Stock Exchange as the country's largest IPO in history—a long way from Quadir working out of his used-car-cum-office in Dhaka. Today Quadir is a professor of practice and the founding director of the Legatum Center for Entrepreneurship and Development at MIT. A few years ago, he sold his stake in Grameenphone for $33 million—before tax, and with over half of the proceeds going to his private backers.

Students who discuss the case in my classes divide into two camps when they learn the terms and timing of the sale. The majority support the decision and are impressed with the millions Quadir made for himself and the good he created for others over that decade of hard work and risk. A vocal minority, however, are upset at how he was pressured by his larger partners to give in, ultimately taking home much less value than he might have had he kept the shares, and less than the value he built. I do not share the latter viewpoint—knowing when to turn created into captured value is one of the arts of being an entrepreneur—but you can judge for yourselves by the end of the story as to whether Quadir was fairly compensated for the social and economic benefit that there is no argument he created.

Nor is there argument that there are two parallel dramas here. One is the drama of *creating* extraordinary value—in overcoming scorn and skepticism to establish a clearly successful venture. The other is the drama of *capturing* extraordinary value—in the scrappy, prolonged effort that Quadir expended in securing his and his private investors' own just desserts.

Almost neighbors with Quadir in Boston today, Ant Bozkaya is also on the faculty of MIT and the subject of one of our Harvard Business School cases.[1] About the time that Grameenphone was finally ready to launch, Bozkaya, four thousand miles away in Turkey, had a similar insight about the opportunity to be a first mover in exploiting Turkey's brand-new electricity deregulation. Bozkaya also risked his time, his savings, and his good name to put together a group of domestic and international giants—gorillas—to form Turkey's first independent power producer (IPP) on one of the giants' large campuses. (An IPP is a way to allow private companies to create power generation plants and sell the excess electricity back to the public utilities.) Unfortunately for Bozkaya, his first IPP lit the way for his partners, as well as numerous latecomers, to usurp his pioneering efforts and make many more millions—without him. Bozkaya was eventually paid for his success, but in this case, my students are of one mind, and Bozkaya himself agrees: his gorillas took almost all the bananas, dropping only one or two for the person who made it happen.

An "Atrocious" Idea

Sitting in his New York investment bank office in 1993, Quadir couldn't help shake the memory of how, as a thirteen-year-old boy in Bangladesh, he was sent to a village ten kilometers away to obtain medicine for an ailing sibling. After walking all morning to reach the village, he learned that the pharmacist was away, and Quadir had to spend all afternoon walking back home, empty-handed. That was far from an unusual experience in Bangladesh at the time—most villages had no telephones or public transportation networks. Even two decades later, when Quadir had a relatively comfortable life on Wall Street, his home country still had only two phones per thousand people, and none outside the cities.

By 1993, he was a world away from his childhood experience, but that was when Quadir first had the idea that his home country might represent an untapped market in mobile communications. In retrospect, the wireless opportunity in poor economies seems obvious to us, but in 1993, it seemed foolhardy. In his mid-thirties, Quadir visited Bangladesh in October that year to assess his idea's feasibility. "I had no background in telecommunications or in economic development," Quadir recalls. "I might have been a Wharton-trained, New York investment banker, but I did not know much about contemporary Bangladesh, as I had been away for twenty years."

Quadir was not surprised that the large swaths of rural Bangladesh had been ignored by local carriers; he just hadn't anticipated how dilapidated and expensive the overall telecommunications infrastructure was. Much of the legacy analog network routinely malfunctioned, waiting lists were years long, and with an average annual income of $220 per capita the $500 installation fee and annual $600 subscription were prohibitive.

Quadir returned to New York discouraged, but two pieces of useful intelligence kept him from abandoning his efforts: parts of the existing analog network would soon be converted to digital, and in parallel, a process of issuing cellular licenses would start in less than a year, in July 1994. Opportunity was just around the corner—he thought.

Quadir knew it would be impossible to move the needle of rural prosperity in Bangladesh on his own from a base in New York. So he went back to Bangladesh to try to enlist Bangladeshi economist Muhammad Yunus, the founder of Grameen Bank, a pioneering microfinance institution that has shown how to help alleviate poverty by providing small loans to the poor to start their own microenterprises. By 1993, Grameen Bank had eleven hundred branches and served thirty-four thousand villages. (Yunus would be awarded the 2006 Nobel Peace Prize for the work of Grameen Bank.) Quadir knew Yunus's buy-in would be a stamp of approval and would open important doors, and he thought the social agendas were completely synergistic. After many attempts, Quadir finally reached Yunus, but he was initially uninterested in Quadir's proposal.

It took Quadir several more attempts in coming months to interest Yunus, but the slowly relenting Yunus remained unwilling to commit the bank's capital, instead offering to write a letter of support. That endorsement was indeed valuable in opening doors, but it wasn't enough to get the project off the ground. This wasn't going to be a venture that Quadir could convince others to take over: if he wanted to launch an economic revolution in rural Bangladesh, he would have to take the reins himself and put together the syndication of partners to finance, build, and operate the network.

In the spring of 1994, Quadir met Joshua Mailman, a wealthy New York social investor. Quadir told Mailman that he was personally willing to commit two years of his life to the cause—one that he believed could transform and empower rural Bangladeshi's economically. Mailman agreed to invest $125,000 in a fifty-fifty partnership with Quadir in order to pay Quadir's living expenses. They named the partnership Gonofone meaning "phone for the masses" in Bengali. At that point in his view of what might be possible, Mailman's investment was the first sign of "faith in me that obliged me to prove I was worth that faith," Quadir recalls. "Giving up was no longer an option."

Mailman's motive was primarily social, but Quadir also saw an opportunity to profit. "A lot of people talk about the social aspects of Grameenphone," Quadir observes, "but they don't quite know that there's a hardcore business aspect of the company, too."

So Quadir left Wall Street, moved to Bangladesh, settled into an apartment, and started planning out the syndication of partners. Quadir reasoned that Grameen Bank, with branches covering the country, could serve as an excellent distribution partner, but he knew that the first priority was a telecommunications carrier with operating expertise and deep pockets to build and run the expensive infrastructure: hundreds of millions of dollars would ultimately be needed. So he started knocking on doors in the United States, but no one got it. Quadir's Bangladesh opportunity, like Ibrahim's Celtel in sub-Saharan Africa, seemed primarily like an opportunity to throw money away: Bangladesh was one of the world's poorest countries, and he could not interest a single US carrier. "We are not the Red Cross," dismissed one. Neither were any US private-equity investors interested, seeing investments in developing countries like Bangladesh as, well, stupid.

Quadir turned to the Nordic countries, which had the highest cell-phone penetration in the world and where Nokia and Ericsson were located. Several Nordic carriers had invested in developing markets and were familiar with some of the normal frustrations that came from dealing with governmental bureaucracies and outdated infrastructure. After several false starts, Quadir was able to convince Sweden's state-run telecom, Telia, to commission a feasibility study.

Telia's support was the trigger to convince Grameen Bank to officially join. As Khalid Shams, deputy managing director of Grameen Bank, later recalled, until Telia's stamp of approval, "the idea just seemed so atrocious . . . but Quadir was very persistent. He was someone who could do the bulldozing."[2] Grameen Bank was finally on board.

The three companies—Gonofone, Telia, and Grameen Bank (through a new established subsidiary, Grameen Telecom)—created a consortium to bid for a wireless license in late 1994, with Gonofone promised 10 percent of the shares. Quadir's dream seemed to be on the verge of becoming reality.

Quadir's euphoria was short-lived. In February 1995, six months after he had first met with Telia executives, Quadir was contacted by the company's headquarters in Sweden. Telia was dropping the project. Dejected,

Quadir was sure that Telia's exit would trigger Grameen Bank's as well. He needed a replacement immediately before his effort could come apart at the seams.

Quadir resumed wooing possible partners in other parts of the world, including Telenor, Thailand's Ucom, and Japan's Marubeni. But he couldn't quite convert the interest into action—especially as Grameen Bank itself had not put any money into the venture yet. Grameenphone was in a holding pattern.

Quadir had no formal office of his own, working out of space he was allowed to use at Grameen Bank and sometimes just his car. That was Quadir's personal low. His own bank account had dwindled to nothing, and his wife was expecting their first child. "When my daughter was born in July 1995," he recalls, "I was at the bottom. I'd abandoned everything in America, and Grameenphone was not yet happening." He couldn't even use his contacts to secure a landline for his apartment in Bangladesh—he had been waiting for more than a year.

Grameen Bank still was unwilling to commit any capital. The moment of truth for Quadir came just a month after his daughter was born, when the Bangladesh Ministry of Posts and Telecommunications invited tenders for three cellular licenses and bids were due on September 30, 1995. So Quadir flew to Norway to make a last-ditch effort to Telenor.

Rather than slamming the door shut, Telenor decided to commission its consulting arm to study the market in Bangladesh, and the consultant indeed concluded that wireless service could be viable for rural villagers. Luckily, as the bid deadline approached, the government extended the date to November 6, which gave Quadir time to complete the feasibility study and submit a final bid.

Telenor and Grameen Bank both found the study persuasive: on October 8, 1995, Telenor officially informed Quadir that it would participate in the bid for a cellular license. With that good news, Grameen Bank did an about-face, committing to invest and demanding a majority stake in the new venture. This curveball flew in the face of Telenor's agreement

to lead the syndication as the main investor, network builder, and opera-
tor. And in the interim, Grameen Bank had invited Marubeni, a giant
Japanese general trading firm, to join the syndication, partly to offset
Telenor's influence.

Just when Quadir could see the light at the end of the very long tun-
nel, dividing the ownership of Grameenphone became, well, divisive:
the gorillas were already jostling each other over the bananas, and the
tiny Gonofone was the partner to suffer most of the fallout. Rather than
the ten percent stake promised by Telia, which Quadir had felt was a
fair reflection of his years of investment, so-called "sweat equity," in the
last-minute arm twisting among the three large partners, Gonofone was
squeezed down to a disappointing 4.5 percent. Grameen Bank (through
a newly established nonprofit, Grameen Telecom) agreed to a 35 percent
stake, with a verbal commitment from Telenor to eventually relinquish
part of its 51 percent majority to Grameen; Marubeni would hold the
remaining 9.5 percent.

In the spirit of the saying "Beware of your dreams; they may come
true," what Quadir had been seeking all along—the financial involvement of Grameen Bank—actually ended up pushing Gonofone and, with
it, Quadir down the pecking order. Disillusioned that his years of sacrifice resulted in less than half of what he expected (which he had to
share with his Gonofone partners), Quadir nevertheless felt ambivalent.
"I always tried to balance my wishes to see the baby be born healthy and
grow independently, with my instincts to keep the baby in my lap," he
recalls. His long-harbored dream to provide cellular coverage for all of
Bangladesh was finally under way. The complex and often tense negotiations for who would own what percentage culminated in an agreement
just hours before the tender submission deadline.

But even that 4.5 percent stake would be challenging for Gonofone to
hold on to. Part of the deal among the partners was to provide $10 mil-
lion up front, and an additional $40 million in tranches to build the net-
work and launch the service, and along the way each partner, including

Gonofone, would be required to invest its part of the $40 million in proportion to its shareholdings. In other words, if Gonofone could not come up with about $1.8 million (4.5 percent of $40 million) over the upcoming one or two years, Gonofone's stake would be further diminished.

Arriving to submit the bid on the morning of November 6, Quadir found chaos. Trade-union activists were blocking the gate, and over a dozen bidders had shown up. To avoid confrontations with the union, the ministry had secretly shifted the venue for bid submission to a different office; Quadir and a Telenor executive put the bid documents in a Samsonite briefcase and submitted the bid personally to the secretary of telecommunications.

It was not over yet. In June 1996, after nearly a year of processing in the government helped by Grameen Bank's lobbying efforts, there were worrying indications that a newly elected government would void the bidding process and start from scratch. Once again, Quadir feared having to throw in the towel. "There was almost no hope," he recalls. "And at that time, I had a wife and a child, and I was thinking I had to cease this fruitless activity. I could not sustain it much longer."

Fortunately, Yunus's personal intervention with the new prime minister proved persuasive, and in November 1996, the government offered cellular licenses to three operators, including the Grameenphone syndication. Since there was already one wireless operator with about five thousand subscribers, the number of cellular operators climbed to four overnight, all having the license to provide services throughout Bangladesh. But Grameenphone was the only one that had specific plans to provide coverage in the rural areas.

Launching the Service

Just one month later, Yunus surprised his partners by declaring in public that the service would go live in just four months, on March 26, 1997,

Bangladesh's Independence Day. Quadir and the partners worked day and night to meet the deadline.

On the declared day, Grameenphone indeed began commercial operations, albeit with more symbol than substance, using six base stations in Dhaka initially serving three thousand urban subscribers and twenty-eight village phone operators (VPOs), women who bought cell phones and rented out usage of the one phone to their poor neighbors. The first two calls from the new cell phones were made from Prime Minister Sheikh Hasina to the Norwegian prime minister and to a VPO on the outskirts of the capital. On the first day, five thousand eager applicants lined up outside Grameenphone's offices, greatly exceeding the partners' modest expectations, and Quadir felt the satisfaction of a vindicated vision.

Once launched, Grameenphone grew rapidly by all measures. In 2000, the company made its first profit of $3 million, which climbed to $28 million, $45 million, and $67 million each year thereafter, with 30 percent profit margins. In 2008 Grameenphone went public and the stock appreciated significantly. Fast forward to the present, and Quadir's baby company is now a grown-up, with $1 billion in 2011 sales and a market value of about $3 billion. At present, Grameenphone covers virtually all of Bangladesh, with close to forty million users and generating rural economic activity via a substantial number of VPOs.

There is no doubt that Quadir's vision has created value for its users: the venture has been lauded as a model for improving economic opportunity and inclusion for citizens in poor countries, through profitable investments in technology. According to economist Jeffrey Sachs, Grameenphone "opened the world's eyes to expanding the use of modern telecommunications technologies in the world's poorest places."[3]

But back in the early ramp-up years following the 1997 launch, things were not nearly that simple for the "baby's" parents, Quadir and his backers in Gonofone. Despite his various roles (chief strategist, chief financial officer, and board member) during and after the launch, Quadir's attempts to have a larger stake in Gonofone were thwarted time and again through 2001. Powerless to change that and also feeling that his "baby" was now a strapping youth, Quadir moved back to the United States to start his next career, including a lecturing stint at Harvard.

But in 2002, Quadir, then a nonvoting board observer, suddenly saw a break in the opposition: its Asian investments in shambles following the financial crisis of 1998, the Japanese trading company Marubeni was interested in selling its 9.5 percent stake. Not legally obligated to allocate any of the purchase to Telenor or Grameen, Quadir confidentially struck a deal with Marubeni. The Japanese company allowed him a few months to come up with $22 million to buy its shares, which would thus up Gonofone's stake to 14 percent.[4]

But persuading some deep-pocketed financier to put up $22 million in a Bangladeshi company proved to be another in a string of extremely difficult tasks, again putting Quadir's persistence to the test. Even in 2003 Bangladesh was *still* seen as an exceedingly risky market, and many of the big-name private-equity investors again scoffed at the deal.

Just as one lone private-equity fund was finally on the verge of signing a deal to back Gonofone's purchase, Marubeni, having patiently allowed Quadir months to round up the funding commitment, decided to inform Telenor and Grameen that it intended to sell its stake to Gonofone.

All hell broke loose. The chimpanzee was about to get some of the bananas that had fallen unnoticed to the ground, and the two gorillas, Telenor and Grameen, were so livid that they momentarily stopped bickering with each other and turned their wrathful gaze on the chimpanzee. Telenor executives immediately flew to Boston, implying legal action. Grameen, far off in Dhaka, was also up in arms and threatened to use every legal means to block the deal. The two large partners each claimed that *it* deserved the right to purchase the Marubeni shares, despite the fact that their "right" had legally expired and that both had passed on opportunities to buy the Marubeni shares before being offered to Quadir.

Concerned that even a decisive legal victory would be a Pyrrhic one, Quadir, ever the pragmatist, spent many months negotiating back and forth among the parties, using all of his investment banking prowess to finesse a deal that all would agree to. Finally, having exhausted the alternatives, Quadir agreed to sell Gonofone's entire stake in the operation, including the option to buy Marubeni's shares, for $33 million. That deal left two owners of Grameenphone, Telenor and Grameen, the former with majority control of 62 percent, and Grameen with 38 percent, as Quadir and the other backers of Gonofone took their cash in late 2004 and left the company entirely.

The gorillas, interestingly, wasted little time in returning to their spats with each other over the bananas, and it has since shown little sign of abating, with Muhammad Yunus publicly berating the foreign Telenor for controlling the lives and income of poor Bangladeshis, and Telenor's executives countering that it was their money and expertise that enabled millions of those lives to be better ones.[5]

Using a variety of techniques to crunch the numbers, my students figure that at the time of Gonofone's exit in 2004, Grameenphone's still privately held shares were worth, on paper, anywhere between $500 million on the low side and $1 billion on the high side. That means Gonofone's stake, including the Marubeni shares, was conservatively worth $70 million, and possibly twice as much—again, on paper. Quadir's personal stake in Gonofone was equal to slightly less than half of that. Yet he had sold at $33 million.

Had Quadir become a fairly wealthy pragmatist, or—how to put it—was he too hasty to capitulate (as some of my students feel)? In very frank discussions as a visitor in my classes, Quadir justifies selling for $33 million as a rational act that took into consideration the on-paper worth of Gonofone's stake in the still-private venture, the uncertainty of Grameenphone's future, and the desire to use his hard-earned wealth in other endeavors, including creating a nonprofit foundation and a center for entrepreneurship and development.

It is not difficult to make an argument for either case; you will have to reach your own conclusion. What would be difficult to conclude, however, is that it doesn't matter. Personal gain—the capture of extraordinary value—is an integral element of entrepreneurship.

A Different Ending . . .

Even though today he teaches cases on entrepreneurship, venture capital, and private equity at MIT, there's one entrepreneurship case Ant Bozkaya avoids discussing: that of his own company, TA Energy.[6] Fifteen years before becoming an academic, Bozkaya had left a steady and prestigious job at a well-regarded, family-owned Turkish company to take advantage of Turkey's deregulating electricity industry. Bozkaya, Harvard professor Bill Kerr, and I chronicled his experience in a Harvard Business School case study, but "I don't like to use it," Bozkaya says. "My students are so harsh on me."

Bozkaya didn't start his career to become either an entrepreneur or an entrepreneurship professor, although today he is an authority on entrepreneurial finance. Born in Turkey, Bozkaya received an undergraduate degree in industrial management and his MBA from Virginia Tech, followed by stints for Andersen Consulting in the United States, the United Kingdom, and Australia. He didn't return to his native Turkey until he was recruited to lead the restructuring of a division of a large, diversified Turkish holding company, his success at which led to his appointment to the board.

That was 1997, at the beginning of the deregulation and privatization of the electricity market in Turkey, which planted the seed for a new business in Bozkaya's mind: "I was one of the very few to see IPPs as sexy. Producing electricity was not considered very innovative, in part because it relied on technology that had been around for almost a hundred years." The IPP business model itself had been implemented in other countries, but the model was new for Turkey, and Bozkaya saw the chance to combine his operational skill with his experience working with both domestic and global resources. His strategy was to start small but end big. He would first partner with one of the major international power development players, which would help build, finance, launch, and operate their first IPP. With the first demonstrated success, so went the script, together Bozkaya and the partner would put together a string of IPPs and ultimately make money by listing the group of IPPs on the Turkish stock exchange.

Turkey's economy at the time was growing, and many multinationals were following the growth to open up Turkish operations. But even multinationals that had been in business for years in Turkey still couldn't assemble the local and global resources and navigate the local bureaucracy on their own, persuade the government to remove regulatory obstacles, and put together a viable consortium to launch an IPP. At the same time, it was clear to Bozkaya that the country needed more electricity and better service, which was very sporadic at best: demand was growing. If he could only bridge the supply and the demand: "My role was not creating a technology or a service, but rather bringing players together and aligning their interests where there is a big opportunity for everyone." Bozkaya thought that he could pull it off, with his management skill and agility and contacts.

To get that first IPP up and running and profitable would require the creation of a "bundle" of contracts with a consortium of six or seven partners to supply the fuel, provide the land, finance the operation, supply the equipment, build the plant, operate the IPP, and buy the produced electricity. To do that, Bozkaya had to play chicken-and-egg: if he could persuade a big company to provide the land and to commit to becoming the IPP's long-term, captive customer, he could then persuade an international supplier of the expensive cogeneration equipment (there were only a few in the world) to come into the deal. Then he could find a partner to build the plant and operate it, all the while committing to purchase gas and oil under a long-term fixed contract with a national utility. Finally, with it all put together, he could find a financial partner to put up the capital to finance the entire project.

To pull it off, he would have to act quickly and near-simultaneously on all fronts to persuade the various partners and negotiate the contracts. This was going to look like months of intense shuttle diplomacy.

Before leaving his executive position, Bozkaya first offered the opportunity to his employer, trying to persuade the conglomerate that the IPP business could be an attractive new venture. The conglomerate did not see it the same way. So Bozkaya resigned his steady job to go after the nascent IPP market. Like Quadir, it was, in hindsight, the time in his life when he was least able to take risks. He was in his mid-thirties with a respected, well-paying job as a senior executive of a major corporation, with a young family. Bozkaya decided to limit his investment of time and money to the equivalent of six months' salary—$80,000—and would pull the plug, so to speak, if that ran out.

Bozkaya first began to line up customers for the electricity. At the time, Turkey was suffering from major electricity blackouts, so Bozkaya's pitch was this: if you'd like to have steady, reliable, long-term electricity service, buy it from me. Even if the rate is not lower than you are paying now, I guarantee you constant service with no outages.

One of his first customers to show serious interest was Coca-Cola, which had a major facility in Turkey, and it agreed to buy 30 percent of the plant's output. Even more critically, his former employer, which had one of its companies on a large, campus-like site, started seeing the light (sorry) and agreed not only to be the IPP's anchor customer, but also to provide the land in exchange for a 10 percent stake in the IPP, with an option to increase its ownership to 40 percent. This was a breakthrough:

Such a powerful partner with skin in the game would provide legitimacy as Bozkaya built the entire bundle.

Bozkaya did not realize it at the time, but he had just invited a gorilla to pick bananas for him from a bush that he, Bozkaya, had found. With customer commitments in hand, he hopped on a plane to London to pitch to Rolls Royce, one of the world's largest turbine manufacturers, to agree to supply and install the requisite turbine in Turkey. Bozkaya was cognizant of the fact that Rolls Royce's acceptance could not be taken for granted, since manufacturers often participated in financing the sale of the equipment, and there were only a few turbine suppliers in the world, so they were in big demand and chose their sites carefully.

Bozkaya's pitch worked, and with Rolls Royce's consent under his belt, Bozkaya next persuaded Shell Oil to agree to supply the oil to fuel the turbines. "I was creating value for everyone," Bozkaya says. "The IPP would buy multi-million-dollar products from Rolls Royce, oil from Shell, and gas from a Turkish supplier. I created value for end users, because I was providing them a reliable electricity supply. I brought in a large engineering company with global experience building IPPs and an international operator who had management experience making all this work." In short Bozkaya was creating a win-win-win situation—for everyone but himself; it just hadn't dawned on him yet.

With the key players lined up, Bozkaya convinced international financial institutions to join together to back the deal, making money from interest payments from the IPP. In just four months of whirlwind activity shuttling back and forth to negotiate contracts, Bozkaya had the first IPP all buttoned up.

Or so he thought. The stun came in the form of a grim meeting with the patriarch chairman of the family conglomerate, now his key customer, land provider, and equity partner. "We don't need you anymore to make this deal happen," the chairman said. "But don't worry, we will be generous. Take a finder's fee of $1.75 million, and leave the rest to us. Or else we are out."

Bozkaya's big vision of a publicly traded string of IPPs dissipated before his very eyes. In a single meeting, Bozkaya went from committed
entrepreneur who had created the opportunity of his career, to a consultant with a fee, admittedly a significant fee, but a pittance compared
with the entrepreneurial venture he had set out to create. "We don't need
you anymore." The words stung. The gorillas would take care of the
bananas, and by the way, "Be grateful that we are throwing a few pieces
your way. But you are a chimpanzee, not a gorilla, and the tree is ours
from now on."

Shocked and even offended, Bozkaya briefly considered calling the
patriarch's bluff and rebuffing the ultimatum, but he quickly realized that
he had from the outset misunderstood the relationship between perceiving an opportunity, creating value, and capturing a stake for himself. "I
messed up because my aspiration for my personal role did not reflect
how my participation and power would evolve," he says now. "In the
first stages of organizing the IPP, I was indeed the first one to bring all
the players together. There was great benefit for all the stakeholders in
my ability to recognize the window of opportunity and know-how to
put the bundle together. But I failed to see that immediately after putting the bundle together, I had nothing more to offer. My contribution
was simply not important; I wasn't necessary." Within just a few months,
Bozkaya's unique value added went from high to zero.

"Once the model is clear, and since the players are major powers with
a lot of internal capacity, financial and human resources, they really *can*
do this by themselves," he says. If he'd known from the start how it
would turn out, he says, he might have just acted as a consultant with his
onetime fee (called a *development fee* in the industry) from the beginning,
rather than aspiring to be an owner.

So Bozkaya, like Quadir, sold for less than he had envisioned, ultimately using his experience, contacts, and credibility to put together
two more IPPs in neighboring countries, getting paid a very respectable

fee as a developer, not a stake as an entrepreneur. "Could I have made hundreds of times more?" he asks. "I don't know."

––––––––––––––

The stories of Quadir and Bozkaya are similar in many respects. Both men created value by identifying opportunities that others ignored or rejected, and both then put together the partners and the resources to parlay the opportunities into valuable, growing businesses. Such value-added brokering is often overlooked or dismissed by academics and policy makers as not "real" entrepreneurship, but it is no less entrepreneurial than the stereotypical high-tech start-up. In fact, in some ways it is more purely entrepreneurial, because it requires no special resources other than unadulterated entrepreneurial ability manifested in the insight and creativity to perceive the opportunity and the skill to put the pieces together. In reality, this manifestation of entrepreneurship is fairly common, such as in movie production and real estate development.

A fundamental problem for the entrepreneur, a problem exacerbated for broker-entrepreneurs, but ubiquitous to some extent, is the fairly significant gap in time between when the entrepreneur perceives value, succeeds in creating it, and finally benefits from it personally (figure 9–1). As a result, entrepreneurs are frequently vulnerable at some point to the gorillas taking away their bananas: the chimpanzee sees the bananas (the extraordinary value), may create some of it, but the gorillas, who are essential in reaching the bananas (creating the value) and doling them out (capturing the value), can take it away at any time.

The challenge for entrepreneurs lies in the fact that their ability to capture value created by the venture frequently occurs much later, and thus they must capture some of the value created long after they themselves have ceased to contribute, that is, after their added value has been consumed, used up, and indeed, they are not longer needed. The incentives for the larger partners (or later investors) to deprive entrepreneurs of their just desserts are powerful. As a result, it is not at all uncom-

FIGURE 9-1

Relationship between value creation by an entrepreneur and changing value of the venture

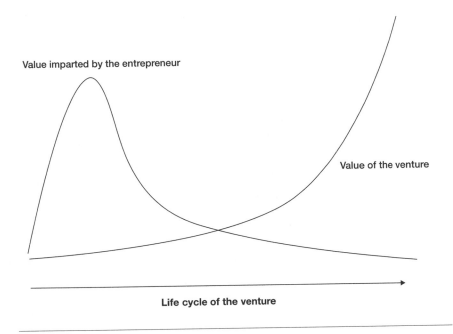

Value imparted by the entrepreneur

Value of the venture

Life cycle of the venture

mon for entrepreneurs to feel shortchanged by latecomers. Of course, the latecomers don't see it as unfair; to the contrary, they often feel quite sincerely that they are being unusually generous if they allow the entrepreneur to be compensated at all. Furthermore, if the latecomers are corporations, most of them do not understand the notion of taking a risk in exchange for uncertain, possibly extraordinary future profit, so they heavily discount the entrepreneur's contribution in economic terms. In this sense, large partners are almost invariably anti-entrepreneurial.

Both Quadir and Bozkaya were able to see their ideas turn into real value—a key element in our definition of entrepreneurship. But the difference between the two is how much value they then captured for themselves. The different ways they played their own hands as they gathered together the partners that were essential for their businesses demonstrate how quickly an entrepreneur can lose a meaningful stake with which to capture value. The first step in capturing significant value is in understanding the rapidly shifting power dynamics among players and what an initially crucial entrepreneur can do to maneuver through the situation. It's not easy.

It doesn't happen by itself. It is part of entrepreneurship—making money (or other significant, noneconomic value) is important. In fact, it's one of the most prevalent ways we gauge just how entrepreneurial someone has been. Seeing the potential for value where others do not and then realizing, in the sense of creating, that value are both essential. But until entrepreneurs have managed to achieve that extraordinary payoff for their effort and risk, they haven't entirely finished the job. They are more—or less—entrepreneurial, partly according to how far they've been compensated for their risk and contribution. People do not believe that an entrepreneur who gives up the right to an extraordinary reward for his or her efforts is quite as entrepreneurial as one who gives away, to charity or other endeavors, cash that has entered the entrepreneur's bank account.

This concept may be difficult for some readers to accept in a period during which we have seen markets fail and people who have made a lot of money seem not to have earned it, a period in which we are searching for a value that transcends unbridled greed. For this reason, I take this topic up in more detail in chapter 12, "Capturing Extraordinary Value."

PART FOUR

MAKING SENSE OF IT ALL

*W*orthless, *Impossible, and Stupid* portrays entrepreneurship as a contrarian process in which an entrepreneur uniquely realizes and reaps extraordinary value by seeing its potential where others do not, largely because the market misses the opportunity or dismisses it as worthless, impossible (unimaginable), or stupid. The particular constellation of factors at that moment is perceived by virtually everyone but the entrepreneur as valueless. But the potential extraordinary value becomes actual because of the entrepreneur's ability to recognize, realize (as in "bring forth"), and then reap the value that no one else anticipates.

Therefore, entrepreneurship *always* surprises us; it is *always* baffling. It is *always* difficult to predict. Attributed to anyone from Bohr to Berra, the quip is apt: "Prediction is difficult, especially about the future."[1] Who could have predicted SABIS's expansion to fifteen countries, seventy-four schools, and sixty-two thousand students? Or Actavis's meteoric rise to number five and a hundredfold increase in employee headcount in just eight years? Or Studio Moderna's dominance of multichannel retailing in twenty Central and Eastern European markets? Or the sale of phones to millions of poor rural subscribers by Iqbal Quadir's Grameenphone? Or Jay Rogers's ability to roll out dozens of crowd-sourced cars within three years? Or Will Dean's $20 million first-full-year revenues from people paying to slither in the mud? Or . . . The list is as long as the history of entrepreneurship, which is itself as long as humankind.

Our reactions (if we are honest)? "I would never in my life have thought of that!" "That's impossible!" "Isn't that amazing?" "I wish I would have done that." "What will people think of next?" "You can make money out of that?!" "That's like making a silk purse out of a sow's ear."

Behavioral scientists have taught us the ubiquity of hindsight bias: The same events that we predict with low probability become "sure things" after the fact. Yet even after the fact, we remain surprised by these examples of extraordinary value creation, testimony, I believe, to the strength of our a priori skepticism, derision, and dismissiveness. We remain amazed (or puzzled or chagrined) at the success of these ventures even when looking at them as *faits accomplis.*

In *Worthless*, I have tried to spread a broad canvas and paint it with a variety of examples of entrepreneurship to shake our Silicon Valley stereotypes. And on the canvas we see that our entrepreneurs are outwardly normal people. Atsumasa Tochisako, Sandi Češko, Will Dean, Sean and Michael Dimin, and Vinod Kapur are what I call *accessible entrepreneurs,* that is, ordinary people with extraordinary accomplishments. "If they can do it, there is no inherent reason why I cannot also." Robert Wessman was seen by his high school peers as someone average at best, never to be voted most likely to succeed. If Wessman can do it, I ask my students, why can't you? The answer, when they push themselves to think deeply about it, is this: it is primarily a question of choice and commitment—of desire and attitude—than of aptitude and skill. The answer resides as much in our willingness to enter into the unknown, to learn from successes and mistakes, and to maintain a flexible persistence, as it does in brilliant inspiration and genius, technical or otherwise (although sometimes they work, too).

But the accomplishments of these ordinary entrepreneurs are anything but ordinary; indeed, there is nothing average about entrepreneurship. Entrepreneurship is not about central tendencies; it is about extremes. Entrepreneurship is not about what is likely; it is about what is possible. It is not about ordinary; it is about extraordinary. The common denominator of all of these accessible entrepreneurs is their contrarian perception, creation, and capture of extraordinary value. It is their recognition, realization, and reaping of more value than anyone else (the market) could have anticipated.

As we will see in the next chapters, the extraordinariness of entrepreneurship has implications and challenges for entrepreneurs and policy makers alike. But "buyer beware:" Lurking behind the intuitively appealing (at least for many) *Worthless* definition of entrepreneurship lie some surprising and even disturbing questions about what entrepreneurship is and is *not*, how aspiring entrepreneurs should face their task, and how societal leaders who envision entrepreneurship as essential for many aspects of society should realize their vision.

CHAPTER 10

Perceiving Extraordinary Value

Opportunities are not fruit on trees waiting to be picked.

Smart people don't start car companies when the automotive industry is collapsing.

At the heart of the perception of extraordinary value is the entrepreneur's contrarian belief that what other people view as worthless, impossible (or unimaginable), or stupid is potentially valuable, possible, or smart. When the world saw the automotive industry falling apart, Jay Rogers saw an opportunity for making cars in a different way; many savvy investors indeed thought the idea and timing were both way off. Fortunately for Rogers, he was capable of persuading enough investors, employees, and partners that even though the idea might have seemed absurd, Rogers would be smart enough to turn it into something useful.

Smart people don't build a financial services company with customers who have neither cash nor credit.

Yet where the US banks saw the unbanked immigrant population as risky and poor, Atsumasa Tochisako saw this unattractive market segment as filled with potentially loyal customers who would, by the way, collectively capitalize a new transnational loan product with their remittances and represent a hitherto untapped multi-billion-dollar market. When most people saw worm excrement, Tom Szaky saw a blockbuster fertilizer product. Where Slovenian consumers saw false promises, Sandi Češko envisioned a multi-channel platform for selling a plethora of products and services. Where others saw a charity at best, Iqbal Quadir saw economic empowerment and financial gain. Where the fishermen saw cheap, rotting fish and Manhattan's chefs saw, well, nothing, the Dimins saw a profit-making supply of quality seafood and a better dining experience.

The Opportunity Illusion

The perception that there is a need or a want or a pain "out there" is at the core of what we typically call an "opportunity." We look at the automotive industry's inefficiency, the waste that is polluting us, or the want for new forms of entertainment or luxury, and we see problems or potential, and we see opportunity in solving those problems or delivering on that potential. So we think about opportunity as something that exists in the marketplace of needs, pains, or wants, something that no one is responding to effectively. There is potential in the situation, a potential that, if we can just unleash it, will generate value for customers, for the world, for the market, or for whomever.

The problem with this view of opportunity is that it objectifies something that is not simply a property of "objective reality." This is what I call the *opportunity illusion* because it conjures up a misleading image of a fruit on a tree waiting to be picked. Popular language reflects this illusion: "You have to reach out and grab opportunities when you see them." "Don't let that opportunity pass you by." "Strike while the iron is hot." It is as if an opportunity is a thing, and the job of the entrepreneur is to see it first. "The early bird gets the worm."

Let's assume that two people look at precisely the same situation and the same facts and come to opposite conclusions about whether there is any latent opportunity there. The old witticism about the two shoe salesmen is apt: one comes back from a trip to a very poor country and says,

"There is no market for shoes; everyone is barefoot." The second shoe salesman comes back from the same territory and says, "There is a huge market for shoes; everyone is barefoot."

Clearly, opportunity is at least partly in the eye of the beholder. *So what makes one person see it and the other not?*

The Entrepreneur's Capabilities

One answer: It partly depends on how the entrepreneur sees him or herself. An opportunity remains a flight of fancy unless the viewer sees that he or she has the capability, assets, or information to make it a reality. It is not an opportunity just to perceive a need or imagine a solution. Before Meron developed the PillCam, gastroenterologists knew perfectly well that there was an objective need for a safer and more convenient method to image pathologies in the small intestine. Imagining—daydreaming about, conjuring up—an ingestible camera that moved itself down the GI tract and sent pictures was also a no-brainer. But what if it turned out that it was impossible to develop, manufacture, approve, and distribute such a camera in reality? The sheer imagining of the solution does not turn a need into an opportunity either. Lots of people can build castles in the sky. Harry Kleiner is recognized as a great science fiction screenplay writer, but *Fantastic Voyage* is not the identification of an opportunity, and Kleiner (at least in this respect) was not the entrepreneur who developed the PillCam.

What turned capsule endoscopy for small-intestine imaging into an opportunity was that a particular person, Gabi Meron, possessed a unique combination of the skills, information, and access to resources (experts, for example, and investors) that would be needed to convert perceived into created value. Having managed two electro-optics companies, Meron understood certain aspects of developing imaging systems. Because he had been an executive in a pharmaceutical company, he could understand the world of medicine and health care. He had managed large, complex projects for the military, so he had leadership skills. After six months of studying the market and talking with doctors and opinion leaders, Meron had special information. And finally, Meron had the initial backing of investors, so he had access to financial resources (although that turned out to be the riskiest aspect of the start-up at times).

A market need, pain, or want without a person to address them is not an opportunity. Opportunities are the interactions of personal capabilities and some characteristics of the objective situation. One without the other is insufficient.

There are three general types of capabilities that interact with external factors to create opportunities: assets, information, and skills.

Assets

Assets come in many forms, including cash, real estate, and intellectual property, and possessing them changes the perception of opportunity. A piece of undervalued real estate is not an opportunity for me if I don't have cash or cannot get a mortgage. In 1998 a friend of mine, Laurent Adamowicz, bought for $55 million a luxury food company, Fauchon, revered by Parisians for decades. Adamowicz's prior experience with luxury brands and food products, and his access to capital as an investment banker, allowed him to see extraordinary value in the underutilized brand, where others were blind to it. That included Fauchon's previous owners, who initially did not even know they wanted to sell the brand until they saw that someone was persistent in wanting to buy it. One of the reasons Adamowicz wanted to buy Fauchon was that the owners, he had learned, had been treating the real estate that Fauchon owned as the more valuable asset and had been undervaluing the Fauchon brand itself. But Adamowicz used his knowledge and experience to get it right: on the day he closed the acquisition, he sold off the buildings, and immediately began redeploying the venture's assets in captivating the upscale New Yorkers and French ex-pats with a new store on Fifty-Sixth and Park Avenue, rejuvenating the market in Tokyo, and refocusing the hundreds of Fauchon's products to generate new sales and market momentum. The end result was an upsurge in the brand's popularity and the company's rapid growth.

Defining opportunity as partly subjective may seem readily apparent to some, but this definition goes against some well-worn and well-accepted descriptions. The so-called Harvard Business School definition, which graces the entrance to the Harvard Innovation Laboratory and is taught to all first-year MBAs at the world's best business school, says that entrepreneurship is "the pursuit of opportunity beyond the resources currently under control."

This definition of entrepreneurship treats opportunity as if it were a "thing" that can be pursued—it is the proverbial early bird's worm. It also implies that identifying objective opportunities precedes figuring out what resources entrepreneurs must acquire in order to address them.

Not so simple. Our examples suggest that the prior possession of, or even belief about, relevant capabilities has a distinct impact on the perception of opportunity. For instance, I may not even notice a market need if I don't think I have the capability of addressing it. To use an analogy, a basketball court is not the same opportunity to someone five feet tall as it is to a seven-footer. The opposite may be true for a Ping-Pong table.

In addition, beliefs about what I can or cannot do can determine which challenges I take on and which ones I overlook. According to Harvard's definition, taken to a logical extreme, it would be entrepreneurship if I sold you the Brooklyn Bridge, took your order and, hopefully, money, and then went and figured out how to acquire it to actually deliver the deed over to you. But if I *did* own or even had a legal option to acquire the Brooklyn Bridge, believe me, I would begin to see opportunities for value creation and capture that I could not even begin to imagine without such ownership. Opportunity exists sometimes *only because of* the resources currently under control, even if it is only the belief or perception that I control certain resources, or because I know I can acquire them. Perception drives opportunity as much as opportunity drives perception. A market need is an opportunity only if you can (and want to, as I will suggest later) address it.

Information

Using information to create arbitrage, buying low in one place and selling high in another, is as old as humankind. The Phoenician traders of the first millennium BC knew that the Persians to the east revered silver and silver artifacts.[1] And they knew that the Iberian farmers (what is now Spain and Portugal) were letting molten silver drain off when they burned their fields. The Iberian farmers saw something worthless, in fact, bothersome. The Phoenicians saw opportunity in the Iberian silver because they knew where and how it was valued as well as how to extract it from ore. According to historians, in order get the silver, the Phoenicians offered a trade to the Iberians: in exchange for getting you to collect this annoying silver liquid and teaching you to manage extraction of silver from ore, we, the Phoenicians, who have a diverse set of powerful deities to protect us, will offer you their protection in return. The Iberians agreed, one result of which was the depletion of most of the silver ore deposits in the Iberian Peninsula. The Phoenicians later added further value by using their skills to turn the silver into beautifully decorated artisan wares, examples of which grace museums throughout the world.

Three millennia forward, Stephen Greer, a successful, self-made scrap-metal trader and the author of *Starting from Scrap* (one of my favorite entrepreneurship books), saw opportunity to turn scrap metal into money by finding out who wanted to buy scrap magnesium.[2] He then traveled into the hinterlands of rural China to find plants trying to get rid of their scrap. His information about both made the oversupply of scrap in one place, and the need for scrap in another, into an opportunity. I could have seen the same need for magnesium, but for me the identical objective reality would not have been an opportunity without information about the supply. Mediating between remote buyers and sellers using special information about supply and demand is one of global society's oldest forms of entrepreneurship.

Skills

Robert Wessman had neither special assets nor special information when he took over Actavis. Nor did he know anything about generic pharmaceuticals. He had neither contacts nor capital. But Wessman did have skill: He knew how to build a team. He knew how to work hard and how to drive his people to achieve more than they believed they could. He knew how to talk reluctant company owners into selling their companies to him and join the Actavis juggernaut. He knew how to move extraordinarily fast. He had an uncompromising competitive streak. So when he saw the failing, illiquid, tiny generic maker in Reykjavik embroiled in ownership battles, he saw opportunity because he had complete confidence in what he, Robert Wessman, could accomplish. I don't have those skills, so if I had been in Wessman's shoes, same place, same time, there would have been no opportunity. And Wessman's belief in his special abilities in integrating acquisitions and exploiting synergies allowed Actavis to buy assets at (what turned out to be) attractive prices, because he and Actavis had the skill to convert worth-less into worth-more.

The entrepreneur's belief that he or she has these capabilities has two effects. One is that it leads the entrepreneur to perceive more value (opportunity) than does the market. Wessman's ability led him to see extraordinary value in the acquisitions he made; he could buy cheaply and enhance the value of his acquisition. Second, it also leads the entrepreneur to take more risk and to persist despite natural resistance (intrinsic adversity) because the entrepreneur believes that he or she can convert that perception to tangible value.

The Entrepreneur's Desire (or, How Do I Know What I Want Until I See What There Is?)

This necessary interplay between some characteristic of the situation or market need and the entrepreneur's capabilities is still not enough for there to be an "opportunity." Let's suppose that it is 1999 and I, Daniel Isenberg, imagine that it would be very useful to have an ingestible video camera. And let's also suppose that I know Gabi Meron and that he and I both believe he has all of the skills, information, and assets to develop and market such a camera. But if he doesn't want to do it, is there still an opportunity? I don't think so, at least not quite the same opportunity as if he did have that desire. The entrepreneur has to want to bridge that gap very badly.

Desire is a complex emotion, as poets and philosophers have observed through the ages. Sometimes desire exists a priori, driving us to search for ways to satisfy it. "I always wanted to start a new company in medical devices and health care," a person might say. "I will study, gain experience, save some cash, and look around for partners. I will develop the abilities. And at some point, I will go out and talk to doctors, patients, health-care providers, payers, and find out what the market's needs are." Atsumasa Tochisako prepared unwaveringly for twenty-five years to launch his venture to provide dignified financial services to poor people.

But it can just as easily work the other way around: Desire may also form as a result of success as well as its cause. Sandi Češko did not initially desire to build a retail powerhouse in twenty-one countries, nor did Jorge Rodríguez, whom you will meet later, desire to build a global compliance and logistics services company. Their desires were fueled by their initial successes.

This is what I call the *discovery of desire*, and I believe it is much more common than we think. One hot summer day, I found my five-year-old son Itai standing in front of the open refrigerator door when we had just moved to Israel. Probably imagining my own mother's voice, I exhorted, "Itai, don't hold the fridge door open!" And operating on the theory that desire drives action, I added, "First think of what you want to eat, and then open the door and look for it."

Set your goals based on your desires, create a plan for achieving them, and execute. Right?

"How do I know what I want until I see what there is?" he replied. In other words, "Why frustrate myself wanting something that is unattainable?" We don't often want what we cannot have or cannot achieve.

Might people who have unique capabilities to profitably solve a problem choose not to? It may be difficult to imagine, but people who see market needs for which they have the skills, assets, or information to uniquely address those needs may not be interested in matching their personal resources with the market. In part because personal desires or wants can conflict with each other, it happens a lot. One of my students had, before starting his MBA program, created a social networking site that had become a smash hit in Brazil: twenty-one million email requests to subscribe to the site were sitting on its servers!! But my student preferred to leave his venture, get his MBA, and let his brother and father keep the company alive while they figured out what to do with all the customer inquiries. Jim Sharpe founded Extrusion Technologies through his acquisition of a small maker of metal parts in Randolph, Massachusetts, and it was his dream to grow the company only to a certain size so that he could cash out and spend time with his family.[3]

One of the stories my students love to hate is when Mei Zhang "abandoned" her growing Beijing-based venture, WildChina, to move to Los Angeles to support her asthmatic son's health and her journalist husband's career.[4] Zhang had launched the tour company in 2000 to help travelers experience China in a different way, through culinary, historical, or ecological tours to the less-trod back reaches of the large country.

Almost immediately after launch, Zhang was forced to confront the near-death experiences brought on by 9/11 and SARS. With grit and persistence, she began to rebuild the company's revenues. But in 2004, when she left her four-year-old "baby" in the hands of a CEO she had hired (one she would later regret as a poor choice), WildChina was still fighting hard to establish a foothold in a tough marketplace. Students in my classes are split right down the middle, but significant numbers of both men and women alike are shocked that Zhang would have left the venture that only she knew how to build. But Zhang's desire had shifted. And desire cannot simply be drummed up at will. It's either there or it's not. (A happy sequel to the story: Zhang has relocated with her family back in Beijing, she is back at WildChina as chairperson, and the venture is growing nicely.)

In each of these cases, the opportunity diminished or disappeared because the entrepreneur's desires changed. The truth is not a simple one: wants, needs, and capabilities develop in a complex interaction in which each pulls and pushes the other (figure 10–1).

FIGURE 10-1

Opportunity is the interplay of capabilities, market needs, and values

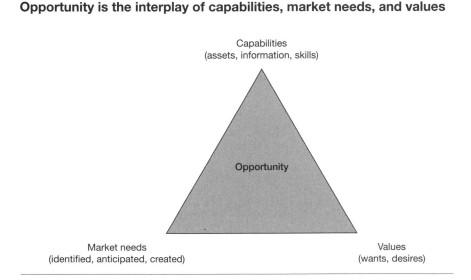

The Entrepreneur's Mind-Set

Are the mix of capabilities, market needs, and desire enough? Maybe in some circumstances, but there is also something in the attitude or mind-set of potential entrepreneurs that fosters contrarian perception. This manifests itself in the propensity to question things most of us take for granted or assume are not answerable. Some people think there is even a genetic influence here, but that debate is not germane to our discussion. Ron Zwanziger, the developer of the MediSense blood glucose monitor and founder of two additional billion-dollar ventures (I have mentioned Zwanziger earlier in *Worthless*), starkly told my Harvard class, "If you want to be entrepreneurs, you cannot think like sheep." Entrepreneurs seem to have developed an independent streak in the way they assess market perceptions (Zwanziger told my students that he thinks there is a genetic predisposition for this tendency, by the way).

Optimism is also a part of that same mind-set, and entrepreneurs are almost certainly unusually optimistic, in particular about the anticipated impact of their perceived capabilities on the market. Sometimes they are so optimistic that they grossly overestimate their chances of success. Some call that propensity irrational optimism because it is not justified by the objective probabilities, and it is true that aspiring entrepreneurs believe they will not fail where others have.

Is irrational optimism good or bad? It is certainly a bad thing for statisticians, whose tools are not created for recognizing the value of anomalies, and investors can mitigate against it by carrying a portfolio. But entrepreneurs can place only one bet at a time, so for them, entrepreneurship is not about central tendencies or what is likely; it is about the outliers and what is possible. Although extreme optimism is not a robust determinant of success, it is probably a necessary prerequisite for achieving it. If success is random, then for sure you and I and the entrepreneur should bet against it. But if as an entrepreneur, I see a game of chance as a game of skill instead, then I have the possibility to make an extraordinary gain. If I have unique information about whether I really can solve a technical problem, or if I have an unusual capability to sell new products to customers who initially may think they are not interested in buying, then the objective probabilities of success change, and the rare, extraordinary outcomes are not random, even if they may remain unusual. That is what extraordinary is, and my optimism may be (relatively) justified. I have at least some ability to turn a game of chance into, at least partially, a game of skill.

What's more, the propensity to think independently, to challenge conventional wisdom, and to act in a contrarian fashion is not quite the same as irrational optimism. By tying their future worth to something that is, initially, worthless, impossible, or stupid, entrepreneurs are in a sense buying low—investing in an idea that is undervalued by others—so that they can later sell high, reaping extraordinary value from it.

Contrarian thinking just as often comprises undervaluing an asset that the market overvalues, and a contrarian mind-set can be either optimistic or pessimistic at different times. The flip side of contrarian optimism is the decision not to buy—or invest in—something that is overvalued. To be successful, it is important for entrepreneurs to perceive when the market may be *over*valuing an idea, to know "when to fold 'em." Or as Shakespeare's Falstaff famously put it, "The better part of valour is discretion." Laurent Adamowicz sold the overvalued real estate of Fauchon at the same time that he bought the undervalued Fauchon assets. Having made twenty-six successful acquisitions, very often at prices significantly lower than market, when the market changed because acquirers were starting to pay premiums for their acquisitions, Robert Wessman stopped buying up companies. Bert Twaalfhoven, founder of over fifty companies, sold his holding company Indivers in 2001 primarily because his growth through acquisition strategy was too expensive as company valuations became inflated.[5] The jet engine supply and maintenance industry he was active in at the time had become too attractive, so it was more lucrative for him to leave. That is *not* optimism, irrational or otherwise. It is a contrarian mind-set.

Finally, there is a further difference between irrational optimism and the contrarian perception of extraordinary value. The difference lies precisely in the creation of the tangible value, not just its anticipation or pursuit. Whereas irrational optimism is about intention and hope, entrepreneurship is about more than intention, just one part of the story.

To the contrary, contrarian perception may be the least important of the triptych of perception, creation, and capture. Imagine, for example, that the idea that people will spend millions to visit space for a few hours turns out to be wrong, or not. Or imagine that space transportation can (or cannot) be used to profitably mine rare minerals. At the time of this writing, space tourism and logistics is one of the more talked-about hot new sectors, and some very successful entrepreneurs such as Elon Musk (of PayPal and Tesla) and Jeff Bezos (of Amazon) are currently heavily invested in the process of finding out if this is the stuff of overzealous imaginations or prescience. It could go either way. Perceiving the possibility is just a part of the story; making it happen, both technically and from a value-creation perspective—getting real customers to actually buy what you are selling profitably—is required as well. In the next two chapters I will argue that creation and capture are required to complete the picture.

CHAPTER 11

Creating Extraordinary Value

An idea is a point of departure and no more.

—Pablo Picasso

Aren't entrepreneurial ideas a dime a dozen? Is the perception of the possibility of creating extraordinary value less important than the actual creation of that value? Can we call something entrepreneurship if no value has been created?

In other words, do entrepreneurs get an A for effort?[1] Few can resist the proposition that the activity of value creation is at the heart of entrepreneurship, although I have seen raised eyebrows when the word *extraordinary* qualifies it (I will get to the extraordinary part in Chapter 12). The words *value* and *creation* are simply too positive, even catchy, to question.

Not so fast: value creation is about outcomes; it says nothing about how we get there. Yet if we eavesdrop, so to speak, on the everyday dialog about entrepreneurs and entrepreneurship, we hear that we constantly confuse effort and effect. We refer to people who keep trying out new schemes as "entrepreneurial": So-and-so has an entrepreneurial spirit because the person keeps proposing new and creative solutions to problems; such-and-such a group in one place or another is so entrepreneurial because its members are always looking for ways to generate a little extra income. These descriptions treat entrepreneurship as about effort, not outcome.

This confusion creeps into the academic dialog as well because many conceptual treatments of entrepreneurship focus on the perception of opportunity and the *intention* to create value regardless of its results. Entrepreneurship is the recognition of opportunity or the attempt to create value, *not* its actual creation. One of my favorite theorists, Israel Kirzner of the so-called Austrian school, views entrepreneurship as the spark of recognition that an asset can be deployed more profitably, and previously unrecognized value is revealed.[2] Kirzner and other thinkers imply that the realization of the potential value is a predetermined outcome of its revelation, the automatic result of its discovery. Harvard's "pursuit of opportunity" is about chase, effort; it says nothing at all about the catch.

Is Anyone Who Tries Hard Automatically an Entrepreneur?

I do not think it is that simple, because some ideas really are whimsical flights of fancy. *Back to the Future*'s Doc Brown pursues the "opportunity" of traveling in time; although we know Doc Brown is a bit off his rocker, we also find him charming, I suppose, because he is playing out our own childhood fantasies. But on the other hand, as contrarian converters of ideas to value, successful entrepreneurs typically recall that along the way, "everyone thought I was crazy." So what distinguishes the truly whimsical and whacky wannabe from the wise and prophetic entrepreneur? Why is Doc Brown pretty nutty, but Elon Musk, pursuing commercial space travel and tourism in his new venture, SpaceX, an entrepreneur?

Results. The catch. I will argue that we can only consider something to be entrepreneurship by its results. I used to wonder why our family Dalmatian engaged in hundreds of futile cat chases. After a while I realized that she was really only interested in the chase. But the catch matters; one reason is that the catch is one way of distinguishing between the exercise of folly and the creation of value.

The Fool on the Hill

Folly and value are opposite ends on a continuum, separated by a line that is at once very thin and easy to miss (our intentions) and at the same time a continental divide (the results). From the perspective of value creation, folly represents the depletion or destruction of value. It is wasted time, effort, money, or alternative opportunities. Can we distinguish a priori between the irrational pursuit of opportunity and the contrarian recognition of value that drives value creation, and therefore, entrepreneurship? A positive answer would be literally priceless.

Yet in the contrarian view of entrepreneurship, this is a particularly important distinction because everything looks like folly before it becomes valued. As most entrepreneurs have felt and many have expressed, from Given Imaging's Gabi Meron to Local Motors' Jay Rogers, "everyone thought I was crazy." Peter Diamandis, founder and CEO of X PRIZE Foundation, commented on television, "The day before every big breakthrough, people thought it was crazy." The observation has been echoed by countless entrepreneurs who created huge amounts of value. Being thought crazy is a common aspect of contrarianism: why would a sane person pour energy, time, and money to acquire or develop a valueless asset? But aren't we as likely to hear this observation from the many who have attempted and failed, who really had "crazy" ideas?

A venture can vacillate between folly and value very rapidly. For well over ten years, Dean Kamen, who had made a large amount of money from previous technology ventures, invested many millions of his own and other investors' money in the vehicle that would ostensibly revolutionize personal transportation, the Segway. We have all seen Segways lately in city tours or airports. In fact, Kamen succeeded in creating a fully operational vehicle that performed as he had envisioned, as well as a large, modern manufacturing plant in New Hampshire. Legendary Silicon Valley venture capitalist John Doerr prophesied that Segway would reach $1 billion in sales as fast as any company in history, and he put his money where his mouth was (or vice versa) as he, Kamen, and others poured $100 million into Segway when it was just a vision.

But that is not yet value creation: we know that value is created when someone exchanges something else of value—usually money!—for that thing. The problem was that Kamen could not sell very many of the expensive contraptions for years, and a lot of the economic value invested in Segway was destroyed (or consumed): the investors surely had negative returns, as did Kamen himself. Had they created a white elephant, a great, amazing, impressive white elephant? In 2003 *Wired* considered Segway to be such a failure of value creation that it ran a scathing article, "Segway's Breakdown: Inventor Dean Kamen Promised That His Superscooter Would Change the World. Then Reality Hit—Hard."[3] In 2009, *Time* labeled the device one of the ten biggest tech failures of the preceding decade.[4] It was a tremendous success as an invention, make no mistake. But even in Kamen's own words, "I wouldn't have predicted the mountain would be so big and that there would be so many hills to cross to get to the top."

Innovative? Extremely! Entrepreneurship? Maybe. Maybe not. The jury is still out, and the balance sheet is not public. We do see increasing numbers of Segways everywhere we go, and the company's website is upbeat, announcing dozens of new partnerships. We even see them on TV commercials (not for Segways). But who knows if a balance of value has been created or consumed? The story of Segway is not unique at all.

Do Entrepreneurs Get an A for Effort?

My late friend Nahum Sharfman was the founder of two successful ventures, Commtouch (NASDAQ: CTCH) and Shopping.com (sold to eBay for $634 million). One day, he told me: "You academics are remembered by the *best* thing you have done in your careers. If you win the Nobel, you are always the Nobel laureate. But we entrepreneurs are remembered by the *last* thing we did. If we failed, no one will remember that once we were worth a billion dollars."[5] And if they do, he said, it will be in a negative context: look at how much he or she lost. "In fact," my friend continued, "having failed after succeeding makes it worse. We have to keep moving." Sharfman was working on a third new venture when he died tragically in a private plane crash.

His friendly jibe at academics aside, Sharfman's point is that results are what matters in entrepreneurship, not laurels. The bar is always raised, often by entrepreneurs themselves.

Actual value creation as an outcome, and not the intention to create value, is essential. If value is not created, then the entrepreneurship is not complete; the market, having judged at the outset that what he or she is doing is worthless, impossible, or stupid, might just as likely have been correct.

So I conclude that entrepreneurs do not get an A for effort. If they did, a lot of goofy efforts would have to be called entrepreneurship.

If entrepreneurs fail to create value, in a well-functioning market their ventures fail as well. Because this is so likely, failure always looms large as a concrete possibility. I recently received an email from an entrepreneur, Nadeem Kassam, whose venture I am invested in.[6] He has been working for six years to build what he (and now some VC investors and partners) believes will be *the* "killer app" for real-time body function monitors, such as heart rate, blood pressure, and so on. I think the product is phenomenal. Just along the way to building the product's proof of concept in those first years, Kassam experienced several "near-death" experiences. Last year, with commercial sales imminent, the venture had to delay product launch by over a year due to challenges in developing the complex suite of sensors, not helped by a patent challenge, and in the meantime the field of great competitors has only become more crowded. Now, just after launch, they have supply difficulties.

Will they pull through? I hope that by the time you are reading this book it will be at the head of the pack! But entrepreneurs *always* live on the market precipice, peering over into the abyss of potential failure. I invested in another venture a few years ago launched by an entrepreneur with a huge exit under his belt—a sure thing, I thought. Two years later I wrote off my entire $30,000 investment because the engineer (not the entrepreneur) turned out to have been an extremely clever manipulator of data and the intellectual property was *worthless* (and we all felt *stupid* that we believed that this *impossible* device could have worked so well!)

The "necessity" of accepting failure as a likely, even a vital, feature of entrepreneurship has become a popular topic. Indeed, from a societal perspective, there is evidence of a positive relationship between the sheer quantities of ventures that fail when they are young (the more the better) and the quality of failure (the quicker and less costly it is to fail, the more venture formation occurs), and the ability of a society to foster successful ventures in sufficient quantities. So to encourage entrepreneurship, society must make failure structurally easy—legally, administratively, and culturally. Labor flexibility and liberalizing bankruptcy make exit from failures easy. Governments that implement these few reforms discover that it does indeed help create a flow of new aspirants; high failure rates and high success rates (more of the latter) go hand in hand with high value creation. In addition to destigmatizing failure so that more entrepreneurs will join the fray, the reforms also help society recycle "scrap" financial and human capital to new ventures.

Some have gone so far as to extrapolate from this insight to exhort society to literally celebrate failure; Singapore has started to give failure awards. But what is good for society might be bad for individuals (and vice versa), and calls to celebrate failure send a flawed message: entrepreneurs should avoid failure, not celebrate it. To some of you, that may sound obvious, but at the Global Competitive Forum 2012 in Riyadh, I attended a session called "The Art of Failure." But failure is anything but art. Picasso said, "Art is the elimination of the unnecessary." Failure, from a societal perspective, is the unnecessary scrap on the floor, the wood chips or the unused paint. Of course, when the *next* entrepreneur comes along, that scrap may be very valuable. Placing value creation at the heart of entrepreneurship emphasizes that the art is the *success* at creating and capturing value, not the failure to do so.

The Long and Winding Road

Because the entrepreneur is relentless in seeking success and dodging failure, any impression that the path to extraordinary value creation is a straight one would be misleading. Although we may simplistically expect, all else being equal, that perception precedes creation which precedes capture, but all else is rarely equal. Value creation is usually a circuitous, messy process that is cleaned up only in telling the tale, not in the doing. More often than not, the perception of opportunity is continually revised and modified as the aspiring entrepreneur engages with real customers and attempts to acquire real resources (cash, people, customers).

There have been some good attempts to present the entrepreneurial path as an iterative, nonlinear one to help make order out of the untidiness of entrepreneurship. The title of Peter Sims's book *Little Bets: How Breakthrough Ideas Emerge from Small Discoveries,* suggests the value of taking small steps that can be redirected along the way.[7] *Just Start,* by

Leonard Schlesinger, Charles Kiefer, and Paul Brown, provides a how-to methodology for taking those first steps toward perception and creation of value.[8] New terms such as *creAction* or *effectuance* have emerged to express the reality that in the uncertain world of the entrepreneur, the forecasting of long-term expenses and revenues can be "misplaced concreteness" and not as useful as jumping in and swimming (starting out by testing with one foot, going in knee deep, etc.).

In 1984, I coined the phrase *thinking-acting cycles* to describe a process that seemed to me to be an aspect of managerial effectiveness and, for that matter, human learning. Thinking, that is, figuring things out, connotes to us (anyway, to me) an armchair activity conducted with a glass of port and classical music in the background. But on second thought, thinking is *inseparable* from action; they are part and parcel of the same process. From birth, we act on our environment (how about a good cry, anyone, to get some food? Or a gurgle of laughter to get played with?) to figure out how to get what we need. We tinker with a new smart phone to get it to work. Concepts form in the cauldron of action; acting and thinking are two sides of a coin. We learn language by using it. We learn dance by dancing. We learn math by solving math problems. While we are learning from doing, we usually do think about what we are doing, and that helps us understand how to do more of it, better. Sometimes, as in learning how to drive or fly, some book learning is needed before we jump behind the wheel. Although in a variety of fields studying the manual in advance is necessary, it is not sufficient, and frequently, it is more effective if it happens in conjunction with practice and experimentation.

Entrepreneurs also figure out where opportunities are by tinkering with the market to learn how to create value. As this learning proceeds, new capabilities (information, assets, and even skills in the form of other people or oneself) are developed, which further shape the perception of opportunity, that is, the perception of the possibility of creating extraordinary value.

The manner in which Sandi Češko grew Studio Moderna exemplifies the iterative nature of perceiving and creating value. Češko initially tested his own perception of opportunity (or lack thereof, in his case) by trying it out on potential customers, that is, by seeing if indeed the product (a molded plastic strip designed to relieve lower back pain) and the selling method (TV) actually led to sales (an exchange of value). His first action was to give a few samples to friends with lower back pain, and they reacted with enthusiasm to the product. With that feedback, Češko invested in refining the product further. Later, he created the first infomercials to see if he could make the selling method work. The process led to experimentation with stores so that customers could see the product before buying it and could then pay in cash. The results of the experiment led to the use of the stores as points of sale and their eventual deployment to sell additional products.

Not only has this process led to tens of millions of euros in revenues for Studio Moderna's first product, the Kosmodisk, alone, Češko has also codified this empirical approach to identifying new product opportunities in an internal software application called PIS (product identification system). Studio Moderna's PIS is an evidence-based method for identifying and introducing new products to Studio Moderna's channels and incrementally ramping up investment in their marketing as the evidence of market acceptance increases. This greatly improves the company's rate of success and also facilitates the churn of perhaps thirty or so new products in and out of the company's catalogs each year. The product offerings and selling channels are adapted to each of the twenty-some different national markets in a way that fits the often idiosyncratic needs of each geography.

Some degree of incrementalism is a fact of entrepreneurial life. Jorge Rodríguez founded PACIV in 1997 in Puerto Rico by jumping into self-employment without any explicit concept of opportunity ("I didn't even know there was a word for entrepreneur").[9] He launched PACIV as a supplier of control system integration services to help pharmaceutical companies comply with the stringent FDA regulations for computers and software in the manufacturing process. Despite not having a vision for PACIV or a clue about so many aspects of starting and running a business, within months Rodríguez was making much more money self-employed than he had while employed at a pharmaceutical company. He began to see a strong match between his skills and the market needs, and he started to envision a bigger organization. He discovered an opportunity without anticipating it, at least consciously.

Rodríguez has continued to push the value envelope. He has entered the US and European markets, and most recently diversified for awhile beyond the pharmaceutical industry by realizing that his (his company's) capabilities were applicable to other process-intensive, highly regulated industries such as food and beverages and water treatment. Even more recently he has told me that PACIV is refocusing again entirely on biosciences.

Česko's and Rodríguez's perceptions of opportunity were driven by the realities of value creation and capture. "How can I know what I want until I see what there is?" becomes "How can I know what there is until I see what I can do?" These entrepreneurs are less driven by a strategic vision than by bumping into opportunities, at least initially.

But let's not get carried away. Years ago, a famous social psychologist, Karl Weick, characterized action under uncertainty by taking the old ready-aim-fire and standing it on its head as ready-fire-aim. Although it was not his most significant academic contribution, the phrase *ready-fire-aim* really caught on like, well, fire. Weick is a delightfully provocative thinker, in person as well as in print.

But many people were enchanted by the catchy ready-fire-aim without critically examining it. Can we specify beforehand whether the egg of entrepreneurial action should come before the chicken of thought? Cinemex, Clutch Group, and Given Imaging are all examples of entrepreneurial ventures that were launched after extended periods of detailed planning. The planning was so effective that all three ventures progressed according to their multiyear strategic plans. In at least *these* cases the months of detailed planning paid off. To be certain, these highly planned entrepreneurs also encountered many surprises, but nevertheless, in these examples of the creation of extraordinary value, thought preceded action. One of them, Cinemex, greatly exceeded the financial projections in its original business plan, a shocking rarity in the world of entrepreneurship.

Bert Twaalfhoven, in his forty-plus-year career as an entrepreneur, blended strategic and opportunistic action at different junctures, becoming more strategically focused on small niches within the jet engine supply chain as his career progressed and as he learned how to succeed.[10] It is clear that his extensive planning helped him opportunistically identify gaps in the market. When I was a venture capitalist in Israel, my partners and I inevitably pushed the Israeli entrepreneurs we invested in to be more systematic and strategic in their approach to creating value, and to avoid what Ronald Cohen, the pioneering founder of Apax Partners, calls "indecent haste."[11]

A Hard Day's Night

Partly because it is an iterative, messy, uncertain process, entrepreneurship requires an unbelievable amount of hard work. PACIV's Rodríguez once tested the resolve of a potential hire who would open up the European market for PACIV as a partner with proverbial skin in the game: "This is tough bloody sh*t . . . the long hours, the focus, dedication and commitment that is needed, it is at the beginning sickening and you need to be prepared mentally, physically, and emotionally." To repeat venture capitalist Todd Dagres's comment, "starting a company is not supposed to be easy."

Bert Twaalfhoven has a list: forty-two crises in his forty-two years as an entrepreneur.[12] These include a court-ordered factory shutdown in the

Netherlands; the time his US–bought car washes stripped the lacquer off high-end French and Italian cars because the water spray was too strong; the time a company purchaser gave Twaalfhoven postdated checks for the company's assets and then disappeared; a factory that burned down overnight; a German minority partner's physically obstructing Twaalf-hoven's entrance into his own factory; and the discovery that his Los Angeles plant was washing cyanide into the Los Angeles–Watts water system. The kitchen of entrepreneurship is a very hot place.

Entrepreneurship is hard. It is perceived as hard, it is experienced as hard, and it *is* objectively hard.

We need to revisit the question: if entrepreneurship is such a good thing, why can't it be easier?

As I have described in chapter 6, *intrinsic adversity*—that is, realizing an idea for a product or service that customers (or investors or partners) don't see the need for—usually means overcoming significant resistance to the notion that the product or service is worth something. The re-sistance may be by customers, investors, key people you want to hire, regulators, and almost anyone else. The more contrarian the idea is, the greater is this natural resistance. In many cases, demand must be gen-erated, and in most cases, market inertia and even antagonism or con-tempt must be overcome. Studio Moderna faced scorn for TV shopping in Slovenia. When an entrepreneur perceives an opportunity in the form of something that is undervalued by the market and whose actual value the entrepreneur wants to realize and then capture, aspiring entrepre-neurs always encounter hurdles. To prevail they need to leap over, crawl around, rearrange, or take down those hurdles.

Making Sense of Entrepreneurial Risk

One cause of this "tough bloody sh*t" is risk, which, I believe, is an-other much misunderstood topic. Second in frequency only to the question "Can entrepreneurship be taught?" is the question I am often asked: "Is entrepreneurship risky?" "Don't MBA programs teach you to be risk averse?" Let's take a closer look at entrepreneurial risk.

Well, doesn't everyone know that entrepreneurship is risky business? Some people, including some economists and most entrepreneurs themselves, see risk taking as the essential ingredient of entrepreneurship and the primary distinction between the entrepreneur and the wage earner.[13] Without risk, there can be no extraordinary profit, or value.

On the other hand, entrepreneurs themselves talk a lot about reducing risk, which some academics call *risk mitigation*. Increasingly entrepreneurs and their educators and investors maintain that the risk-taking entrepreneur is a thing of myth.

Can the *Worthless* perspective shed some light on the role of risk in entrepreneurship? Let's first take a slightly more abstract look at the process of extraordinary value creation. One reason for the difficulty in creating value is that in order to do so, the entrepreneur has to go against the grain, has to deliver something that is new to the market, and at a profit. Naturally, there is a lot of uncertainty in actually doing that: all the effort may not lead to the new product or service, and then there is the challenge of getting people to buy it. Again abstractly, activity A (all the effort and investment and time) may not lead to outcome B (a product people buy with profit and in sufficient quantities to make it worthwhile); in fact, it is a statistical long shot. Creating that new product may lead to insufficient sales or no sales at all. Getting people to buy something new is getting them to behave differently, and behavior change is always a little like climbing a cliff—it requires effort. The cliff the entrepreneur faces is a world in which the chances of A leading to B are far, far less than perfect. There are big unknowns standing in between the status quo and creating value from a valueless idea.

The probability that an entrepreneur will successfully navigate any one hurdle (such as developing an ingestible prototype, in the case of Given Imaging) is itself less than 100 percent. When you line up all the hurdles that must be surmounted to get the PillCam to where it can be bought and sold, that is, to where value creation is proven, the list is daunting: gaining regulatory approval, raising sufficient capital, getting key opinion leaders to adopt and promote the invention, getting insurers to reimburse its use. The probability of an entrepreneur's overcoming any of these is less than 100 percent, and in general, the probability of overall success is not the probability of the weakest link, but the combined probabilities of the success of each of the links. A 70 percent probability has to be multiplied by itself for each of ten independent steps along the way, yielding a combined chance of about 1 percent. (A more sophisticated modeling of the combined probabilities of success would yield a higher number, but not much higher.)

That is risky. Part of the argument between "entrepreneurship is risk" and "entrepreneurship is mitigating risk" comes from confusing games of chance where outcomes are random, with uncertain games of skill in which outcomes are uncertain but are influenced by the player's abilities. Entrepreneurship is not a crap shoot (game of chance); it is a poker table (uncertain game of skill). You are dependent to some extent on the luck of the draw, but how you play your hand over time is what creates champions, and as discussed earlier, the entrepreneur's assessment of his or her unusual capabilities determines whether the entrepreneur sits down at the poker table at all. So the entrepreneur's strategy for dealing with the inherent riskiness of the venture is a crucial consideration.

Risk Optimization

The *Worthless* perspective offers a synthesis, which I call *risk optimization* because it implies that there is indeed an investment of time, effort, and resources and that this investment is an effort whose results are uncertain. This process entails uncertainty and risk, both of which are essential for creating extraordinary value. Risk is the result of the initial investment. Uncertainty is in the external environment. As Cohen writes, "as an entrepreneur, you are always trying to take advantage of uncertainty; that entails the risk of things not running out as you expect."[14] If entrepreneurs avoid risk, they will not be able to create and capture extraordinary value, but will instead only capture ordinary value (or none). So if they are not able to take risk, they will merely stay put and play it safe. It is difficult to win the pot if you keep your cards in your hands.

Yet, many entrepreneurs disparage the notion of entrepreneur as risk taker and insist that they in reality *do* play it safe. I climbed three mountains when I was in high school and college in Oregon. One time it was with my neighbors, the Krakauers, including the now-famous author and climber, Jon Krakauer, when he was sixteen. I think many mountain climbers and other extreme sportsmen would also claim that they play it safe by "mitigating risk": they buy the best equipment, check it carefully, and comply with rigorous safety protocols. They go one step at a time, making sure that each step is certain before taking another one.

That is what we did in climbing Mount Jefferson, on which over the years there have been many climbing accidents, including fatalities. I vividly recall one guy we met just near the icy top. He was climbing without any gear and had a deformed leg, which forced him to use a cane. He had no foul weather gear. We were risk takers. He was a gambler. The cards he had been dealt made it much less likely he'd succeed, and he played them badly, violating many rules. He made it up and down, miraculously, but for those three hours he was indeed a fool on a hill. If mountain climbers really wanted to mitigate risk and play it safe, they wouldn't climb mountains—hill climbing is much less risky. The risk is an essential part of the reward. (Even though the Krakauers signed my name in the summit log book, I chickened out a few hundred feet from the top and waited for them to get back.)

To reach any summit, you must do more than have your head in the clouds; you must have your feet solidly on the ground. Value creation is certainly not unmitigated gambling, and indecent haste leads to indecent waste. Entrepreneurship is grounded in producing results, in engaging in an activity that people will pay for at a profit for the seller.

But seeing only the risk-mitigation side of the coin implies that risk is a bad characteristic that needs to be reduced. You mitigate disease, pain, hunger, poverty. You don't mitigate love, pleasure, or wealth. When entrepreneurs expose themselves to the possibility of failure it is usually a choice that they make, not a disease they contracted that needs to be alleviated.

Thinking in terms of the *optimization of risk* instead of risk taking or risk mitigation helps synthesize these two important aspects of how extraordinary value is created. Risk optimization is a continuous accordion-like process of alternatively "de-risking" and "re-risking" the venture as the activity focuses on the creation of actual value.

Here is a schematic version of how risk optimization works: the entrepreneur sees a possible intersection of needs, wants, and capabilities—market requirements, personal motivation, and individual capabilities. In short, an opportunity. Gabi Meron encountered the idea of the Pill-Cam and thought it was insane himself at first, but as he studied the problem of imaging the small intestine, he realized that if an ingestible camera could be developed (with a very complex spec), gastroenterologists would use it and payers would reimburse for it. He also saw that he had a lot of the requisite capabilities. And he had the desire and ability to work extremely hard at a minimal salary to make it happen.

The overall venture risk goes down, and the perception of opportunity goes up, as aspiring entrepreneurs see that their special capabilities most likely allow them to create and capture extraordinary value. It is this view of the special capabilities that lessens the risk in the situation *for the aspiring entrepreneur;* the same situation remains very risky for the person without the special capabilities. A lot of research shows that this self-perception of the entrepreneur is not entirely objective, but nevertheless is one of the drivers of the entrepreneurial choice. As Meron puts it, "I was absolutely sure I could pull it off." Research and experience suggest that his confidence should have been much less than "absolute," but this is how entrepreneurs think.

At that point, the entrepreneur re-risks the situation, ups the ante so to speak. Meron increased the level of risk in two ways: one was in accelerating the timetable for developing the PillCam and bringing it to market with FDA and other regulatory approvals. The second was in committing to enter three major markets simultaneously, namely, the United States, Europe, and Japan. These were the biggest and toughest markets, and rather than approaching market expansion incrementally, Meron persuaded his board to attack all three in parallel, using different strategies for each market. The venture only had about $1 million left in the bank at that point, so this really was re-risking. Then, having increased the risk by embarking on three major markets in parallel, Meron subsequently lowered the risk of the Japanese penetration by looking for local partners to provide regulatory expertise and to finance the entire operation.

Whereas Given Imaging's board at the time wanted to mitigate risk by breaking risky investment into several smaller pieces (sometimes called "staging" the investment), we later see that an apparently risky strategy of making one large incremental investment was in fact safer because the FDA approval (and revenues) was delayed by a year, and the CE approval allowed Given Imaging to generate its first revenues from the European market. The riskier and bolder plan also made it easier for Given to raise a lot more capital from venture capitalists, who were sold on the large potential that could be realized.

Having reduced much of the risk in product development by proving that a camera with the basic elements of the PillCam could image a pig's small intestine, the risk, or uncertainty, became focused on two areas that remained further from Meron's control: financing the effort and facilitating physician adoption. As it turned out, Meron's greatest difficulty was in securing ongoing venture capital from investors who were skeptical of the execution challenges, less so of the market. When he had sufficient financing to bring Given Imaging through FDA application and approval, Meron's efforts focused on the remaining sources of risk.

Back and forth: risk, de-risk, and re-risk. The point is that the ebb and flow of risk is inexorable; in part it is there because of the choice to be in a particular risky situation—to climb a mountain rather than a hill, as it were. In part it is there because to stay on the extraordinary side of value creation, the entrepreneur tries to maintain a certain, optimal amount of risk in the venture. He or she neither does away with it, nor rushes into it blindly.

What makes entrepreneurs take all that risk in the first place? One big piece is the prospect of the capture of extraordinary value, the topic of the next chapter.

CHAPTER 12

Capturing Extraordinary Value

You need incentive and fear of losing your shirt. If you don't have
that fear, you're not being driven to enhance yourself.

—**Carl Bistany, CEO, SABIS Educational Systems**

Extraordinary value capture—personal gain—is increasingly being mar-
ginalized in the way we think and talk about entrepreneurship, as witnessed by the burgeoning popularity of terms such as *social entrepreneurship, entrepreneurial leaders,* and *corporate entrepreneurship.* The question
I will address in this chapter is whether personal gain, that is, the capture
of value, should be reinstated as a core element of that dialog. Is a venture without value capture less entrepreneurial than one with both value
creation and value? Isn't extraordinary value creation sufficient? And
isn't extraordinary value capture a by-product of extraordinary value
creation?

As I will argue, I have gradually come to the difficult conclusion that the
burning desire for extraordinary value capture is almost a sine qua non
for the supreme effort required to convert the value from imagined into
tangible value. Personal gain is the simplest and most powerful motiva-

tion. If a person does not feel deeply that "This must pay off for me," there will rarely be extraordinary value creation. It is no coincidence that entrepreneurs work extremely long hours and sacrifice their personal lives to overcome market indifference or disdain. They will often tell you that it is not about the money, but without the alignment of the potential of big profit and accomplishing the impossible, the process of entrepreneurship cannot sustain itself and breaks down. Because my primary focus on financial gain bothers some people, I will concede that sometimes—but not nearly as often as we think—non-financial can substitute for financial gain.

Entrepreneurship is a complex phenomenon. The proposition that value capture is a requirement for entrepreneurship raises a few interesting questions that I will try to answer while demonstrating that when the prospect, *as well as the actuality,* of value capture is absent, the activity we might otherwise call "entrepreneurial" is significantly less so.

Nor is value capture an automatic result of value creation, as the experiences of Iqbal Quadir and Ant Bozkaya (and countless other entrepreneurs) demonstrate. Both had to struggle with powerful partners to get their rewards. We may disagree about how much they deserved, but the reward did not come easy because, in part, dividing the excess value created is frequently a bone (or banana) of contention. Similar tussles face almost every entrepreneur at some point in the process, as there are no objective criteria for the appropriate compensation for the level of risk taken in creating the value in the first place. That is crucial because frequently entrepreneurs bring in partners and abdicate at least some of their control over determining who deserves what.

For example, Zipcar, now well known in the United States, is spreading to other countries (where the concept originated, but was peripheral). Zipcar was founded by Robin Chase as an innovative scheme for providing affordable transportation for urban dwellers, starting with "asset-poor" university students and urban dwellers in Boston. In its first years, Zipcar's growth was rapid, but incremental, not the leaps-and-bounds of exponential growth VC–type investors look for. It took a longer time than expected and several major injections of capital for the company to achieve scale. But over time, Zipcar convinced a hesitant market and has become a reasonably big success, as well as an inspiration to other entrepreneurs on how other underutilized capital assets, such as apartments, can be profitably shared. Today Zipcar has over half a million users in the United States, and a fleet of eight thousand cars. In April 2011 Zipcar went public on NASDAQ, becoming a billion dollar company for a while. In fact, it created so much value that the average worth (in stock) of *each* of its cars exceeded $120,000.[1]

Most of the recognition for founding the company and popularizing the concept has indeed gone to Chase, who is a popular speaker at universities and conferences. So how much of the billion dollar value do you think founder Chase captured for herself? Well, according to SEC filings, the directors on the board made millions. Stephen Case, a director who invested very near to the IPO, beneficially owned about $100 million worth of stock. Scott Griffith, who joined Zipcar as CEO four years after it was founded, was worth about $15 million.

But what does entrepreneur Chase have to say? "What I got in stock was just a very small fraction of the value I created," Chase told me, "less than one percent of the stock when the company went public. The CTO [Chase's husband], who was extremely important in the entire concept and there for the first seven years, got much less, a very raw deal."[2] A contributing factor toward her slim reward was what Chase calls "the costliest handshake of my career": At the very first meeting with her cofounder Antje Danielson, who had seen car-sharing in Europe, Chase and Danielson shook hands on a 50–50 deal. But Danielson stopped working at Zipcar ten months after the handshake to have a child, and did not play much of a role in getting the service into the market. "You have no idea at such an early stage how much value partners are going to contribute going forward," cautions Chase. Point of note: Chase honored her handshake with Danielson, even if it was an expensive one.

Keurig coffee makers now grace the shelves of every major retailer in the United States, including Target and Costco. In 2006, Green Mountain Coffee completed the acquisition of Keurig for about $160 million. The details are confidential, but the venture capitalists and management, who built the company from a frustrated team of equipment developers years behind schedule to a major innovation in home living, made a killing.[3] Very little—perhaps just a few hundred thousand dollars (my own guess, based on conversations with some of the protagonists), according to a few insiders—was left for Keurig's founder, John Sylvan.

This is not necessarily to imply that the entrepreneurs were short-changed; it is to emphasize that value capture is an important issue, and cannot be taken for granted as a logical outcome of value creation. Keurig's value-capturing shareholders would probably argue that most of the value in Keurig was created not by the inventors and founders, but by Nick Lazaris, who took over as CEO early on, commercialized the product, and built the company into the retail innovator that it became. Another lesson: entrepreneurship is not necessarily about founding a company. It is about extraordinary value creation and capture.

Without personal value capture, entrepreneuership is weakened and entrepreneurs are impoverished, literally and figuratively. Quadir, Bozkaya, Chase, and Sylvan are better and more skillful entrepreneurs if they reap the value that they create.

Even though we intuitively equate ownership with entrepreneurship, more entrepreneurs than you might expect are frustrated by the mismatch between value creation and capture.

Ownership Matters

"To the non-entrepreneur, the personal guarantee may not sound like a big deal, but we slept every night with that on our minds," recalls Stephen Greer, the Hong Kong–based scrap king.[4]

Jorge Rodríguez, founder of PACIV, worked in the 1990s for Eli Lilly in Puerto Rico as a control system engineer. His skill at preventing and addressing FDA audits, with their very punitive warnings or punishments, earned him a "rock star" reputation throughout the company. In 1997 when he left Lilly to strike out on his own, Rodríguez was making about $45,000, a very respectable paycheck for a young engineer a few years out of college.

"In my first six months running my own company," Rodríguez recalls, "my dividend payment corresponded to a fifty-percent salary increase. It was ridiculous. In my second year, I had made my yearly salary for seven years! I used to keep track of that and say to myself, 'OK, if I close the company today, I do not need to work for ten years.'"

At first Rodríguez was a one-man operation, performing the identical services that he had provided as a salaried engineer for the same company, but now he was making a lot more. One reason for his higher billing rate was that he was now a variable cost that could be cut when needed and used only when required, which allowed him to extract a premium over his salary (risk taking leads to value capture). And Rodríguez worked much harder because he was more motivated to do so, so much so that he spent up to eighteen hours a day, seven days a week, on the job. Over time, Rodríguez began to hire more engineers and has since become a global player, with offices in Indianapolis, Ireland, Puerto Rico, Italy, and the United Kingdom, employing over 90 people (at its peak, 150) and serving many large and demanding multinational customers. Rodríguez himself has personally netted over $20 million in pretax dividends. That is the capture of extraordinary value.

This may sound obvious to many, but ownership does matter. What makes the statement less obvious have been attempts to broaden the definition of entrepreneurship to include value creation inside large corporations ("intrapreneurship"), the establishment of interesting non-profit ventures ("social entrepreneurship"), innovation inside government agencies, and so on, where there is no significant personal stake for those expected to be entrepreneurial. Good scientists, inventors, engineers, intellectuals, and educators are considered "entrepreneurial." Entrepreneurship has become synonymous with initiative, resourcefulness, creativity, leadership, and almost everything good. I have heard the terms *parentrepreneur* and *artrepreneur*.

Some may argue that the definition of extraordinary value capture and its relationship to entrepreneurship are arbitrary issues of semantics and opinion. To be sure, people can define entrepreneurship in any way they want, but it does not mean that they should. In fact, determining what makes for a good definition is a complex topic that I won't delve into here. Suffice it to say that definitions have to pass the test of serving a useful purpose, even if in just making communication easy and effective. But when you stretch the definition of a word to be increasingly all-encompassing, it loses its utility. That is happening to the word entrepreneurship as its meaning rapidly becomes diluted. These days audiences chuckle with recognition when I observe facetiously that people do some good things (i.e., create value) that are *not* entrepreneurship.

The second characteristic of a good definition is that it has consensual validity, that people pretty much agree on what the word means, and can point to the same thing when using the word.[5] The requirement that entrepreneurship include some form of ownership meets both criteria: it is useful and consensual. Entrepreneurs own a stake in the fruits of their endeavors, which means that they benefit personally from the value created. If the value is extraordinary, their personal benefit is extraordinary.

But ownership also matters experientially.[6] Greer, as he moved from owner to executive, back to owner, and then back again to executive after his company was acquired, writes: "The reason I had woken up every day in the past was to make sure that [we] would survive and thrive . . . but being a manager isn't the same as being a partner . . . the current in my veins just didn't pump with the same vigor."[7] Ownership feels different from nonownership, and the experience leads to different behaviors, such as extremely high motivation and hard work.

My eldest son, Itai, who once stood at the fridge looking for what he wanted, is now a thirty-year-old aspiring entrepreneur in Israel. He is not a communications engineer or medical device developer; Israel has earned a well-deserved reputation as one of the world's highest concentrations of technology-based entrepreneurship. Itai is what I tongue-in-cheek call an entertainment engineer; he creates and runs nightclubs.

Tel Aviv has also built in recent years a reputation as one of the clubbing hot spots in Europe, and Italian, French, and British party lovers will sometimes hop on a plane for a weekend of uninhibited fun. As actress Claire Danes recently proclaimed on Conan O'Brien's talk show, "Tel Aviv is the most intense party town I have ever been to." On any given night at any of a dozen or so of the bigger clubs, anywhere between five hundred and fifteen hundred young people dance and party until 4 or 5 a.m. On weekends, there is sometimes an "after" that starts when the clubs officially close, and it ends in the morning. Somehow these partyers also hold down full-time jobs. Speaking of which, one of these clubs might have fifty or more people on the payroll for marketing, bartending, operations, and security.

The business model of the clubs is to make money from the bar, where profit margins are very high (the bars sell, as far as I can figure out, water with a dash of alcohol and a smidgeon of flavor, and a generous portion of romantic hope, none of which has a significant material cost). Risk is optimized in several ways. One is that most of the expenses vary with the amount of revenues. So, for example, each night is outsourced to an independent contractor—called the manager of a line, or specific night—who is responsible for all of the aspects of that night, including bringing in the beautiful people and getting them and their admirers to spend on drinks. To do that, the line manager must hire a marketing team. The line manager's income, and thus the ability to pay the people working for the manager, is a percentage of the spend at the bar. No spend, no income. High spend, high income. So there is risk, and there is reward. The job of line manager contains numerous elements of what we would call entrepreneurship: reward based on effort, the possibility of failure, and the need to create value (a nightclub experience on the manager's particular night that causes people to buy).

But what is missing from the equation is ownership, that is, the opportunity to capture really extraordinary value. The line manager in the club does not typically have ownership in the club itself, although there are exceptions, but in principle and often in practice, ownership and management are distinct. Crossing the boundary from line manager to owner, although it is a very thin boundary from the perspective of activity, has a major impact on the new owner's attitude, behavior, and experience.

I witnessed this firsthand when Itai left one club as a very successful line manager for years and started setting up his own first club, which was quickly followed by a second. The actual activities he is engaged in are almost the same as what he did before, but his ownership makes a huge difference in his feelings, motivations, and concerns. He is also taking financial risk as well as putting his name and self-concept on the line as a capable nightclub operator.

But there is greater opportunity for him to capture value, so that he looks for (pursues, perceives) value where others do not. That has included, for example, seeing the potential of an underutilized but famous former regional police headquarters (awaiting a permit for conversion to condos) in a section of town not known for its clubs. Within a month, the lines of impressive-looking people stretching around the block suggested that it was one of *the* hottest spots in hot Tel Aviv. He also saw the potential of an old, underutilized central post office building not far away and is in the process of duplicating the success.

Itai's functions have broadened to some extent beyond those of a line manager, but they are not significantly different, and he has partners who play important operational, financial, and logistical roles. Itai does not do everything by himself, of course; that is why there are sixty people on the payroll. But the fact of ownership per se has changed his mind-set, his aspirations, and his experience more than his actions. His success or failure will be visible, not to mention that he will have creditors to face if he fails financially. His success or failure will have an impact on his future options: success will make it easier for him to find space, partners, and capital for future clubs, in addition to giving him added self-confidence. Without the prospect of value capture, this would not be happening, and until he actually captures extraordinary value, he will not be a success. When the extraordinary amounts of money start flowing into Itai's bank account, he will be a real entrepreneur.[8]

"And Where All the Children Are Above Average"

With dry wit, the well-known tagline from Garrison Keillor's mono-logues on *A Prairie Home Companion* points to the average experience of being extraordinary. Why is extraordinary a necessary qualifier? OK, you might say, it makes sense that perception, creation, and capture are all three essential aspects of entrepreneurship. But why *extraordinary*? Why can't entrepreneurship be the creation of ordinary value? many have asked me.

I have become convinced that the creation and capture of ordinary value can never be considered entrepreneurship, for two reasons, one practical and one conceptual, realizing full well that this statement will be controversial for some. On the practical side, value capture must be extraordinary because without it, most people will find it difficult to jus-tify the risk, hard work, sustained effort, stress, and investment. Extra-ordinary is what motivates all of the people in this book. The "blood does not pump in your veins" for ordinary value.

But a second, conceptual reason has to do with the nature of value and the surprising confusion between its consumption and its creation. In entrepreneurial pursuit, ordinary value creation often translates into value consumption or even destruction, and therefore is not entrepreneurship.

Let me explain that because it is perplexing conclusion. Most of us would agree that intentionally tearing up and throwing away money (or any other tangible form of value) is the destruction or consumption of value, at least economic value, and that this act is the antithesis of value creation. Value consumption and destruction are not that different, but throwing away a $20 bill, for example, is closer to value destruction, whereas using that $20 bill instead to see a movie or buy a meal is closer to value consumption. In the former case—throwing away the bill—there is presumably no exchange; the $20 is simply wasted. In the latter case, the $20 is used, or consumed, in exchange for an experience or nourishment.

I witnessed this firsthand during a charity auction when two of my students competed for a $10 bill, which one of them eventually won for $75, with the proceeds ($65) going to the charity. Witnessing the event left a lasting impression on me: After nine intense months of learning almost everything about making money at Harvard Business School, these guys were competing to give it away! Did the winner sacrifice his wealth as a way of donating to the greater cause of the charity, and gaining the personal satisfaction of helping others? In fact he prevented others from donating by winning the bidding. If creating value for the charity were his objective, he would have stopped the competitive bidding process before the end and proposed that he and his rival declare a draw and both donate their highest bids to the charity. No, paying $75 for a $10 bill was the consumption of value, not its creation.

We all consume value daily in much less exhibitionistic ways. We pay $20 to see a movie, have a sandwich, or take a taxi instead of a bus. Successful entrepreneurs often spend the value they capture from their business, sometimes ostentatiously, buying fabulous houses, boats, professional sports teams. But spending their money that way is clearly not entrepreneurship. That's simply consuming the value that entrepreurship created.

Consuming value isn't limited to how we spend our personal resources. You consume value anytime you knowingly invest time, effort, or resources in option A, fully aware that doing something else (option B) will certainly make you more money, all else being equal.

Now let's carry this logic to the choice between establishing a company to work for yourself, on the one hand, and working for someone else to earn a salary, on the other. Let's say you turn down a job offer with a Wall Street investment bank for a $100,000 salary (option A) to instead buy and run a flower store in Manhattan (option B) with the intention of just getting by, say, at best earning the same $100,000 you would have gotten with the bank but more likely earning $80,000. This is not extraordinary value creation and capture—it is value loss, destruction, or consumption. It may be that you consume the $20,000, that you "buy" something important to you with it, just as you would pay $20 to see a movie: You "paid" (gave up) $20,000 for the pleasure of owning your own flower shop. No one would argue that you do not have every right in the world to give up a better or more certain salary to buy your freedom from a stupid, over-controlling boss, or to set your own hours (at least, so you thought before you bought the flower store), or to handle flowers, which is something you always wanted to do. It is your decision whether the price is worth it.

But buying your independence for $20,000 is not entrepreneurship, for the same reason that paying $20 to see a movie is not entrepreneurship. It is only entrepreneurship if there is a much larger upside potential that somehow you can, and believe you will, convert that $20,000 investment into much more than $20,000. The conclusion that owning your own flower shop is not in and of itself entrepreneurship holds, whether the difference is $20,000, $200, or $2. Owning a flower shop might make you a small-business owner—not an entrepreneur. Unless or until there is a perception of the possibility of capturing extraordinary value, owning a flower shop can never, in and of itself, be entrepreneurship. If you own your own flower shop and deliberately set out to turn it, say, into a national chain with the goal of selling the company for many times your original investment, then we are starting to talk about extraordinary value creation.

My friend Jim McCann did just that. In 1976, McCann bought a flower shop on First Avenue and Sixty-Second Street in New York. He ended up creating 1-800-flowers.com, the largest retail flower-delivery business in the world, with about $1 billion in revenues. McCann bought that first little flower shop knowing that he wanted to build a big company that was worth something: "I bought it not because I wanted to be a florist, because I knew nothing about that [no expertise!—DI]. I bought it because there was a boom in plant and flower buying, but no one was looking at the business with McDonald's eyes, of being big [contrarian!—DI]. It was hard to keep good staff then, because selling flowers wasn't cool [worthless!—DI]—they wanted to work in established finance businesses downtown, like Lehman Brothers and Bear Stearns [both of which went bankrupt recently—DI]."

McCann kept on working his salaried job at nights because he had a wife and young kids and wanted to plow all his earnings from the flower shop into growing the business. He had fourteen shops within a decade.

Where did McCann's ambition come from? "My father was a painting contractor," he says, "and he and his brothers were also talking about how they could grow the business, and get bigger and bigger. And I had read about Walmart and McDonald's, so why not me?"

The great feat is to create and capture the value. It is no great feat to consume, lose, or destroy it, although it may be a lot of fun and may contribute to society. But spending money for whatever purpose is not entrepreneurship. David Siegel, founder of Westgate Resorts, had the right to ostentatiously use his hard-earned millions to have fifteen servants and housekeepers on staff and a bowling alley in his new Florida mansion, Versailles, the largest mansion in the United States, as featured in the critically acclaimed movie *Queen of Versailles*. Any entrepreneur can consume his or her hard-earned money in numerous ways, or not at all. Some of the ways may be socially beneficial—Siegel also created scholarships and donated to charity. The Giving Pledge founders, Bill Gates and Warren Buffett among them, pledge to donate 50 percent of their net worth to charity while they are alive. Most of them are self-made entrepreneurs who captured tremendous amounts of value from ventures they created and made extraordinary personal gain from. But whether value consumption is conspicuous or charitable, it is value consumption, not creation, and it is not entrepreneurship.

For value to be extraordinary, the entrepreneur must create it from assets that others undervalue (or don't even notice), and that means, in the pure case, taking something that is worthless, impossible, or stupid, and creating and capturing value from it. The striving for extraordinary value is continual; when it stops, so does the entrepreneurship.

Money Can't Buy You Love

So far, my examples have equated value with money—money is a pretty good proxy for value, but there are good reasons to challenge any perfect equivalence. Some might argue, for example, that nonmonetary (what the economists sometimes call psychic) rewards can be as powerful motivators as financial ones and can create the same behaviors. Indeed, the personal satisfaction and public recognition for solving a social problem such as reducing AIDS or alleviating poverty can be tremendous.

Furthermore, money is not the universal yardstick that we often assume it is. For people at different stages in life, in different societies, and at different income levels, one million dollars in cash can have completely different meanings. And if money were an objective yardstick, serial entrepreneurs with successful exits and millions in cash in their accounts should be less motivated because each incremental dollar of gain has less personal usefulness for them.

On the other hand, money is a remarkably powerful motivator, and when all is said and done, it is as fundamental as other basic needs, such as food, safety, power, and sex because it can be consumed to acquire most of those things, directly or indirectly. What's more, to succeed as an entrepreneur requires an all-consuming drive. The only nonmonetary way I have come up with of describing that drive is: "the extreme sense of personal accountability for results." If nonmonetary rewards can give a person an extreme sense of personal accountability for results, then in that case, it is possible to be an entrepreneur without the monetary motive.

It is rare—but not impossible—to achieve this without money. But because it represents such a universally fungible form of value, the prospect of financial success or failure is still the most direct and reliable—not the only—way to create an extreme sense of personal accountability for results. I have personally been involved in launching both economically and noneconomically motivated enterprises, and the experiences of ownership of a financial stake and ownership of a nonfinancial (psychic) stake are very different. It is difficult to engender an extreme sense of personal accountability for results without real, tangible, practical ownership, the proverbial skin in the game, the difference between the pig and the hen.[9] Most people who have experienced both will confirm this. And nonowners are much more susceptible to self-delusion, to the mirage of value creation and value capture.

My Kingdom for a Horse

The night that my student paid $75 for a $10 bill, the proceeds went to a social venture that was created by his classmate, another one of my former students, Avichai Kremer, who had that school year founded one of the best cases of a social, not-for-profit entreprise that I know of. His story is not about money, and it is difficult not to call what he did entrepreneurship, so it can be a useful example, albeit a heartrending one.

Within days of being definitively diagnosed with amyotrophic lateral sclerosis (ALS) on March 15, 2005, Kremer—at the time a first-year Harvard MBA student—decided to act. He was aware that his intact physical capacities would rapidly degenerate over the coming two or three years, with death from asphyxiation certain to follow three or so years later, even while his mental capacities would remain the same as those that got him accepted at Harvard Business School to begin with. By that March 15, Kremer also already knew too well that not only were there no cures or even treatments for ALS, but the cause or causes of the disease (or diseases) remain even today a mystery, at least partly because pharmaceutical companies do not consider the market large enough to justify the risky R&D investment required, although that viewpoint is changing.

Determined to devote the remainder of his life to the declared purpose of finding a treatment that he himself could benefit from, Kremer convinced a hard core of a dozen or so Harvard graduate students and professors to devote dozens, then hundreds, and then thousands of hours to building a philanthropy to stimulate hithterto underfunded research on ALS. The result was Prize4Life, which has been recognized by the US White House as well as the Israeli prime minister's office as a leader in the search for ALS cures and treatments. Through Prize4Life, Kremer has inspired dozens of research teams, hundreds of volunteers, and thousands of donors to support the cause, raising $9 million as of 2012. The "prize" part of Prize4Life has started to work as well, with the first $1 million challenge prize awarded in 2011 to Steward Rutkove, a researcher from Beth Israel Deaconess Medical Center in Boston, following five smaller prizes for innovative conceptual approaches proposed by over one thousand researchers from around the world.

Seven years after creating Prize4Life and having defied the three- to five-year life span of ALS patients, Kremer received the Israeli prime minister's 2011 award for entrepreneurship and innovation in Israel, the land of entrepreneurs. I was fortunate enough to attend the ceremony. Kremer was unable to move from his wheelchair to receive the prize because ALS incapacitates a person gradually; the prime minister had to leave his podium and awkwardly rest the prize on Avichai's unmoving arms.

Prize4Life is using money to create significant noneconomic value. But has the social entrepreneur Avichai Kremer captured any of that value? What does it even mean to capture value in his case, if it is not monetary? Would he have been motivated differently had he himself not been a potential beneficiary of an ALS treatment?

Here is what Kremer recently wrote to me (he uses an antenna on his forehead to activate a mouse—he cannot move his hand to type or his vocal chords to speak):

> For a man facing death money is insignificant. Shakespeare knew it when his Richard the III said: "My kingdom for a horse!" Hope is the currency of value. A purpose is another. Purpose to still make a difference even if there's a chance you won't be around to enjoy it. I get both from Prize4Life.
>
> Would I do it if I wasn't a patient myself? Probably not, unless someone close to me was a patient—the same reason you're helping me. Money is a powerful incentive, and a very convenient one being able to trade it for almost anything, but it can't be traded for everything (like an ALS cure) and in those cases, a higher form of value capturing kicks in. But your argument still holds (only with intangibles). So hope is certainly a driver of value: I hope I'll personally benefit from the cure I hope to find. It's my "horse" if you will, that will carry me away from the ALS battlefield.
>
> The personal motivation of finding a cure for me certainly started the journey, but as time passes, two things happen: 1. My

condition deteriorates. 2. The more time and effort I invest in the endeavor, the more it becomes my life's mission, and gets a life and importance of its own . . . When these two things happen, the hope to capture personal value starts to mix with the sense of purpose.

In parallel with Avichai's establishing Prize4Life, Kremer, Robert Brown, and I established a for-profit venture, AviTx Inc., with the mission of identifying and commercializing treatments for ALS.[10] This is not a normal for-profit venture: the objective is to treat ALS, not to make money; making money is a mechanism for motivating and disciplining all of the players. So we raised a few hundred thousand dollars from wealthy entrepreneurs who believed in our mission and who do not expect to make money, either. In fact, we are very clear with ourselves and everyone else: the purpose is to treat ALS, not Alzheimer's disease and not multiple sclerosis. If we encounter a drug candidate whose purpose is to treat Alzheimer's but not ALS, we will not pursue it, even if it means losing money and potentially not curing a different horrible disease. We are prepared to subordinate the profit of our venture to its social mission, and as long as we are clear with ourselves and our shareholders, there is no problem with our suboptimizing our profit. The irony is that we have made some money because we licensed one treatment to a top-tier pharma for further testing. But I have to be honest: we are volunteers and don't work very hard at it. Not having a lot of skin in the game matters.

"A Crack, Jerk, and a Leap"

Implications for Leaders, Entrepreneurs, and the Rest of Us

Let me recapitulate the thesis of *Worthless* in slightly different words. We have seen that entrepreneurship is defined by three elements: the perception, creation, and capture of extraordinary value. The only way to create and capture such extraordinary value is to perceive its potential where many others do not. Since those others—the market—view a situation as valueless, it is very difficult to distinguish a priori between assets (or ideas) with latent potential for value and truly valueless assets (or ideas). They both seem, at best, equally worthless, impossible, or stupid to most people.

Some characteristics of entrepreneurs, in particular their perception of their own capabilities, information, or assets, lead them to perceive the presence of latent extraordinary value. That self-perception and the possibility of extraordinary value capture (personal monetary or non-monetary gain) motivate the entrepreneur to confront different types of adversity and embark upon the difficult and risky venture of creating extraordinary value where the market initially sees none.

A Little Theoretical Background

Most people observe the contrarian entrepreneur at the beginning and think that the person is either wasting his or her time or completely daft. Somewhere along the path toward value creation, a change takes place, and it begins to be clear that the idea was not so crazy after all, that the market was wrong, and that some novel value exists now where it did not exist before. We can really only know it is entrepreneurship with some degree of confidence after the fact. It is surprising. It boggles, baffles, and stumps us as our dozens of examples have shown. There are many thousands more out there, in every country and society, at least as far as I have traveled and observed.

A detailed discussion of economics or psychological theory lies beyond the scope of *Worthless,* but here I will invoke the economist Joseph Schumpeter, whom many people see as a father of entrepreneurship theory because of his insights on the importance of creative destruction in economic cycles. In 1993 Schumpeter scholars discovered an article Schumpeter wrote in German in 1932 but never published. With not one mention of creative destruction, the article was simply titled "Development." In it Schumpeter equates economic development, of which he sees entrepreneurship as the driver, with a process that he claims is fundamentally unpredictable, occurring in a "leap" or a "jerk" and reflecting novelty that is discontinuous in nature: "Neither are these changes uniquely determined. The change transmuting one imprinted form into another one must represent a crack, jerk, or a leap . . . the new [state of affairs] must not be reachable by adaptation in small steps." (Later he writes, "cannot be decomposed into infinitesimal small steps.")[1]

Entrepreneurship is unpredictable. The entrepreneur jerks and leaps and does not crawl, inch, or saunter. Schumpeter rejects incrementalism as too smooth and inappropriately overdetermined to apply to economic development. He argues that economic development is the outcome of a process that is by its very nature indeterminable from existing models or beliefs: there is a "fundamental impossibility of extrapolating trends . . . The triad, 'indeterminacy, novelty, leap' remains unconquerable."[2]

These are striking words from an economist! Two decades later Schumpeter elucidated his "principle of indeterminateness" to the annual gathering of the world's leading contemporary economists: "Without committing ourselves either to hero worship or to its hardly less absurd opposite, we have got to realize that, since the emergence of exceptional individuals does not lend itself to scientific generalization, that there is an element that . . . seriously limits our ability to forecast the future."[3]

Entrepreneurship—and entrepreneurs—cannot be forecasted. They are unpredictable and exceptional. Moreover, as I have shown, when true entrepreneurship is just forming in an effort to actually create value, it is met with apathy, resistance, ridicule, derision, scorn, and hostility—until after it succeeds, of course.

Implications for Society's Leaders

What does this mean for society? There are at least three groups of people who are potentially affected by the ideas presented in *Worthless:* leaders in society who believe, as I do, that significantly more entrepreneurship is a good thing and want to create more of it; the potential entrepreneurs of the world; and all the rest of us.

There are important implications of the *Worthless, Impossible, and Stupid* thesis for public and private leaders, by which I mean not only publically elected officials, but also heads of corporations, university heads, cultural and artistic icons, successful entrepreneurs who want to give back, heads of private foundations solving social problems, and educators. But because of the inherently exceptional and discontinuous nature of entrepreneurship, it is challenging, and probably counterproductive, to make simple or programmatic policy prescriptions. But it is also unnecessary to leave the evolution of entrepreneurship entirely to random processes. Following are a few directive thoughts.

Leaders and governments cannot—and should not— try to tell entrepreneurs where the opportunities are

It is both futile and counterproductive to attempt to tell entrepreneurs what to do or where the opportunities are. You should not select sectors, regions, or types of companies in which to develop entrepreneurs. You should not specify sustainable, green, social, knowledge-based, or innovative opportunities, despite the societal importance of all these endeavors. Pushing entrepreneurs into identified sectors or types of businesses pulls the extremes toward the center, fosters mediocrity (and, thereby, less value), and depletes the collective entrepreneurial reserve. Entrepreneurs themselves need to identify where the opportunities are, very often exactly where everyone else, including policy makers, thinks the opportunities *are not*.

Governments (and other leaders) will defeat their goal of fostering entrepreneurship if they assume the role of the entrepreneur in the messy process of identifying wherein lies the potential for creating extraordinary value. Cluster strategies, which include top-down prioritizations or competitive strategies aimed at incentivizing venture creation in specific sectors, err if they try to imply that certain sectors have more opportunity than others. Not only are these strategies unnecessary, but they also risk dulling the sum total of entrepreneurial spirit in a society, rather than honing it.

A famous development economist has created a sophisticated methodology for mapping sectoral adjacencies to point entrepreneurs and government policy makers toward opportunities. So, for example, an economy that has strength in coffee production should move toward cacao or industries that use the same skill sets as coffee production. A country that produces oil should encourage entrepreneurs to move into oil by-products. According to the *Worthless* view of entrepreneurship, *if* fostering more entrepreneurship is a policy objective, such sectoral prescriptions are misguided and potentially harmful. And unnecessary: coffee entrepreneurs certainly do not need to be told to look for opportunities in cacao or other adjacencies—if there are opportunities in adjacencies, no doubt the entrepreneurs will be there way before the rest of us. If they cannot figure that out, then they will never be very good entrepreneurs.

Another famous policy expert visited Iceland in 2010 and argued that for Iceland to be competitive as a nation, government policy should favor the creation of clusters around Iceland's natural assets, specifically fishing, natural beauty, and geothermal energy, three resources Iceland has aplenty. That would seem to make sense, and some businesses in Iceland have been created around those assets. Fortunately, there is no shortage of Icelander entrepreneurs who did not listen to the experts and who instead pursued their own, idiosyncratic perceptions of opportunities, producing world leaders in generic pharmaceuticals (Actavis), online games (CCP), and prosthetic devices (Ossur), creating lots of value and thousands of jobs. Israel, where military technologies have spilled over into market leadership in data communication and security, for example, has also "allowed" the emergence of market leaders in cutting tools (Iscar) and home carbonation systems (Soda Stream). Boston is home to a completely illogical cluster of high-end, customized bicycle manufacturers.

None of these ventures is easily predicted by what makes sense to policy makers—all of them are surprising. Not only do these successes create extraordinary value, but they also inspire yet more potential entrepreneurs to identify opportunities where others don't see them. If these entrepreneurs had listened to the competitiveness experts, they might not have pursued the opportunities that were being overlooked or downplayed by others.

Israel's innovation program, for example, has as a matter of policy shunned prioritizing sectors in which to encourage entrepreneurship.[4]

Instead, for decades it has provided incentives for entrepreneurs to step forward with their own ideas.

In fact, entrepreneurship in regions *frequently* defies policy predictions and programs and other attempts to create better environments for entrepreneurship. If you examine averages of conduciveness to entrepreneurship, for example, you'll find that California is outranked by Arizona, Louisiana, Idaho, Wyoming, and Tennessee, which are more entrepreneurial (in terms of new company establishment) than the home of Silicon Valley, which has the highest concentration of venture capital investment in the world. Massachusetts, which follows California as number two in venture capital investment, is in the bottom quartile.[5] Bolivia, Ghana, Angola, and Uganda are more "entrepreneurial" than Israel, which after California and Massachusetts is the third-largest regional recipient of venture capital funds.[6]

You *can* foster a more enabling environment

The preceding discussion is *not* an argument that government is irrelevant. To the contrary, government is essential in numerous ways, for example, in creating the most conducive legal and regulatory environment and in providing an infrastructure to remove physical and communication barriers, to name just two of many. Nor should government avoid setting social priorities, highlighting problems (poverty, pollution, crime, etc.) that should be addressed; that is government's prerogative and responsibility. But for entrepreneurship, government should be at most a market maker, seeing itself as a potential consumer of value-creating solutions to those problems and as a market pull, not as a pusher of entrepreneurship. If there is value to be created and captured, let the entrepreneurs sniff it out; it is counterproductive to try to stick their noses too far into it.

I believe that in collaboration with other public and private leaders, government can do a lot to cultivate an environment in which naturally contrarian entrepreneurs are more likely to flourish. To do this, government can influence six domains that make up the *entrepreneurship ecosystem:* policy, culture, finance, education, support organizations and infrastructure, and markets.

I have written about entrepreneurship ecosystems extensively elsewhere.[7] Here, I will just point out a few specific examples of ways that government can influence these important domains:

- Public leaders can introduce policies that increase the flexible redeployment of labor if entrepreneurship fails, liberalize bankruptcy laws, and, perhaps, decrease taxes on capital gains.

- Leaders can highlight success stories as a way of inspiring entrepreneurs and can encourage an environment that values unconventional thought and action.

- Leaders can allocate funds toward solving social problems (e.g., energy efficiency, personal security, or health), and these will naturally attract entrepreneurs.

Entrepreneurship-friendly government is absolutely *not* necessary for any individual entrepreneur to be successful. I usually tell entrepreneurs in challenging environments, "Treat the environment as hostile, similar to the ash spewing from a volcano—there is nothing you or anyone else can do about it in the short run, but you have to know that it is there to succeed." But for their parts, if public and private leaders want entrepreneurship to be a key part of the society and economy, government and public leaders must adopt a mind-set laser-focused on reducing the barriers to entrepreneurship.

Entrepreneurship has a social price

Nothing is free, and there is a societal cost to entrepreneurship as well, which many of us prefer to ignore or gloss over. By virtue of going against the grain, entrepreneurs create social and economic friction—Schumpeter did not use the term creative *destruction* by coincidence—and leaders need to think honestly if encouraging entrepreneurs to challenge the status quo is a price they are willing to pay for the benefits of entrepreneurship. Since it is the entrepreneur's "job" to challenge accepted wisdom and rules in the search for extraordinary, hidden, or overlooked value, which can be a challenging and an annoying characteristic, entrepreneurs chafe and irritate, often interpersonally and certainly in terms of markets and social structures. You cannot be an entrepreneur without a mind-set that challenges both the beliefs that others hold dear and the behaviors that are deeply entrenched. Metaphorically, societies cannot pour concrete for sidewalks and expect entrepreneurs to stay off the grass if the entrepreneurs perceive that they have found a useful shortcut. A society composed primarily of entrepreneurs would be very interesting, but almost intolerable because the level of social and economic friction would be too great.

Singapore is well known for its statist approach to capitalism—an approach supported by strong cultural conformity to social norms and obedience to authority. Many of the norms are formalized as laws that a more open society would find intrusive. There is a famous tourist T-shirt: "Singapore Is a Fine City: No Littering—Fine $1000; No Smoking—Fine $1000; No Urinating in Lifts—Fine $500 . . ." Singapore is also known for being prosperous but having insufficient entrepreneurship. It is the one area criticized by Singaporeans in a published national competitiveness report: "Disappointing performance on entrepreneurship . . . remains relatively low."[8]

Authoritarian societies such as Saudi Arabia and the United Arab Emirates espouse entrepreneurship as strategic for their economic development and for job creation, but cultural norms, as well as political processes, actively discourage people from challenging accepted or conventional ways of doing things. Speaking out against authority or openly flaunting convention or questioning the rules is extremely frowned upon and sometimes even punished.

Israel, in contrast, is known for its chaotic culture in which people are often publicly abrasive and competitive (although often in a paradoxically cooperative way, as others have observed). Visitors notice this almost immediately, as it is reflected in everyday life—taking a bus or driving on the road, not to mention quarrelsome politics. Arguments and harsh comments are commonplace, driving is aggressive, and contentiousness is often lauded. Military service is known for its relatively flat and participative culture, in which low-ranking soldiers can and do express their opinions to superiors and exhibit an irreverence that is unheard-of in other armies. Tel Aviv is now ranked as one of the most diversity-tolerant cities in the world.[9] It is not at all out of the ordinary for the most junior employee in a high-tech venture to tell the CEO exactly what he or she is doing wrong (I experienced that myself as the founding CEO of a company there). As Silicon Valley's Guy Kawasaki put it with hyperbole years back: "Israel has five million people, six million entrepreneurs, and fifteen million opinions. Singapore has five million people, six entrepreneurs, and one opinion."[10] A culture that allows broadly for challenging and independent thinking creates an atmosphere where entrepreneurship can thrive.

Reducing adversity should not necessarily be a policy objective

It is natural to think that if something is easier, more people will do it, and so making life easier for entrepreneurs is so logical that it has become almost axiomatic as public policy. But in *Worthless* I have suggested entrepreneurship thrives in adversity, and thus the goal of adversity reduction is simplistic and probably wrong. More likely, whether adversity is conducive or inhibitive depends on the type of adversity, and some types of adversity may be necessary for entrepreneurs to thrive. As I have noted, in the United States there is a strongly negative correlation between areas that are famous for their entrepreneurial intensity, on the one hand, and small-business friendliness, on the other hand, although I am sure the causal paths are complex and it is unjustified to conclude that by making it easy, those states drive out entrepreneurs.

Entrepreneurs ubiquitously complain about how the environment gets in their way. But just because entrepreneurs voice frustration with the shortage of financial resources and human talent does not necessarily mean there is a problem or a market failure. Entrepreneurs will *inevitably* acutely experience the insufficiency of resources, even in the best of times and in the best of circumstances.

From a societal perspective, intrinsic adversity is a necessity to be tolerated—the friction and resistance of the market are signs that the entrepreneur may be onto something good and is pursuing a valuable opportunity and that the potential for value creation may even be great. Entrepreneurs should feel that the difficulties come from the markets—for their products, for capital, and for talent. I have seen this time and again: as entrepreneurs strive to create extraordinary value, usually it becomes more difficult, not less so, to compete for critical resources. Customers, capital providers, and talent are, and should be, naturally selective of the opportunities that are most beneficial for *them*. That means rejecting those that are the least beneficial.

This is a battle that policy makers must leave for the entrepreneurs to fight. Although they do complain, with understanding and experience entrepreneurs tackle these battles with relish, because they know that winning them means extraordinary value creation and capture.

Extrinsic adversity, however, is a bad thing that exists when the product, labor, and capital markets do not function freely to allow the natural selection of new products and services by the markets. External adversity exists when forces external to these markets—bad roads, bad courts, corruption, bad governance, poor connectivity, labor inflexibility, inappropriate bureaucracy, poor rule of law—get in the way, impeding or distorting those markets. So from a policy perspective, *this* is the battle that policy makers *should* fight.

Relatedly, *opportunistic adversity* is a good thing because it provides the impetus for extraordinary value creation and capture. That is not to say, of course, that social ills and unsatisfied human needs are good. But they do exist, and significant value is created when entrepreneurs successfully overcome them—an important success for society and for growing large ventures. Opportunities for entrepreneurs to capture extraordinary value this way will drive value creation: the X PRIZE Foundation we saw in a previous chapter is one example.

But that does not mean that government should push entrepreneurs in the direction of solving these problems. *There is no need to push entrepreneurs anywhere.* By prioritizing the allocation of resources to addressing social problems—health care, security, education, or the environment— entrepreneurs will be naturally drawn to these areas. Opportunities pull entrepreneurs, whether incentives push them there or not. Incentives can sometimes prime the pump, but they cannot substitute for the ongoing flow. And entrepreneurs know how to discover undervalued opportunities—that is what they do; that is their forte.

Encompass all varieties of entrepreneurship, not just start-ups

Most policies serve to emphasize start-ups to the exclusion of other forms of extraordinary value creation.[11] The policy emphasis should be on removing the barriers to extraordinary value creation, period—not just for small or large ventures, or young or old ventures. One reason that policy makers conflate start-ups and entrepreneurship is because of a misconception that entrepreneurship is ownership, innovation, or youth employment. However, there is nothing in the perception, creation, and capture of extraordinary value that says that start-ups are intrinsically better at it than existing enterprises, or that the redeployment of existing, undervalued assets may not sometimes be a better way to create extraordinary value.

Robert Wessman took a failing Icelandic company with ninety-some employees and a small revenue stream and turned it into a world leader.

Bert Twaalfhoven acquired existing technological assets in the jet engine supply chain and redeployed them commercially. His first successful venture copied a commercial business model from the United States and brought it to Europe. Carl Bistany took a third-generation family company with five schools and oversaw its growth to seventy-four. Whereas ownership is essential, the founding of a company—the common image of the entrepreneur—is not.

The test is the creation and capture of value, not necessarily the creation of value from scratch. And conflating entrepreneurship with starting up new ventures leaves a lot of potential value untapped; remember, entrepreneurship is creating value from assets that are undervalued, whether they are new or not. Family businesses in emerging markets are often breeding grounds of extraordinary value creation. Purchasing existing and underperforming brands, real estate, manufacturing capacity, or distribution channels and infusing them with new growth can generate tremendous amounts of value. Rescuing distressed assets from banks or venture capital funds is a potential source of value creation. The start-up movement that is sweeping the world, as evidenced by Start-Up America and numerous other national start-up campaigns (the bubble may burst or the pendulum may have swung back by the time this book comes out), somehow suggests that creating an asset from nothing is better than re-purposing an existing one. As a result, there is a rich opportunity for policy to specifically target high value creation from existing assets. Scale-up is at least as important as start-up.

Not surprisingly, because they sniff out opportunity where others smell nothing, entrepreneurs understand that extraordinary value creation is not just about starting a new venture. MBA courses in acquisitions and turnarounds are among the most sought-after courses in business schools. The increase in popularity of "search funds" often founded by newly minted MBAs is further evidence.[12] Prospective entrepreneurs "get" this intuitively, and it is counterproductive for policy makers to detract from this understanding by overemphasizing start-ups to the exclusion of other forms of value creation.

Nor is small necessarily beautiful. The research on employment creation, often cited by policy makers as evidence that small companies create jobs, is much more nuanced.[13] According to the most commonly cited Kauffman Foundation study, net job creation seems to be the most prevalent among a small portion of rapidly growing medium-sized firms, as well as smaller portions of large, established firms and start-ups. Other more extensive research has shown that young firms, not small firms, create jobs.[14] There are huge numbers of small and old firms that don't create jobs. They don't create value, either. Extraordinary value-creation creates jobs.

Be willing to tolerate income inequality

In 2012, a few thousand Facebook shareholders in California witnessed the tangible quantification of their heretofore paper wealth: current estimates are of a thousand new millionaires, a few dozen new billionaires, and a few dozen or a hundred in between. We are talking about new liquidity of tens of billions of dollars, although as of this writing, Facebook's share price is being traded significantly below its IPO price.

California's economy is about $2,000 billion, that is, $2 trillion. One estimate of the GDP of Silicon Valley is about one-tenth to one-twentieth of that; let's say about $150 billion.[15] Facebook was worth about $107 billion after its IPO, with about half of the company's ownership located in the Silicon Valley community.[16]

Facebook's IPO is a very big economic event in the local economy. The population of the San Francisco Bay area is about 8 million. Add in 1 million for San Jose and a few million for the other people in the overall region. Let's say we are talking about 10 to 12 million people (if we are more conservative, we can take the 3 million population estimates of the valley itself; it does not change the overall picture). If there are 10 new billionaires, 100 new ten-millionaires, and 1,000 new millionaires in the area, a little simple arithmetic shows that massive inequality will be the immediate result of Facebook's shareholders' wealth creation and capture. About 1 out of 10,000 people will immediately become unfathomably wealthier than the other 9,999.

Suddenly, almost literally overnight, a minuscule number of individuals created and captured extraordinary value, and their wealth is vastly outstripping others who have not done so. By the way, I have personally witnessed this happen in Israel, where the hundreds of tech acquisitions and IPOs created incredible personal wealth in just a few years for a very small segment of the population. Of course, they and the Facebook founders and first staff earned it with their own brains, sweat, and risk-taking.

The Facebook inequality is the direct result of one of the most amazing examples of entrepreneurship of our decade. As a world expert on urban economics writes, the US cities in which inequality is highest "reads like a who's who of major knowledge economy centers. Huntsville (a center for semiconductor and high-tech industry) and Silicon Valley come in at first and second place. College Station-Bryan, Texas, is third; Boulder, Colorado, named by *BusinessWeek* as the number one place for new start-ups, is fourth; Durham, North Carolina, in the famed Research Triangle, is fifth; and high-tech Austin, Texas, is ninth. New York (11th), Los Angeles (12th), Washington, DC (16th), and San Francisco (18th) all number among the top twenty metros with the most unequal wages."[17]

Is that inequality of wealth, the direct result of entrepreneurship, good or bad? Without much difficulty, we can anticipate some of the impact of such a tsunami of cash pouring into the hands of so few in any small region. Certainly there will be some short-term trickle-down effects: retailers will sell more, high-end restaurants will fill up, travel agencies will flourish, accountants and wealth managers will increase business, and real estate values and agents' commissions will go up. Nannies will be in demand. Car dealers will sell more BMWs, Porsches, and Ferraris.

There will be a greater demand for personal services such as landscaping, house cleaning, and high-end concierges.

People with nice houses for sale will get better prices faster; maybe some foreclosures will be avoided. Because people will pay more taxes, underwater municipalities' fiscal health will improve (eventually). There will be more angel investors, so start-ups will have more options for raising money, and the region will become more of a destination for opportunity-seeking entrepreneurs. Many people who did not see themselves as entrepreneurs will be inspired to try. Some of the newly rich will make charitable donations to help the less fortunate, probably with some concentration in the region because people often like to donate close to home where the problems are acutely felt.

I have seen these sorts of outcomes with my own eyes. That is the good news. But painful social outcomes can be anticipated as well. People at the bottom of the local pyramid will find it more difficult to afford their real estate taxes as their properties get reassessed; they will find it harder to buy houses for themselves as increased property values also trickle down. Education may get worse as the newly rich send their kids to private schools. They may find that they cannot afford to stay in the previously reviled "inner city" and are pushed out into the suburbs.

In the best-case scenario, the positive trickle-down of wealth will take many years until it drips down to the bottom of the income scale. How all these changes will affect the economists' measures of inequality in the region is uncertain. But no doubt, the common statistic thrown about these days to indicate inequality—the ratio of income of the highest 1 percent to, say, the lowest 10 percent—will skyrocket immediately and stay very high for a long time. The sudden wealth of a few will increase average wealth somewhat, but the median (a more conservative measure of a central tendency) will hardly budge. Wealth will stay concentrated, perhaps even more so than before the entrepreneurial success. Furthermore, as we have seen in Boston, any region that enjoys a boom in entrepreneurship attracts talented people away from other regions, impoverishing the people-losing regions in terms of human capital.

If we want extraordinary value creation and capture, and if the Facebook example is any indication of some of the societal impacts of successful entrepreneurship, and if we really want more entrepreneurship in our regions, we will need to be willing to tolerate pretty severe income inequality for a significant period. I believe that the net societal effect will be positive over the longer run, largely because it will inspire more people to try their hands at it and there will be more proximal resources available for them to do so. As asserted earlier, entrepreneurship is an equal opportunity employer.

But it would be a mistake to dismiss some of the short- or medium-term pain that entrepreneurship might create. In most open societies, economic development can be likened to a Slinky toy moving downstairs, in which there may be a big discrepancy over time between the most wealthy and the least, but the former eventually drags the latter along. I believe the entrepreneurship will increase the linkages and shorten the time frame. But some very severe discrepancies will exist, at least for awhile. The challenge for public leaders is to make sure that the two ends do indeed stay linked and do not create a tear in society's fabric, without dragging down entrepreneurial aspirations, either.

For Entrepreneurs

The *Worthless* perspective on entrepreneurship has implications at the micro level, for individuals like you and me and for our own entrepreneurial aspirations and prospects. We find no shortage of books, magazines, blogs, conferences, and speakers telling you the right way to succeed and what you should and should not do. Some of the better book titles include *Breakthrough Entrepreneurship, Just Start, Poke the Box,* and *Heart, Smarts, Guts, and Luck.*[18] David Gumpert has over the years written a practical series of books, although you might find the pairing of two of his books, *How to Really Create a Successful Business Plan* and *Burn Your Business Plan!,* puzzling (presumably, aspiring entrepreneurs are supposed to create the plan before burning it).[19] And the list goes on.

When I was teaching entrepreneurship at Harvard Business School, the conventional career advice given by most professors to MBA students was to go out and get a decade or so of industry experience under their belts before starting out on their own.

A recent *Wall Street Journal* piece, "So, You Want to Be an Entrepreneur?" has this checklist for making the entrepreneurial choice:

1. Are you willing and able to bear great financial risk?

2. Are you willing to sacrifice your lifestyle for potentially many years?

3. Is your significant other on board?

4. Do you like all aspects of running a business?

5. Are you comfortable making decisions on the fly with no playbook?

6. What's your track record of executing your ideas?

7. How persuasive and well-spoken are you?

8. Do you have a concept you're passionate about?

9. Are you a self-starter?

10. Do you have a business partner?[20]

This advice makes as much sense as any, I suppose. *Harvard Business Review* has published my own, surprisingly popular test (which I wrote half tongue in cheek), which has been taken by tens of thousands of people (see the sidebar "Should You Be an Entrepreneur? Take This Test").

Should You Be an Entrepreneur? Take This Test

So some of your friends are doing it. The government is encouraging you to do it. President Obama is talking about it. People who do it are on the front pages and on the web almost every day. So should you do it? Should you join the millions of people every year who take the plunge and start their first ventures? Take the two-minute Isenberg Entrepreneur Test and find out.[a] Just answer yes or no. Be honest with yourself. Remember: the worst lies are the ones we tell ourselves.

1. I don't like being told what to do by people who are less capable than I am.
2. I like challenging myself.
3. I like to win.
4. I like being my own boss.
5. I always look for new and better ways to do things.
6. I like to question conventional wisdom.
7. I like to get people together in order to get things done.
8. People get excited by my ideas.
9. I am rarely satisfied or complacent.
10. I can't sit still.
11. I can usually work my way out of a difficult situation.
12. I would rather fail at my own thing than succeed at someone else's.
13. Whenever there is a problem, I am ready to jump right in.
14. I think old dogs can learn new tricks.
15. Members of my family run their own businesses.
16. I have friends who run their own businesses.
17. I worked after school and during vacations when I was growing up.
18. I get an adrenaline rush from selling things.
19. I am exhilarated by achieving results.
20. I could have written a better test than Isenberg (and here is what I would change . . .)

a. Adapted from Daniel Isenberg, "Should You Be an Entrepreneur? Take This Test," *HBR Blog Network*, February 12, 2010, http://bit.ly/HBR_ER_Test).

Such lists are, of course, meant to be helpful, and they can be. But if entrepreneurship is about defying conventional wisdom to create and capture value, then that should include defying conventional wisdom of how to succeed as an entrepreneur. Indeed, if you by now agree with me that entrepreneurship is about creating and capturing extraordinary value, then there are countless ways to accomplish this, and some of these will naturally go against the grain of the best, or at least the most seasoned, advice in the world. (Even mine.)

There is something about entrepreneurship that is impossible to codify. It is characterized by Schumpeter's "novelty," "leaps," and "jerks."

Opportunity Revisited

One of my favorite spoofs of my own profession is a four-minute investment pitch to a Silicon Valley angel group that an actress, "Rachel Sequoia," gave. Sequoia surreptitiously appeared (barefoot) to pitch her start-up concept, ShareTheAir108 (so named, because, as Rachel says, "ShareTheAir" was already taken).[21] Rachel followed all of the start-up rules to a tee. She pitched ShareTheAir108 as an innovative idea to capture air from tourist destinations (e.g., Rome), extract the essence, and then manufacture and package each essence in large quantities in the United States and sell it as Rome air to consumers everywhere. When customers would open the jar, they would have a "Rome experience" without having to travel there. Each jar of air would be very profitable; hence ShareTheAir108 would become a very big venture.

Rachel was a perfect start-up entrepreneur. She had a clear product concept, a compelling value proposition, and a novel business model. It was so perfect that some of the audience of angel investors thought she was legitimate; reportedly, Rachel even received investment inquiries.

There is something futile about building rule boxes for entrepreneurship, when entrepreneurship is about creating and capturing value outside the box. Ironically, the entrepreneur's "job" begins just as the rules begin to gel, and that job is to break, ignore, or change those rules, or at least the rules of the marketplace.

There are many rules inside the rule box: listen to your customers, create a business plan, change your business model when the present one does not seem to work, take small steps rather than large leaps, or raise as much money as you can when it is available. Yet we now know that in many circumstances, doing exactly the opposite works, sometimes even better. Indeed, outside the rule box lies the worthless "rule scrap," which entrepreneurs sometime turn into value. Scrap heaps by definition stink and look ugly, but they present many great opportunities for buying low, converting, and selling high. One current slogan is "cash for trash." Entrepreneurship is not about central tendencies or averages; it is about creating value from deviance, from the residuals, from what's left over after the market takes its bite.

To create extraordinary value, you do have to think counter to the market. You do have to perceive that there is value to be made where others do not or cannot. But belief alone is insufficient: you need to test your contrarian perception against the reality of the marketplace. Did you really create the anticipated extraordinary value? You will only know if and when people will actually pay for it.

All such concepts have some element of risk in moving from idea to market, and all are inherently uncertain. Usually the greater the uncertainty is, the greater the extraordinary value creation and capture. Ronald Cohen puts it succinctly: "Successful entrepreneurs have an appetite for uncertainty."[22] With rare exceptions, you will encounter opposition, derision, resistance, or apathy, because the market does not see value in uncertainty—it sees either nothing or the prospect of failure and the destruction of value.

This leads to what I jokingly call the First Law of Opportunity: a really big opportunity will always have at least one really big—and smart—detractor, someone who is wise and experienced and whose opinion you

The Two-Minute Opportunity Checklist for Entrepreneurs

1. Does your business idea soothe someone's pain, discomfort, frustration, or dissatisfaction?
2. Are there lots of those people out there?
3. Do these people (or companies or governments) have money to pay for it?
4. Will they be able to decide quickly to buy your product or service?
5. Does your idea exploit something outstanding or unique about you?
6. Do you have important assets that no one else has (money, access to customers, technology, leadership skills, execution, location, salesmanship, etc.)?
7. Can you think of at least two people who might join you?
8. Do their skills complement yours?
9. Do they have the same values that you do?
10. Do the majority of people whose opinion you highly respect think your idea is a good one?
11. Does at least one person (and not more than three people) whose opinion you highly respect think your idea is a *bad* one?
12. Is there something about the idea or its implementation that compels you to really devote yourself to it?
13. Can you sneak by the big competitors without them noticing you for a while?
14. Can you find a potential customer who will take your calls, give you feedback, try out a pilot?
15. Can you start up without huge gobs of money?
16. Can you keep your fixed costs low during launch?
17. Does your idea lend itself to small, incremental steps that can inexpensively generate valuable information as well as at least a little cash?
18. Can you think of something that Isenberg has forgotten? (And it is . . .)

Adapted from Daniel Isenberg, "The Two-Minute Opportunity Checklist for Entrepreneurs," *HBR Blog Network*, March 4, 2010, http://blogs.hbr.org/cs/2010/03/the_2minute_opportunity_checkl.html.

respect. If not, then it probably is not a big opportunity. Listen to very smart people, *some* of the smartest of whom will not think very highly of your opportunity. Take into account their criticisms. Weigh their comments and warnings for their merit. Then think for yourself.

But don't conclude from my law that every disparaged idea is in fact a gold mine. Some scrap *is* toxic, and some trash *does* stink. Most entrepreneurial ideas can never be turned into tangible value. The hard part, for which again there is no formula, is to distinguish a priori between real and imaginary worth, that is, between folly and value. Although I have published a checklist for entrepreneurs to quickly screen an idea to see if it has value (see the sidebar "The Two-Minute Opportunity Checklist for Entrepreneurs"), it should be taken with a big grain of salt. Most big opportunities defy ordinary logic in some way. If only there were a recipe for that—in and of itself, it would be extraordinarily valuable!

There are many ways to attempt to test the reality of your contrarian perception of value, but there is no way to completely remove risk from the process. You do not necessarily have to innovate, be an expert, be young, or even start a company from scratch. You don't necessarily have to be passionate (see below). You may or may not need a business plan. You may or may not need to take a lot of financial risk. You may work well with a partner or two from the early stages, bring one in later, or basically be the top dog yourself the entire time.

The Limits of Entrepreneurial Passion

When I ask people what makes for successful entrepreneurship, high on the list is passion. Many aspiring entrepreneurs who meet with me to get some feedback conclude their pitch with something along the lines of, "And it is an idea that I am really passionate about!" They believe that their passion about an idea gives them a greater chance of success and thus makes it more valuable. Maybe, but I doubt it.

Lest the reader be confused, passion is not the same as a belief that you have special information, skills, or assets that can address, uniquely, a current or anticipated gap in the market. And let's also rule out the semantics: if what they mean by *passionate* is that they are willing to risk lots of time and some savings and to forego other opportunities, then I agree, these are necessary (but insufficient) for successful entrepreneurship.

But willingness to work hard and take risk is not passion; it can be one *result* of passion, but it is not itself passion. Passion consists of a powerful and overwhelming emotion, usually love or hate. It is irrational, even delusive, and it causes us to distort reality, to see things that are not there, and to be blind ("blind passion") to things that are. One of the terms associated semantically with passion is *cacoëthes,* an irresistible urge or mania, whose Latin roots mean "bad" and "character." Yes, the emotion of passion is indeed a tremendously powerful motivator, but as likely as not, passion motivates us to make mistakes, to act in "bad character."

Much of entrepreneurship is passion*less.* Contrast the espoused passion of the novice with Abhi Shah coolly combing through thirty-eight "great" ideas before he began to settle on the legal-process-outsourcing concept behind Clutch Group. Imagine Gabi Meron coolly spending six months studying capsule endoscopy from every different angle, building a long-term plan but also trying to address every possible flaw in this radical new idea. Think of the dispassionate Sandi Češko testing the Kosmodisk on some friends to test his own skepticism.

That is why I often tell entrepreneurs, all else being equal, to leave their passion in the bedroom. That is where the dim lights, soft music, flowers, and candles create a distorted reality that can be very beneficial! But entrepreneurship is about objective, extraordinary value creation. Dreaming about what is possible is one side to the story, but only one side, and that story is woefully incomplete without hard-headedness, in part to avoid getting decapitated by leaving your head in the clouds. As a venture capitalist, I had the job of helping passionate entrepreneurs inject systematic planning, thinking, and organization building into their ventures.

In reality, both seeing (imagining) big value where others do not see it and executing in detail to create that big value are based on mutually incompatible psychological processes, which, like oil and water, don't mix. So entrepreneurs need to learn to mix the hot oil of seeing value where others do not and the ice-cold water of clear-headedness. If I had to choose, I would probably choose clear-headedness, but the trick is to mix the two incompatible tendencies.

Implications for the Rest of Us: When Entrepreneurs Learn to Dance

With uncanny regularity, I get asked if it is really possible to teach someone to be an entrepreneur. "Aren't entrepreneurs born, not made?" Indeed, there is some growing evidence that there are genetic factors that might be loosely related to entrepreneurship—nonconformity, stimulation seeking, and the like. But it is not fair to ask an educator like me whether you can teach entrepreneurship!

Can you teach a person to dance? "Of course!" is the almost universal reply. Sure, not everyone will be a Baryshnikov, but yes, you can teach dance—if the person really wants to learn. I know—I have been through it. When I was fifty-four, I acquired a burning desire (I think the word *passion* is appropriate here) to learn salsa. I had no predisposition to dance, no dance training; nor were there any dancers in my family. Luckily, my passion made me blind to the fact that salsa dancing is really very complex! Although I am fit and like music, there was no reason a priori to think I would become a good salsa dancer. Except that I really wanted to learn.

So I took countless, easily over a hundred, group and private lessons and watched thousands of hours of salsa videos. I was horrible, and the process was very painful. One of my teachers in Puerto Rico told me, "Shut yourself in a dark room for a weekend, and just listen to the music." I tried that. I danced socially two, sometimes three, nights a week, and I dropped into salsa clubs in Japan, France, Israel, Puerto Rico, Colombia, South Africa, Germany, and China to dance when I happened to be there. I participated in national salsa congresses, which are multiday fests with thousands of dancers, performances, and competitions. (I have never competed.)

Today, six years later, after a little blood and a lot of sweat and tears, I am a very good salsa dancer—not great, but very good. I dance the most complex genre of salsa (On2), and I can hold my own on the dance floor with some of the best *salseras* anywhere. In Puerto Rico, I gave a presentation to 150 company presidents on how salsa changed my life, complete with an onstage demonstration.

Learning entrepreneurship is both easier and more difficult than learning salsa. It is more difficult than salsa because in salsa there is a clear goal and there are clear rules. (By the way, the best salsa teachers teach you to learn the rules rigorously in order to break them later.) In entrepreneurship, breaking the market rules is the way to be successful. Can you teach people how to break rules? My dancing looked like jerking and leaping, but can you teach entrepreneurs to jerk and leap into extraordinary value creation and capture?

We need real stories

Can you teach unconventional wisdom? There are many parts to the answer to this question, but I will focus on just one of them—stories. If you suddenly discover that someone has done something that you previously thought was impossible, it can have a dramatic impact on your motivation to try; even more so if you also see how they accomplished it. If someone tells you that there really is a needle in a haystack, then you will be much more willing to search for it there and you will be less likely to give up until you find it.

This is the power of studying real-life cases of entrepreneurs and why I have presented so many in detail here. As I mentioned before, the mere experience of seeing these ordinary entrepreneurs (because they are like you and me) accomplish extraordinary things has stimulated dozens (maybe more) of my students to make the entrepreneurial choice. I have taught entrepreneurship to about a thousand MBA students, and hardly a week goes by without someone from Babson, Harvard, or Columbia contacting me for advice on a new venture. There is no question that their having studied the cases of Česko, Rodríguez, Zwanziger, Bistany, Tochisako, and all of the others has had an irreversible impact on their aspirations. I hope that *Worthless, Impossible, and Stupid* will have a similar impact on you.

You do have to exercise some caution with stories, for two reasons: whereas professionally written teaching cases are usually based on meticulous historical research, entrepreneurs' autobiographies are usually replete with revisionist histories and post hoc explanations of success, often written many years after the events took place, descriptions that may bear little resemblance to the messiness in which reality actually unfolded.

More importantly, sometimes people reach the wrong conclusions from seeing how particular entrepreneurs succeed in particular situations. It is only natural if we see entrepreneur doing A, and then B happens, to conclude that that doing A leads to B, and further, that not doing A will lead to not-B. But this is an optical illusion and usually is a poor guide to the future. I am always careful to tell my students after the sequel to each case discussion, after they find out what really happened, that just because (for example) Robert Wessman in desperation threatened to sue the director of marketing approvals in Germany doesn't mean it is always the right thing to do, or the only thing to do. Just because the entrepreneur in the case did what he or she did does not mean that if the students do the same thing, they will get the same outcomes. And it does not mean that if they try something different, that it won't work. The examples only show the range of possibilities. As long as you treat them correctly, studying a broad range of possibilities is extremely useful.

Entrepreneurship in large corporations will remain elusive

Making large companies more entrepreneurial is a coveted objective of many corporate leaders, like shared value creation or corporate social responsibility, also very much in vogue. Our definition of entrepreneurship suggests that this goal will remain elusive. Simply put, it is the rare large company in which extraordinary value creation and extraordinary value capture line up. People who make money for the company don't get much of it, and often, the people who get the money don't earn it. Senior executives capture most of the extraordinary value without creating it, and lower executives create most of the extraordinary value without capturing it. Many large corporations have the value creation-capture equation backward!

It is extremely rare for large corporations not to severely restrict extraordinary value capture by their employees. How many companies have made their employees, those who create the products and services that go on to make the company billions, wealthy? The answer is the start-ups primarily, and then only in their early years, such as the Facebook Thousand. Ten years from now, new Facebook employees will get stock options and bonuses that at most may double their salaries.

The legendary Shigeru Matsumoto, the inventor of Donkey Kong, Super Mario Brothers, and the Wii, is reputed to share a $1 million salary with five other directors from Nintendo. Matsumoto is clearly an amazing inventor, innovator, and value creator. These great achievements have made billions of dollars for his employer. But he is not an entrepreneur—there is no extraordinary value capture. In most corporations, few corporate employees—except the elite executives—will capture any but a tiny piece of the tens or hundreds of millions of dollars of value they help create. Ironically, the investment banks, private-equity firms, and hedge funds that we love to hate these days were some of the few corporations that really allowed people to capture extraordinary value, although some might question whether they created very much of that value.

In an interesting recent example, Lenovo, the leading PC maker, announced proudly that its CEO, who owns 8 percent of the company's stock, took his $5.2 million permanent bonus and gave $3 million to ten thousand workers, for an average of $300 each.[23] Pricewaterhouse-Coopers, a global professional services firm with close to $29 billion in annual sales, ran an internal contest and chose two ideas that became the basis for new business centers.[24] The award: $100,000 funding to implement the idea. That is 0.0003448 percent of the company's revenues. Big gorillas do not intentionally or willingly share their tasty bananas with little chimpanzees.

WPP, based in the United Kingdom and the leading advertising and marketing services company, may be a rare exception to the rule. Ironically, WPP has come under harsh criticism precisely for its entrepreneurial practices. In a blunt column in the *Financial Times,* CEO and founder Martin Sorrell describes how in 1985 he borrowed about $500,000 to buy 15 percent of the small company and rapidly grew it by acquiring famous advertising houses, such as Ogilvy, JW Thompson, and Young and Rubicam.[25] He had worked at Saatchi & Saatchi and made his move to entrepreneurship when he was forty.

With about $16 billion in 2011 revenues, since 1986 WPP has increased shareholder value forty-six-fold, achieved global market leadership, and outperformed the FTSE equity index during the recession. Sorrell himself has continued to invest a large portion of his compensation in the company, rarely selling shares, and now owns a $200 million stake, about 2 percent.

But shareholder controversy over his "capture of extraordinary value" has caused Sorrell to have to defend WPP's entrepreneurial practices:

> The most wounding comment, made anonymously, is that
> I deserve a "bloody nose" because I have been behaving as an

owner, rather than as a "highly paid manager." If that is so, mea
culpa. I thought that was the object of the exercise, to behave like
an owner and entrepreneur and not a bureaucrat . . . Our biggest
challenge remains to ensure that the company continues to behave
with the mind and heart of a small company, particularly as it
continues to grow—it is already 20 per cent larger than its next
biggest competitor and double the size of most others. We have to
ensure that WPP remains an entrepreneurial, performance-based
company to maintain its global leadership. That is why we target
an incentive pool of 15–20 per cent of our operating profits before
bonuses and taxes for distribution to our top-performing people.
Last year that totaled more than $500 million, a just reward for
record performance.[26]

WPP seems to be oriented toward the perception, creation, and capture of extraordinary value. It is the large-company exception to the rule.
It is not a coincidence that WPP's policy of allowing its employees to
capture some of the extraordinary value that they create has come under
attack. Whereas we tolerate and even admire individuals who make the
entrepreneurial choice, our society does not tolerate entrepreneurship
among the big.

As a result, powerful forces are in place to keep entrepreneurship out
of big companies. Employees who figure this out, who realize that it is
they who are seeing the gaps in the market and the novel ways of approaching them, are the ones creating the extraordinary products, opportunities, business models, and sales channels. These employees either
have already left or are hankering to leave to start their own companies.
If senior executives do figure out that there is a misalignment between
value creation and value capture, they will have political difficulty sin-
gling out small groups of individuals for huge (I mean, *huge*) rewards,
and their shareholders will cry foul as well. So I believe the pursuit of entrepreneurship inside large, established corporations will remain futile,

in part because even though large corporations may create extraordinary value, value capture will continue to be a problem.

Part of the confusion stems from how we use the term *entrepreneurship* as it applies to activities in large companies. A list of the characteristics of entrepreneurial leaders by a very famous US business school includes vision and influence, assembling and motivating a business team, handling uncertainty, efficient decision-making, and identifying opportunities. For the life of me, this list looks like plain old good leadership, and there is nothing particularly entrepreneurial about it; there is nothing about the contrarian perception, creation, and capture of extraordinary value.

I think we have it backward again: entrepreneurs have to be good leaders, but good leaders do not have to be entrepreneurs. Jack Welch was a great business leader, but he never mortgaged his house or took out a personal loan to finance GE, as did Wessman and Sorrell. He never slept at night with the prospect of forfeiting on a personal guarantee (like Stephen Greer and most other entrepreneurs have done) because of GE's failure to repay it.

Paradoxically, one of the only ways that I know of for large companies to become somewhat more entrepreneurial is to encourage the best people to leave and strike out on their own. Most companies will protest that this is a waste of the most expensive talent, a lost investment. Over the years, Bert Twaalfhoven's companies became well known as stepping stones to independent entrepreneurship and wealth; Twaalfhoven tracked the entrepreneurs' progress and made no secret of the fact that many of his stars left and made millions, billions in some cases. What kinds of people do you think are attracted to join a company known as a breeding ground for successful entrepreneurs?

"Daring Greatly"

I want to end on a positive note. I have tried to be contrarian myself, at the risk of being too provocative, even annoying at times. Thank you for tolerating this and getting so far. If I tell you what you already believe, then you may like me or feel comforted, but the value created by the ideas in this book will be limited. For this book to contain extraordinary value, it must call into question some of the widely held beliefs that we cherish. At a minimum, it must make us think. It has certainly done that for me. Entrepreneurship has become a romantic pursuit for many, but there is no substitute for clearheadedness, even when you don't like what you see. Beauty may be the vision of a new product or service, but truth is in its realization.

And if truth be told, with all of my questioning, I believe that entrepreneurship is an extremely valuable endeavor for individuals and societies, even if only a few individuals succeed at it. Much collective value will be created by many more trying than actually succeed. Failure to create and capture extraordinary value—remaining in the realm of the ordinary—may have other benefits such as happiness, insight, and understanding, not to mention mastery and self-control. I failed at one business venture, and although I do not wish to repeat the experience and do not wish it on anyone else, I learned some lessons from my own failure that I could never have learned from success. Just to give you one example, I learned that a high-flying venture that everyone thinks is on the fast track to success can unravel with unbelievable speed; I would never have learned that from the long time it takes to build a success.

Indeed, success usually takes a long time to create, with many obstacles and near-death experiences along the way. Almost every entrepreneur who has indeed created and captured extraordinary value will recognize himself or herself in the classic words of Theodore Roosevelt:

> It is not the critic who counts: not the man who points out how the strong man stumbles or where the doer of deeds could have done better. The credit belongs to the man who is actually in the arena, whose face is marred by dust and sweat and blood, who strives valiantly, who errs and comes up short again and again,

Cast of Characters

Space does not allow me to write about all of the entrepreneurs who have influenced my view of entrepreneurship and on whom I have published cases. These individuals include Mary Gadams (RacingThePlanet, Hong Kong), Frank Sanda (Japan Communications Incorporated, Japan), Shane Immelman (LapDesk, South Africa), Eirik Chambe-Enge (Trolltech, Norway), Sanjay Nayak (Tejas Networks, India), Andrew Prihodko (Pixamo, Ukraine and Switzerland), Bento Koike (Tecsis Wind, Brazil), Ebtissam Algosaibi (Erum Jewelry, Saudi Arabia), Joel Silverstein (Vivaldi Food Products, Hong Kong), Nik Nesbitt (Kencall, Kenya), Jim Sharpe (Xtech, USA), and many others. These are the individuals and their ventures that, because of my own close relationships with them, have revolutionized my view of what entrepreneurship is and is not, what it can be and what it cannot be. I hope they will have a similar impact on you.

Laurent Adamowicz	CEO and founder of Bon'App, a food data analytics company built around a mobile calorie-counter application; former owner of Fauchon; now based in Cambridge, Massachusetts.
Carl Bistany	CEO and board member of SABIS, one of the leading, for-profit education management companies in the world, active in fifteen countries and four continents, including North America and the Middle East. Subject of Harvard Business School case study.
Ant Bozkaya	Founder of a series of independent power producers in Turkey and other emerging economies; originally based in Turkey. Subject of Harvard Business School case study.
Sandi Češko*	Cofounder and CEO of Studio Moderna, a Slovenia-based multichannel retailer and TV shopping leader in twenty countries of Eastern and Central Europe. Subject of Harvard Business School case study.
Miguel Davila, Adolfo Fastlicht, Matt Heyman	Cofounders and co-CEOs of Cinemex, the leading multiscreen cinema developer and operator in Mexico; company sold to Loews for $300 million. Subject of Harvard Business School case study.
Will Dean	Cofounder and CEO of Tough Mudder, an extreme obstacle course challenge management company based in Brooklyn. Subject of Harvard Business School case study.
Sean Dimin and Michael Dimin	Founders and CEO (Michael Dimin) of Sea to Table, a direct marketer of sustainably harvested fresh and fresh-frozen fish and seafood from the waters of North and Central America, direct to chefs' kitchens; based in New York City.
Stephen Greer	Founder and CEO of Hartwell Metals, a global scrap-metal trading company based in Hong Kong and Southeast Asia (since acquired).

Mo Ibrahim	Founder and CEO of Celtel, a leading wireless provider covering sub-Saharan Africa; Celtel sold to Zain for $3.4 billion. Subject of Harvard Business School case study.
Itai Isenberg*	Founder and CEO of The Junkyard, Israel's leading nightclub (and author's eldest son).
Vinod Kapur	Founder and CEO of Keggfarms, developer of for-profit poverty solutions in India and other poor economies, based on the Kuroiler super chicken and Keggfarms' unique microenterprise concept. Subject of Harvard Business School case study.
Avichai Kremer*	Founder and chairman of Prize4Life, a nonprofit to incentivize the finding of treatments for amyotrophic lateral sclerosis (ALS, Lou Gehrig's disease); based in the United States and Israel. Subject of Harvard Business School case study.
Oliver Kuttner	Founder and CEO of Edison2; winner of the $5 million Progressive X PRIZE for cars; based in the United States.
Gabi Meron*	Founder and former CEO of Given Imaging (NASDAQ: GIVN) in Israel, which created the field of capsule endoscopy for imaging the gastrointestinal tract; based in Israel. Subject of Harvard Business School case study.
Iqbal Quadir	Founder and former director of Grameenphone, pioneer of rural wireless telephony in Bangladesh. Subject of Harvard Business School case study.
Jorge Rodríguez	Founder and CEO of PACIV, provider of single-source solutions of control system, instrumentation, and regulatory compliance services; based in Puerto Rico. Subject of Harvard Business School case study.
John (Jay) Rogers*	Founder and CEO of Local Motors, developer of crowd-sourced cars and innovative manufacturing platforms for other equipment manufacture; based in Phoenix. Subject of Harvard Business School case study.
Abhi Shah	Founder and CEO of Clutch Group, the leading legal process outsourcing company; based in Bangalore; New York; Washington, DC; and Chicago. Subject of Harvard Business School case study.
Atsumasa Tochisako	Founder and CEO of Microfinance International, provider of financial inclusion products where such services have been previously unavailable; based in Washington, DC; company active in more than a hundred countries. Subject of Harvard Business School case study.
Bert Twaalfhoven	Founder and former CEO of more than fifty companies, focusing primarily on the commercial jet engine supply chain; based in the Netherlands. Subject of Harvard Business School case study.
Robert Wessman	Former CEO of Actavis, now the fourth-leading generics pharmaceutical maker; originally based in Iceland. Subject of Harvard Business School case study.
Mei Zhang	Founder and chairperson of WildChina, award-winning provider of cultural tourism in China. Subject of Harvard Business School case study.
Ron Zwanziger	Founder of three leading health-care ventures, two of which produced the number one and number two products for blood glucose monitoring; sold ventures for $2 billion; currently CEO of Alere (NASDAQ: ALR). Subject of Harvard Business School case study.

*I have or have had in the past a very minor equity or past business relationship with this entrepreneur.

because there is no effort without error or shortcoming, but who knows the great enthusiasms, the great devotions, who spends himself for a worthy cause; who, at best, knows, in the end, the triumph of high achievement, and who, at the worst, if he fails, at least he fails while daring greatly, so that his place shall never be with those cold and timid souls who knew neither victory nor defeat.

I am sure my admiration for entrepreneurs who are "marred by dust" from the arena and who strive valiantly has shown through the words and pages of this book.[27] Entrepreneurship is not about the likely or the average; it is about the possible, the extraordinary. It is about victory. The entrepreneurs who have graced these pages have shown me, and I hope you, a higher possibility.

NOTES

Preface

1. Edward B. Roberts and Charles E. Eesley, *Entrepreneurial Impact: The Role of MIT* (Hanover, MA: Now Publishers, 2011).

Introduction

1. The Actavis headquarters have since moved to Switzerland.

Chapter 1

1. Daniel Isenberg, "Entrepreneurs: Stop Innovating, Start Minnovating," *HBR Blog,* November 19, 2009, http://blogs.hbr.org/cs/2009/11/entrepreneurs_stop_innovating.html.

2. Daniel J. Isenberg, "Robert Wessman and Actavis's 'Winning Formula,'" Case 9-808-127 (Boston: Harvard Business School, 2009).

3. Ibid.

4. James L. Heskett, "Cinemex," Case 9-898-109 (Boston: Harvard Business School, 1999).

5. Daniel Isenberg, "Entrepreneurship Outperforms Innovation," *Bloomberg Business-Week,* www.businessweek.com/debateroom/archives/2012/02/entrepreneurship_outperforms_innovation.html.

Chapter 2

1. Daniel J. Isenberg, "Inverness Medical Innovations: Born Global (A)," Case 9-806-180 (Boston: Harvard Business School, 2009), and "Inverness Medical Innovations: Born Global (B)," Case 9-806-177 (Boston: Harvard Business School, 2009).

2. Vivek Wadhwa, Raj Aggarwal, Krisztina Holly, and Alex Salkever, "The Anatomy of an Entrepreneur," Kaufmann Foundation Report, 2009, www.kauffman.org/uploadedfiles/researchandpolicy/thestudyofentrepreneurship/anatomy%20of%20entre%20071309_final.pdf.

3. Naveen Jain, "Rethinking the Concept of 'Outliers': Why Non-Experts Are Better at Disruptive Innovation," *Forbes,* July 12, 2012, www.forbes.com/sites/singularity/2012/07/12/rethinking-the-concept-of-outliers-why-non-experts-are-better-at-disruptive-innovation/.

4. His venture started out with a different name.

5. Gujarat is a state in Western India whose natives have a reputation for being industrious and enterprising. It is one of India's more prosperous states.

6. Author interview with Jerry Rao, March 2007.

7. Daniel J. Isenberg, "Clutch Group (India): Should Abhi Shah Grab This Opportunity?" Case 9-809-065 (Boston: Harvard Business School, 2010).

8. *Rocky,* directed by John G. Avildsen (1976; Los Angeles, CA: United Artists, Metro-Goldwyn-Mayer, United International Pictures).

9. X PRIZE Foundation, "Who We Are," www.xprize.org/about/who-we-are.

Chapter 3

1. G20 Young Entrepreneurs' Alliance, organization home page, www.g20yea.com, accessed July 25, 2012.

2. Youth Enterprise Council, "Empowering, Inspiring and Educating the Entrepreneurs of Today and Tomorrow," organization web page, http://theyec.org/organization; and www.youthentrepreneurshipact.com.

3. Daniel J. Isenberg, "Microfinance International Corporation: No, Not *Another* Microfinance Case*," Case 9-808-104 (Boston: Harvard Business School, 2009).

4. Simplistic and persistent stereotypes are that the Japanese culture is the antithesis of entrepreneurial. Having worked for 15 years with the Japanese, I have a different viewpoint.

5. Vivek Wadhwa, Krisztina Holly, Raj Aggrawal, and Alex Salkever, "Anatomy of an Entrepreneur: Family Background and Motivation," Kauffman Foundation Report, July 7, 2009.

6. Robert Fairlie, "Kauffman Index of Entrepreneurial Activity 1996–2011," Kauffman Foundation, March 2012.

7. "Researchers Find Risk-Taking Behavior Rises until Age 50," *University of Oregon Communications,* November 10, 2011.

8. Viva Sarah Press, "Study: Highest Work Vitality Comes at Ages 50–59," *Israel21,* July 11, 2012, http://israel21c.org/news/study-highest-work-vitality-comes-at-ages-50-59/.

9. Frederic Delmar and Scott Shane, "Does Experience Matter? The Effect of Founding Team Experience on the Survival and Sales of Newly Founded Ventures," *Strategic Organization* 4, no. 3 (2006): 215–247.

10. Ironically, I have long since forgotten where I put the article, although I do use its facts with great effect.

11. Sarah MacBride, "Silicon Valley's Dirty Secret: Age Bias," *San José Mercury News,* November 27, 2012, www.mercurynews.com/jobs/ci_22072709/silicon-valleys-dirty-secret-age-bias.

12. Ibid.

Part Two

1. Rossana Weitekamp and Barbara Pruitt, "Kauffman Foundation Study Finds More Than Half of *Fortune* 500 Companies Were Founded in Recession or Bear Market," Kauffman Foundation web page, June 9, 2009, www.kauffman.org/newsroom/the-economic-future-just-happened.aspx.

2. I personally know about dry venture capitalists; I was a general partner of a venture capital firm in Israel for five years.

3. Bessemer Venture Partners, "Anti-Portfolio," www.bvp.com/portfolio/antiportfolio.

Chapter 4

1. "Toyota Expects Its First Loss in 70 Years," *New York Times,* December 22, 2008, www.nytimes.com/2008/12/23/business/worldbusiness/23toyota.html.

2. Local Motors has since increased prices.

3. Kirby Garlitos, "2009–2012 Local Motors Rally Fighter," *TopSpeed,* August 9, 2011, www.topspeed.com/cars/local-motors/2009-2012-local-motors-rally-fighter-ar114008 .html.

4. Barack Obama, "Advancing the Manufacturing Sector," speech given at Carnegie Mellon University, Pittsburgh, June 24, 2011, www.youtube.com/watch?feature=player _detailpage&v=j_2zD-hs0aU.

5. Disclosure: I have made a few small investments in Local Motors.

6. Daniel J. Isenberg, "SABIS—A Global Educational Venture from Lebanon," Case 9–809-167 (Boston: Harvard Business School, 2009).

7. Winnie Hu, "Group Picked to Run Queens School Was Ousted in Chicago," *New York Times,* July 13, 1999, www.nytimes.com/1999/07/13/nyregion/group-picked-to-run -queens-school-was-ousted-in-chicago.html?pagewanted=all&src=pm.

8. KIPP, "The KIPP Foundation," organization web page, www.kipp.org/about-kipp/ the-kipp-foundation.

9. FindTheData, "FAQ's for SABIS International Charter (District): How Much To- tal Revenue Does the SABIS International Charter (District) School District of Spring- field, Massachusetts Have?" http://public-school-districts.findthedata.org/q/17240/948/ How-much-total-revenue-does-the-Sabis-International-Charter-district-School-District-of -Springfield-Massachusetts-have.

10. From SABIS company documents and personal observations in Springfield, MA.

11. Anna Fifield, "A Lesson in Academic Acumen," *Financial Times,* April 15, 2009, www.ft.com/intl/cms/s/0/ce34fe72-2955-11de-bc5e-00144feabdc0.html#axzz20axLBRE5.

12. J. Tooley, *From Village School to Global Brand* (London: Profile Books, 2012).

13. Ronald Cohen, *The Second Bounce of the Ball* (London: Weidenfeld and Nicholson, 2007), 42.

14. Massachusetts Department of Education, "The Massachusetts Charter School Ini- tiative," www.doe.mass.edu/charter/reports/2001/01init_rpt.pdf.

15. Hu, "Group Picked to Run Queens School Was Ousted in Chicago."

Chapter 5

1. Szent-Gyorgyi's original statement was "Discovery consists of seeing what every- body else has seen and thinking what nobody has thought."

2. Fred Smith articles, http://www.evancarmichael.com/Famous-Entrepreneurs/764/ summary.php.

3. Daniel J. Isenberg, "Given Imaging Ltd.—First We Take Manhattan, Then We Take Berlin?" Case 9-808-033 (Boston: Harvard Business School, 2009).

4. Jordan Siegel and Christopher Poliquin, "Tough Mudder's Global Expansion," Case 9-712-415 (Boston: Harvard Business School, 2012).

5. "Why the Marathon Is the Last Thing That New York Needs," *Bloomberg Business- Week,* October 31, 2012, www.businessweek.com/articles/2012-10-31/why-the-marathon -is-the-last-thing-new-york-needs.

Chapter 6

1. Daniel J. Isenberg, "Studio Moderna—A Venture in Eastern Europe," Case 9-808-110 (Boston: Harvard Business School, 2009).

2. All the growth is derived from *organic growth,* in other words, through growing the existing business lines rather than through acquisitions.

3. "About Meetup," company web page, www.meetup.com/about.

4. Scott Heiferman, "The Pursuit of Community," *New York Times,* September 5, 2009, www.nytimes.com/2009/09/06/jobs/06boss.html.

5. Barbara Peterson, *Blue Streak: Inside JetBlue, the Upstart That Rocked an Industry* (New York: Penguin Books, 2004), 69–126.

Chapter 7

1. Daniel Isenberg, "Intelligent Evolution: New Ecosystems for Entrepreneurs," Babson Entrepreneurship Ecosystem Project web page, May 25, 2011, http://entrepreneurial-revolution.com/2011/05/intelligent-evolution.

2. H. Rocha and R. Sternberg, "Entrepreneurship: The Role of Clusters: Theoretical Perspective and Empirical Evidence from Germany," *Small Business Economics* 24 (2005): 267–292.

3. Mary Hallward-Driemeir and Lant Pritchett, "How Business Is Done and the 'Doing Business' Indicators: The Investment Climate When Firms Have Climate Control," World Bank Policy Research Working Paper 5563, February 2011.

4. Daniel J. Isenberg, "Will RacingThePlanet Ltd. Reach the Finish Line?" Case 9-807-148 (Boston: Harvard Business School, 2009).

Chapter 8

1. Marico Innovation Foundation, "IIA 2006: Innovation for India Awards 2006," Marico Innovation web page, www.maricoinnovationfoundation.org/awards/ii_awards_2006/pictures.html.

2. Daniel J. Isenberg, "Keggfarms (India)—Which Came First, the Kuroiler™ or the KEGG™?" Case 9-807-089 (Boston: Harvard Business School, 2008).

3. Richard Harth, "Chicken and Egg Question (and Answer) for Rural Uganda," *ASU News,* September 4, 2012; https://asunews.asu.edu/20120904_ugandachickens.

4. Daniel Isenberg, "An Indian FOPSE," *Innovations: Technology, Governance, Globalization* 3, no. 1 (2008): 52–55.

5. Richard Harth, "A New Breed: Highly Productive Chickens Help Raise Ugandans from Poverty," ASU Biodesign Institute, July 20, 2011; www.biodesign.asu.edu/news/a-new-breed-highly-productive-chickens-help-raise-ugandans-from-poverty.

6. Ibid.

Chapter 9

1. William R. Kerr, Daniel J. Isenberg, and Ant Bozkaya, "TA Energy (Turkey): A Bundle of International Partnerships," Case 9-807-175 (Boston: Harvard Business School, 2011).

2. Daniel Isenberg, Carin-Isabel Koop, and David Lane, "Iqbal Quadir, Gonofone, and the Creation of GrameenPhone (Bangladesh)," Case 9-809-099 (Boston: Harvard Business School, 2009).

3. Jeffrey D. Sachs, *The End of Poverty: Economic Possibilities for Our Time* (New York: Penguin, 2005), 264.

4. Including options and other bonuses, Gonofone's full stake was somewhat higher.

5. Sheridan Prasso, "Nobel Peace Prize Winner Itching for a Fight," *Fortune,* December 5, 2006, http://money.cnn.com/2006/12/04/news/international/yunos_telenor.fortune/index.htm.

6. The names of the venture and of the family conglomerate are disguised, in the HBS case (Kerr, Isenberg, and Bozkaya, "TA Energy [Turkey]") and here as well.

Part Four

1. www.peterpatau.com/2006/12/bohr-leads-berra-but-yogi-closing-gap.html.

Chapter 10

1. M. Aubet and M. Turton, *The Phoenicians and the West: Politics, Colonies, and Trade* (New York: Cambridge University Press, 2001).

2. Stephen H. Greer, *Starting from Scrap: An Entrepreneurial Success Story* (Short Hills, NJ: Burford Books, 2010).

3. Daniel J. Isenberg and Paul Marshall, "To JV or Not to JV? That Is the Question (for XTech in China)." Case 9-807-118 (Boston: Harvard Business School, 2009).

4. Daniel J. Isenberg and Shirley Spence, "Leadership at WildChina (A)," Case 9-807-046 (Boston: Harvard Business School, 2009), and "Leadership at WildChina (B)," Case 9-807-128 (Boston: Harvard Business School, 2009).

5. Daniel J. Isenberg, "Bert Twaalfhoven: The Successes and Failures of a Global Entrepreneur," Case 9-807-165 (Boston: Harvard Business School, 2009).

Chapter 11

1. "A for effort" is an American idiom referring to getting a top grade of A in class because you tried hard.

2. Israel M. Kirzner, *Perception, Opportunity and Profit: Studies in the Theory of Entrepreneurship* (University of Chicago Press, 1979).

3. The article was written by Gary Rivlin and published in March 2003, www.wired.com/wired/archive/11.03/segway.html.

4. 24/7 Wall St., "The 10 Biggest Tech Failures of the Last Decade: Failure to Launch—Segway," *Time,* May 14, 2009, www.time.com/time/specials/packages/article/0,28804,1898610_1898625_1898641,00.html.

5. Despite my friend's calling me an academic, I have also been an entrepreneur and investor.

6. MyBasis, www.mybasis.com.

7. Peter Sims, *Little Bets: How Breakthrough Ideas Emerge from Small Discoveries* (New York: Free Press, 2011).

8. Leonard A. Schlesinger and Charles F. Kiefer with Paul B. Brown, *Just Start: Take Action, Embrace Uncertainty, Create the Future* (Boston: Harvard Business Review Press, 2012).

9. Daniel J. Isenberg, "Can PACIV (Puerto Rico) Serve European Customers?" Case 9–808-099 (Boston: Harvard Business School, 2009).

10. Daniel J. Isenberg, "Bert Twaalfhoven: The Successes and Failures of a Global Entrepreneur," Case 9-807-165 (Boston: Harvard Business School, 2009).

11. Ronald Cohen, *The Second Bounce of the Ball* (London: Weidenfeld and Nicholson, 2007).

12. Personal communication with Bert Twaalfhoven, 2012.

13. I use the term *risk taking* as the investment of some resource at time *T* with an uncertain return at time *T* + 1, and thus there is an inherent possibility of losing the investment. I use *investment* in the most inclusive sense, encompassing effort, money, time, reputation, opportunity costs, and so on. There are different definitions of risk; see, for example, Frank H. Knight's classic *Risk, Uncertainty, and Profit* (Boston: Houghton Mifflin, 1921).

14. Cohen, *The Second Bounce of the Ball,* 106.

Chapter 12

1. Dividing the peak market capitalization of $1 billion by the number of cars, 8,000, yields over $120,000 per car.

2. Personal communication with Robin Chase, 2012.

3. Paul W. Marshall and Jeremy B. Dann, "Keurig," Case 9-899-180 (Boston: Harvard Business School, 2004).

4. Stephen H. Greer, *Starting from Scrap: An Entrepreneurial Success Story* (Short Hills, NJ: Burford Books, 2010).

5. A process that epistemologist Donald Campbell referred to as "ostensive"; see William R. Shadish, Thomas D. Cook, and Donald T. Campbell, *Experimental and Quasi-Experimental Designs for Generalized Causal Inference* (Boston: Houghton Mifflin, 2001).

6. I will continue to use the term *ownership* to include any significant financial stake in the venture's results.

7. Shadish, Cook, and Campbell, *Experimental and Quasi-Experimental Designs for Causal Inference,* 243.

8. Lest there be any confusion, in discussing value capture, I do not see a need to distinguish between capital gains from the sale of stock or dividends and way-beyond-market bonuses. They are all legitimate means of value capture, each with its own implications in terms of taxes, timing, and accounting.

9. "The hen lays eggs, but the pig has skin in the game." Sorry, but that is a common American idiom.

10. We were joined later by Elkan Gamzu, Peter Finn, and Meridith Unger.

Conclusion

1. Joseph Schumpeter, "Development," *Journal of Economic Literature* 43, no. 1 (2005): 108–120.

2. Ibid.

3. Thomas McGraw, *Prophet of Innovation: Joseph Schumpeter and Creative Destruction* (Cambridge, MA: Belknap, 2007).

4. With some recent, relatively minor exceptions.

5. Daniel Isenberg, "Everything You Know About Silicon Valley Might Be Wrong," *HBR Blog,* August 31, 2011; http://blogs.hbr.org/cs/2011/08/everything_you_know_about_sili.html.

6. For example, Daniel Isenberg, "How to Start an Entrepreneurial Revolution," *Harvard Business Review,* June 2010, 40–50.

7. Ibid.

8. Christian Ketels, Ashish Lall, and Neo Boon Siong, *Singapore Competitiveness Report, 2009* (Singapore: Asia Competitiveness Institute and National University of Singapore, November 2009).

9. "The Five Most Improved Places for Gay Tolerance," *(London) Independent,* September 17, 2008, www.independent.co.uk/life-style/love-sex/taboo-tolerance/the-five-most-improved-places-for-gay-tolerance-932635.html.

10. Visa Veerasamy, "Guy Kawasaki, on Entrepreneurship in Singapore," April 17, 2011, www.visakanv.com/blog/2011/04/guy-kawasaki-on-entrepreneurship-in-singapore/.

11. Daniel Isenberg, "Focus Entrepreneurship Policy of Scale-up, Not Start-up," *HBR Blog,* November 30, 2012; http://blogs.hbr.org/cs/2012/11/focus_entrepreneurship_policy. html.

12. A "search fund" is typically a few hundred thousand dollars provided by several private individuals to two or three search fund managers, who use the cash to support their usually prolonged search for a company that the group would then acquire control of with additional funds, and the managers would manage, grow, and sell.

13. Dane Stangler and Robert E. Litan, "Where Will the Jobs Come From?" Kauffman Foundation, November 2009, www.kauffman.org/uploadedFiles/where_will_the_jobs _come_from.pdf.

14. John Haltiwanger, Ron Jarmin, and Javier Miranda, "Who Creates Jobs? Small vs. Large vs. Young," NBER working paper, August 2010; www.nber.org/papers/w16300.

15. Thayer Watkins, "Origins of the Silicon Valley," San José State University Department of Economics, www.sjsu.edu/faculty/watkins/sivalley.htm.

16. Mohannad Aama, "How Many Shares Does Facebook Have Outstanding?" *Wall Street Dispatch,* May 18, 2012, www.wallstreetdispatch.com/how-many-shares-does-facebook-have-outstanding-483.html. At the time of this writing, the total market value of Facebook was down to about $90 billion.

17. Richard Florida, "The Inequality of American Cities," *The Atlantic Cities,* March 5, 2012, www.theatlanticcities.com/jobs-and-economy/2012/03/inequality-american-cities/ 861/.

18. Jon Burgston, *Breakthrough Entrepreneurship: The Proven Framework for Building Brilliant New Businesses* (San Francisco: Farallon Publishing, 2012); Leonard A. Schlesinger and Charles F. Kiefer with Paul B. Brown, *Just Start: Take Action, Embrace Uncertainty, Create the Future* (Boston: Harvard Business Review Press, 2012); Seth Godin, *Poke the Box: When Was the Last Time You Did Something for the First Time?* (Do You Zoom, 2011); Anthony K. Tjan, Richard J. Harrington, and Tsun-Yan Hsieh, *Heart, Smarts, Guts, and Luck: What It Takes to Be an Entrepreneur and Build a Great Business* (Boston: Harvard Business Review Press, 2012).

19. David E. Gumpert, *Inc. Magazine Presents How to Really Create a Successful Business Plan: Featuring the Business Plans of Pizza Hut, Software Publishing Corp., Celestial Seasonings, People Express, Ben & Jerry's* (Boston: Inc. Publishing, 1996); David E. Gumpert, *Burn Your Business Plan! What Investors Really Want from Entrepreneurs* (Needham, MA: Lauson Publishing, 2002).

20. Kelly K. Spors, "So, You Want to Be an Entrepreneur," *Wall Street Journal,* February 23, 2009, http://online.wsj.com/article/SB123498006564714189.html.

21. Spiralmoonmedia, "'Share the Air' Presentation," posted March 23, 2011, www .youtube.com/watch?v=wyrFWbGiGOc&feature=player_embedded#!.

22. Ronald Cohen, *The Second Bounce of the Ball* (London: Weidenfeld and Nicholson, 2007).

23. Laura Northrup, "Lenovo CEO Turns Fairy Godmother, Hands Over Bonus to Employees," *Consumerist,* July 23, 2012, http://consumerist.com/2012/07/lenovo-ceo-turns-fairy-godmother-hands-over-bonus-to-rank-and-file-employees.html.

24. Dan Schawbel, "How Big Companies Are Becoming Entrepreneurial," AOL TechCrunch, July 29, 2012, http://techcrunch.com/2012/07/29/how-big-companies-are-becoming-entrepreneurial/.

25. Martin Sorrel, "Mea Culpa: I Act the Owner That I Am," *Financial Times,* June 5, 2012, www.ft.com/intl/cms/s/0/ea12c3e6-aeee-11e1-a8a7–00144feabdc0.html#axzz20KAsnrRL.

26. Ibid.

27. See the sidebar "Cast of Characters" for a partial list of these individuals.

INDEX

ACKNOWLEDGMENTS

Developing a case study on someone who is devoting his or her life to realizing a dream is an intimate process, and I am fortunate that so many people opened themselves to me, divulging their secrets and exposing their vulnerabilities, doubts, and aspirations. In some instances I got to know their families. I made some fast friends in the process, and to all I owe a deep debt.

But it was not in my plans to write a book about these experiences until my eldest son, Itai, who himself has since chosen the path of the entrepreneur, called me up one day and told me, "Dad, I can't stop thinking about these entrepreneurs you tell me about. Where is your book?" Itai's suggestion came at the right time, and within a few days, I had started writing, having decided that I could make a unique contribution to the general knowledge of entrepreneurship by telling these stories and helping others learn from them. It took four years, but special thanks go to Itai and his persistent and loving nudging. Indeed, from all of my four kids, my start-ups, Itai, Tal, Amir, and Lihi, I have learned so much about life and leadership (and other things), and I want to thank them individually and collectively for contributing to who I am as a person. There is no substitute for being a parent, and it is a unique color in life's rainbow.

Although he cannot be "blamed" for any of this book's content, I owe a special thanks to Len Schlesinger, then president of Babson College, who created a new position for me at Babson in 2009, has supported me in many ways, and has encouraged me to test my insights about entrepreneurship in a novel and ambitious venture at Babson, which we call the Babson Entrepreneurship Ecosystem Project (BEEP). This book is not about BEEP, but the insights and experiences that form this book underpin everything that BEEP is trying to accomplish.

I also thank "Tillo" Rodriguez, a Puerto Rican coffee entrepreneur, who used some of his "captured extraordinary value" to build an idyllic vacation home in the Dominican Republic, which he graciously invited me to use to work on this book.

A few more acknowledgements are in order:

To my current and former students, who ask me tough questions and learn from our encounters; especially to those who keep updating me on their often-surprising accomplishments and endeavors. You make it worthwhile. (I just wrote to some of my former students and learned that ten of them have created about three thousand jobs in the past six years.)

To my former wife Tsvia, who was my support for many years as I was an entrepreneur, a venture capitalist, and a partner of entrepreneurs and who convinced me to move back to Israel in 1987, where I became part of the entrepreneurial revolution there.

To my student Avichai Kremer, who by turning his ALS (Lou Gehrig's disease) into an opportunity to change the world has taught me more about loving life than I imagined possible.

To my writing collaborator and first line editor Karen Dillon, who was a joy to work with and kept me honest, and without whom this book would *never* have been completed. Thanks!

To my Harvard Business Review Press editor Jeff Kehoe, who stood by me with calm encouragement and professional guidance.

Finally a word of thanks to my long-deceased parents, Irvin Isenberg and Cynthia Isenberg, to whom I dedicate this book, with love, appreciation, and longing.

ABOUT THE AUTHOR

Daniel Isenberg is currently Professor of Entrepreneurship Practice at Babson Global, where he founded and directs the Babson Entrepreneurship Ecosystem Project to help cities and countries foster high-growth entrepreneurship. Prior to joining Babson, Isenberg was on the faculty of Harvard Business School, where he taught numerous courses in entrepreneurship including the popular course, International Entrepreneurship. He has also taught entrepreneurship at Columbia University, Insead, and The Technion, Israel Institute of Technology.

Beginning in the 1980s, Isenberg became involved in every aspect of entrepreneurship—first as chief operating officer of Technion Entrepreneurial Associates, a group of Boston-based technological experts dedicated to fostering entrepreneurship in Israel, and later as an entrepreneur, professor, venture capitalist, angel investor, researcher, and policy adviser to over a dozen cities and nations.

Born and raised in Woods Hole, Massachusetts, Isenberg holds a PhD in social psychology from Harvard, where he authored scientific papers on human cognition and interaction. He is a frequent participant in the World Economic Forum at Davos, a member of the Global Agenda Council for Fostering Entrepreneurship, and a frequent speaker on entrepreneurship and entrepreneurship policy at the G20 and other global forums. Isenberg is a regular blogger for the HBR Blog Network and has written feature articles for *Harvard Business Review*, including the hugely popular "How to Start an Entrepreneurial Revolution." He has also published over thirty case studies on entrepreneurship.

Isenberg has four grown children, three of whom are entrepreneurs. He is an avid salsa dancer, wine collector, and a renowned expert at not catching fish.

Karen Dillon is the former editor of *Harvard Business Review*. She is now a contributing editor at *Harvard Business Review* and a coauthor, with Clayton Christensen and James Allworth, of the *New York Times* best-seller, *How Will You Measure Your Life?* It was at HBR that she first worked with Daniel Isenberg on the "Big Idea" article, "How to Start an Entrepreneurial Revolution."

Prior to joining HBR, Dillon was deputy editor of *Inc.* magazine, where she first became interested in the world of entrepreneurs, chronicling both successes and failures with equal fascination. She began her career as editor and publisher of the critically acclaimed monthly, *The American Lawyer*, spending four of her years there with its British affiliate, *Legal Business*. Her editing and writing have been honored by the National Magazine Awards and the *UK Press Gazette*.

A native of Reading, Massachusetts, Dillon is a graduate of Cornell University and Northwestern University's Medill School of Journalism. In 2011 she was honored as part of Ashoka ChangemakeHER's inaugural celebration of the world's most influential and inspiring women.